DOCUMENTS IN MEDIEVAL LATIN

DOCUMENTS
IN
MEDIEVAL LATIN

John Thorley

Ann Arbor

THE UNIVERSITY OF MICHIGAN PRESS

2001 2000 1999 1998 4 3 2 1

Library of Congress Cataloging-in-Publication Data applied for

ISBN 0-472-08567-0

Printed in Great Britain

Contents

Preface

This book is intended for those who know some Latin and who want to tackle historical documents written in Latin from the medieval period. Those who have studied Latin to GCSE level, or who have gone through Eileen Gooder's *Latin for Local History*, will be able to use the book. But those who have a more advanced knowledge of Classical Latin and who wish to become familiar with the rather different styles and vocabulary of documents in Medieval Latin will also find the book useful.

Examples have been chosen from most types of Latin document which are of direct relevance to those interested in British history. Poetry and theological and philosophical works have not been included, partly because most historians will not be directly concerned with these genres, and partly because they have their own particular styles and vocabulary which require specific study.

The book is arranged to some extent chronologically, in that the first section of texts (Chapter 2) is taken from the Anglo-Saxon period, the following three sections (Chapters 3-6) are from the period after the Norman Conquest, mainly pre-Renaissance but with some court rolls from the 17th century, and the final section (Chapter 7) is from the period after 1500.

There are in all about 80 texts (including sub-sections), ranging from the 6th to the 18th centuries. With each text there is a short commentary on linguistic points and also on the historical context of the passage. The latter is intended not only as an aid to understanding the passage, but also as an introduction to the kind of research which such sources can generate. The source given for each text is in most cases a fairly accessible published version rather than the manuscript source. In many cases further information on the texts can be found in the publications quoted. All passages are translated at the end of the book.

As far as the difficulty of the Latin is concerned, the easiest texts are probably the grants, deeds, and other legal and ecclesiastical documents of Chapter 3, partly because they are heavily based on formulaic phrases. The most difficult are the historians to be found in Chapters 2 and 6, together with some of the texts in Chapter 7.

It is not a good idea to try to work through the book from beginning to end. Interests vary, and the book is designed to help those interested in different kinds of documents to tackle first just those in which they are interested. Each chapter is therefore planned as a self-contained unit. If you get a taste for all kinds of Medieval Latin record, all to the good.

A knowledge of Medieval Latin is an invaluable aid for those seriously interested in British (and, of course, European) history up to the early 18th century. Much that was written in Latin has not been translated into English and probably never will be in the foreseeable future, and a knowledge of Latin gives access to the detailed study not only of the medieval historians but also of the numerous deeds, charters, court records and other less official papers which have survived in great quantity from the medieval and early modern periods. Even in the case of Bede, who has been translated many times, to understand his original Latin gives an insight into his literary qualities and his elaborate thought patterns. In the later chroniclers so many details have scarcely been used by modern historians and are a mine of information for both social and political historians. For those interested in local or family history the monastic cartularies, manorial records, ecclesiastical documents, deeds, wills, inventories and court rolls from the relevant areas are accessible for the most part only to those who can read Latin. And for those with an interest in early cartography and exploration in the 15th to the 18th centuries an ability to read Latin gives direct access to much information on maps which is still only partially available in translation.

And to acquire a competence in reading historical records is not such a daunting task for anyone with a reasonable degree of linguistic ability; in studying Medieval Latin nowadays we are at least spared the need to write it or converse in it. One does need a sound grasp of the basics of Latin grammar, since without that foundation fair reading competence cannot be achieved. Beyond that it is mainly a matter of becoming familiar with the modes of expression and the vocabulary of the types of document in which you are particularly interested, and it is hoped that this book will help in achieving this.

I wish to record my thanks to those who have contributed to the compilation of this book: to Richard Hall of the Cumbria Record Office in Kendal for his help with the Kendal Quarter Session records in Chapter 5; to my brother Martin Thorley for discovering our possible ancestor in passage 3(a); to Brian Tear for pointing me in the right direction on records of medieval Lincoln; to John Todd, editor of the Lanercost Cartulary, for permission to use passage 3(g) from the Cartulary; to Joyce Hunter of Lincoln City Library for referring me to the inscription from Gainsborough in passage 7(m); to Professor Danuta Shanzer of Cornell University, New York, for many helpful points on linguistics; to the Essex Record Office for its agreement to my using several documents from Hilda E.P. Grieve, *Examples of English Handwriting 1150-1750*, published by the Essex Record Office in 1954; and to David Iredale and John Barrett of the Moray Record Office for their agreement to my use of documents from their book *Discovering Old Handwriting* (Shire Publications 1995).

In dealing with texts from so many different places and on such a range of subject matter it is inevitable that I have made errors. I hope these will not detract too much from the primary aim of the book, which is to enable those interested in medieval history to improve their ability to read material in the original Latin.

1

Introduction

Medieval Latin: the language

Medieval Latin is not in essence a different language from Classical Latin. During the Roman Empire the use of Latin spread over most of Western Europe and after the collapse of the western Empire in the 5th century AD it continued to be used over many centuries during the medieval period, mainly as a written language but also by many, especially within the church, as a spoken language, even though by the 9th century and probably earlier nobody spoke what could accurately be described as Latin as their mother tongue. In the medieval period Latin was used for purposes which were not envisaged in the time of the great classical writers, and there were therefore inevitably changes in the idiom of the written language, though it remained essentially recognisable as Latin and was indeed called Latin by all its users. These changes were not always in the direction of simplification, and it would be a mistake to assume that Medieval Latin is always easier (however one may define the word) than Classical Latin; in fact much that was written in Medieval Latin was linguistically and stylistically very complex. But the language remained very definitely Latin, and Cicero, Caesar and Vergil would readily have understood most Medieval Latin, even though the vocabulary in specialist fields would have puzzled them.

Medieval Latin was, then, the Latin used for most records, for the writing of most history, theology and philosophy, and also for a large quantity of poetry and other literature by the educated population of Western and parts of Central Europe from the fall of the western Roman Empire in the 5th century AD until the Renaissance, though in some countries, including Great Britain, its use continued for some purposes until the 19th century. In essence Medieval Latin was a composite product, only partly the result of the natural development of the spoken language from classical to early medieval times; it was in fact more the product of the Christian church, and we shall briefly trace how this development occurred.

During the 4th century Christianity became the official religion of the Roman Empire, and from then on the Latin used in the western church became the basis for most written Latin. The essential texts of the church were the Missal and the Latin bible, though the Latin Fathers also had considerable influence on Latin style as well as on theological interpretation. All these texts were, of course, written in what one might call the ecclesiastical literary style of their day, which was itself influenced both by the contemporary spoken language and by the literary models of the preceding centuries, with a heavy admixture of specifically Christian vocabulary.

Until the end of the 4th century numerous Latin translations of the bible were available (the Itala or more accurately the Old Latin versions), and the Missal itself was not in a standardised form. However, after the publication of the Vulgate ('Common') Bible, which is the usual title given to St Jerome's Latin version of the Old and New Testaments, completed in AD 404, the older Latin versions gradually fell out of favour and the Vulgate did indeed become the 'common', most widely used Latin version of the bible. This was certainly the case in Britain; since Christianity was not re-introduced from the continent until 597, it was Jerome's Vulgate which was consistently used from this point. In fact Jerome's Vulgate was a very mixed piece of work. For most of the Old Testament he did indeed provide a new Latin version from the Hebrew, but for the New Testament he did no more than correct the Old Latin versions by comparing them with the Greek (and the Vulgate version of books other than the gospels may not be by Jerome at all). The Vulgate cannot therefore be classed as a work of great stylistic beauty, but it nevertheless became over a period of time the standard version of the bible in Latin.

The Latin Missal probably has its origins as early as the late 1st century AD when Christianity took a firm hold in Rome. It seems to have taken some time for a standardised liturgy to emerge, and there were in fact variant versions in use until the invention of printing made the dissemination of a standardised form much simpler. But most of the essential elements of the later standardised form of the Mass itself were already in existence by the 4th century, and probably a fairly uniform liturgy was already becoming common to most churches by that time, around the time of Jerome's translation of the bible. The language and style of the Mass are therefore little different from Jerome's Vulgate, and the two texts formed a coherent linguistic framework for the language of the church, reinforced by the works of the Latin Fathers which were an integral part of the education of all churchmen.

1. Introduction

So it came about that, although the essential texts of the church were not strictly standardised even after the publication of the Vulgate, they represented a common linguistic tradition which was disseminated over most of Western Europe by the time the western Roman Empire began to disintegrate in the 5th century AD. Amid the confusion which followed in the wake of the collapse of the western Empire the church and its Latin liturgy and bible maintained an administrative structure and a common language across Western Europe which was to persist for over a millennium. Sections of the Missal and the bible were read and heard in Latin every day in all the churches of Western Europe until the Reformation brought the vernacular languages of Northern Europe into the liturgy, whilst in most of the rest of Europe Latin continued to be the liturgical language of the church until the latter half of the 20th century. It is not surprising therefore that the grammar, syntax and style of the Missal and, progressively, of the Vulgate and its commentators became the standard of literary Latin for the whole of the medieval period.

The Latin of the church was still in many ways recognisably the Latin of Cicero and Caesar, though four centuries of natural linguistic development and the Christian context had brought changes. And, of course, Latin did continue to change after Jerome's Vulgate, in particular as a result of its use as the language of law and administration. In medieval Britain, the legal and administrative systems were firstly Anglo-Saxon, and then after 1066 Norman, and the vocabulary of these systems was made to fit the grammatical structures of Latin. But since Latin had become essentially a literary language, later changes had little impact on the structure of the language itself, and the influence of the Missal and the Vulgate remained a stabilising factor.

As far as morphology is concerned (i.e. the ways in which nouns, adjectives, pronouns and verbs change to indicate their grammatical function) the Latin of the Missal and the Vulgate, and therefore of most Medieval Latin, is virtually identical with that of Cicero and Caesar, so that anyone who has learned these basics of Classical Latin will find all the familiar endings there in Medieval Latin, with the occasional change of spelling (mainly Classical **ae** written, and pronounced, as **e**).

In syntax (i.e. the way sentences are constructed) there are some changes. The following list is not exhaustive, but indicates some of the most common differences from Classical Latin:

13

- **quod** or **quia** (and sometimes **ut** or **quoniam**) are often used to mean 'that' in indirect statement, where Classical Latin had used the Accusative and Infinitive construction, though in fact the Accusative and Infinitive construction did continue to be used quite frequently in Medieval Latin, so one has to be familiar with it;
- less rigid rules for the use of the subjunctive (though it occurs very frequently, partly because it was often used in Indirect Statement after **quod** or **quia**);
- an increased use of prepositions where Classical Latin used a simple case of the noun, in particular the use of **ad** and the accusative instead of a simple dative, and **in** with the ablative in expressions of time instead of the simple ablative;
- **suus** is often used for 'his', 'her', 'its' or 'their' without distinction from **eius** or **eorum/earum**;
- present participles are used more frequently, often where Classical Latin would have used a perfect participle or a temporal clause;
- the perfect and pluperfect passives are often formed with **fui** and **fueram** instead of the Classical Latin **sum** and **eram**;
- the infinitive is commonly used to express both purpose and indirect command, instead of the Classical Latin **ut/ne** with the subjunctive;
- many new abstract nouns are introduced, mainly 3rd declension nouns in **-io** and **-tas**.

In vocabulary there was, as we have seen, a great influx of words associated with the church, and also increasingly in Britain of words associated with English (or Scottish) law and administration. Many of these have a precise and technical usage whose full meaning will often require some research to establish; for instance **soca** means 'soc', but what exactly is soc? At least such words are usually quite clearly non-classical. More disconcerting for those who have read some Classical Latin are those words which do occur in Classical Latin but whose meaning is different (or, more precisely, extended into other areas) in Medieval Latin; for instance, in Medieval Latin **placitum** is far more likely to mean 'a plea in court' than to have to do with 'pleasing', **villa** does not usually mean 'a country house' but either 'a manorial estate' or 'a town' or 'a village', **prior** means 'a prior' (in a monastery) as often as 'former', and **presentes** is more likely to mean 'this (present) document' than 'those (who are) present'.

Medieval Latin was used for a multitude of purposes by people varying greatly in their level of competence in the language. Many writers, especially of theology, history and philosophy, were very fluent stylists, mainly following the syntax of the Vulgate but frequently making use of classical models, though even at this sophisticated level of literary production there was a wide range of linguistic expertise. Other writers, especially those who drafted local records, wills, court rolls and the like, were sometimes (though by no means always) rather restricted in their knowledge of Latin grammar and not at all confident outside a few set formulaic phrases. The linguistic range is indeed great, but it is worth remembering that the historical importance of a text is not necessarily related to the quality of its Latin.

It is worth noting at this point that in Britain after the collapse of Roman authority both Early Welsh, the language of the native Celtic population, and Anglo-Saxon, the language of the Germanic invaders, quickly became literary languages, and were used in the production of many forms of records and literature. Latin was always used within the church, but alongside Early Welsh and Anglo-Saxon. After the Norman Conquest Anglo-Saxon quickly lost status and Norman French was used for some official records, but Latin was the main written language for anything of major importance and certainly predominated within the church. It could indeed be argued that it was the regular use of Latin in the two centuries or so after the Norman Conquest that prevented Norman French taking a hold as the language of administration in Britain.

In the later stages of Medieval Latin, in Britain from the early 16th century, the Renaissance brought a greater awareness of the classical Latin authors, and many users of Latin were very much influenced by these authors. Most scholars and senior churchmen prided themselves on their ability to write good Ciceronian Latin, and frequently on maps and monuments the writers of the text were very keen to display their command of 'good' Latin. But such classical scholarship was far from universal, and local records of all types are for the most part little affected by this classicism.

Medieval Latin: the content

There is a vast amount of surviving material written in Medieval Latin. All the countries of Western Europe, and some countries of Eastern Europe, used Latin for most of their records and communications until the Renaissance. In this book we shall be concentrating very largely on material produced in Great Britain and of particular relevance to historians, but this still offers a vast range of surviving material, much of it incidentally still in manuscript form, unedited and unpublished. The following list focuses upon material from Great Britain, but it is no more than a brief illustration of the kinds of text which are available.

(i) Historical writing

The writing of history was carried on all over Europe, usually focused on reigns of monarchs or the national or regional history of the church or of individual religious establishments. Britain produced its fair share, much of it of high quality both historically and linguistically.

(a) Historical narrative, e.g. (all written by monks)

- Gildas (fl. c. 540), *De Excidio Britonum*. Actually not strictly a history but rather a denunciation of his times with a historical introduction, and written in highly rhetorical Latin full of biblical allusion. Not an easy work.
- Bede (673-735), *Historia Ecclesiastica Gentis Anglorum*, down to 731; also numerous other works.
- William of Malmesbury (c. 1095-1143), *Gesta Regum Anglorum*, a history of England from 449 to 1120; also *Gesta Pontificum Anglorum*, a history of the church in England from 597 to 1125.
- Geoffrey of Monmouth (d. c. 1155), *Historia Regum Britanniae*, covering the history of Britain from pre-Roman times to his own day. His style is lively and fluent, but the historical accuracy of much of his narrative is highly dubious, as William of Newburgh (see below) pointed out.
- Henry of Huntingdon (d. c. 1155), *Historia Anglorum*, down to 1154.
- William of Newburgh (near Byland Abbey in North Yorkshire; d. perhaps in 1198), *Historia Rerum Anglicarum*, from 1066 to 1198. A particularly accurate and well written account.
- Matthew Paris (d. 1259, a monk of St Albans), *Chronica Majora*, covering the period from Roman Britain to his own day. Well researched and written in a lively style.

(b) Biography

Mainly lives of saints, e.g.

- Adamnan (628-704), *Life of Saint Columba*
- Eddius (fl. 700), *Life of Saint Wilfred*

1. Introduction

- Bede (673-735), *Life of Saint Cuthbert*
- William Fitzstephen (d. c. 1190), *Life of Thomas Becket*

(c) Monastic chronicles

Most religious houses kept their own chronicles. Some (by no means all) are well written histories, e.g.

- Jocelyn of Brakelond (d. 1211, a monk of Bury St Edmunds), *Chronicles of St Edmondsbury*
- Richard de Morins (d. c. 1242), *Annals of Dunstable*

(ii) Charters, records and other official documents

Most states in medieval Western and Central Europe made extensive use of Latin in keeping records of all kinds. The general pattern across Europe is that modern languages gradually replaced Latin, certainly from the Renaissance and in several cases earlier. In Britain, as we have noted, the situation is rather different in that Anglo-Saxon and Welsh were both literary languages long before the Norman Conquest, and in England and Wales until 1066 both were used extensively alongside Latin (though Latin predominated in church matters). Moreover the use of Latin persisted in Britain long after the Renaissance. Latin was still used in most court records, and very visibly in many funerary monuments in churches (see (iii) below), until well into the 18th century and often later.

The different types of records may usefully be defined as follows, though some of the categories may overlap:

(a) royal charters. These range from the Magna Carta to the granting of town markets, and are usually in a fairly elaborate formulaic style;

(b) court rolls. Manor and borough court rolls were kept by every manor and borough court, and most of these are still in city, county or former borough record offices. Church courts were also held and their records are often retained by diocesan offices. All these types of court records frequently contain detailed accounts of individual cases, which provide a fascinating, and often amusing insight into the society of the day;

(c) legal documents, e.g. wills, leases, writs, bonds, property deeds, deeds of gift. These documents often employ set formulae, which can be elaborate and complex;

17

(d)   the cartularies of religious houses form a distinct category of records. They consist of all the documents which the community considered of importance to the legal and religious life of the house, and therefore contain land deeds of various kinds together with important documents from the church authorities;

(e)   diocesan records, e.g. bishops' registers of parishes, diocesan accounts and all kinds of legal documents. Usually, as one might expect, in good Latin;

(f)   parish records, mainly records of births, marriages and deaths, but also often accounts and legal documents. The Latin is often very restricted and formulaic (and bad!), though some registers were obviously kept by very able latinists;

(g)   financial accounts and inventories. These were kept by the national Exchequer (the Pipe Rolls), by all courts and church authorities, and by more wealthy private individuals, though few from the latter group survive in Latin. Most are in highly formulaic style.

(iii) Maps and monuments

Cartography developed very rapidly after the discovery of America, which coincided with rapid developments in printing technology. Large numbers of maps, from small areas such as the English counties to world maps, were published from the early 16th century onwards. Many contain descriptions of considerable length in Latin, often in good literary style (they were, of course, published documents, aimed at the educated and wealthy). During the 17th century modern languages gradually replaced Latin on maps, but some maps even after 1700 have Latin texts. Many maps from the 16th and 17th centuries still survive and are avidly collected. It is worth noting that few translations of the Latin texts on maps have so far been published.

Monuments in Latin are found mainly in churches and cathedrals. Latin was frequently used on funerary monuments until the late 17th century, is not uncommon in the 18th century, and is even occasionally found in the 19th and 20th centuries. Shorter inscriptions were usually composed locally and often display quaint spelling; longer inscriptions are usually in quite elaborate style and can be syntactically complex. Monuments from the 18th century often show clear signs that the writer has had a good classical education, and was keen to display it.

1. Introduction

(iv) Other prose literature (of particular relevance to historians)

This includes:

- letters. Large quantities of letters on church and state matters have survived. More personal letters have also survived, mainly from well known people whose correspondence was deliberately preserved. Examples are those of Erasmus (c.1467-1536), the renowned Dutch scholar who spent several years in England, mainly in Cambridge, and who wrote in a very fluent, elegant, and often amusing style;
- itineraries. These were a popular literary genre, often describing pilgrimages, though the finest British example is the *Itinerarium Cambriae* of Giraldus Cambrensis (c. 1146-1220), which is a very detailed description of the people and places of Wales;
- technical and descriptive works and manuals on the arts, various crafts, and education.

*

The following categories are perhaps of less direct relevance to historians, though very important in their own right as the product of the thinking of their time, and hence of some importance also in establishing the intellectual context of a period. One has to add that they are also written in more complex Latin.

(v) Poetry

Medieval Latin lyric poetry, epic poetry and hymns were European rather than national in character. France and Germany were perhaps the most prolific producers of poetry in Latin, though there were poets in Britain. A considerable amount of lyric poetry has been transmitted in anonymous collections, such as the Carmina Burana (from the Abbey of Benediktbeuern in Bavaria) and the Arundel Collection. The main categories of poetry are:

- religious poetry and hymns;
- epic poetry, mostly imitating Vergil;
- love poetry, most of it from the 11th, 12th and 13th centuries. Peter of Blois (c. 1135-1212; Blois is in France, about 30 miles north east of Tours), one of the better known writers of love poetry, was

19

secretary and chaplain to Henry II, and after Henry's death in 1189 became secretary to his wife, Eleanor of Aquitaine. In this capacity he was involved in the efforts to free her son, Richard Lionheart, from his captivity in Germany;

- other lyric poetry such as satire, accounts of battles, descriptions of nature (birds were a favourite theme), introspective poetry.

(vi) Theology and philosophy

Large quantities of commentaries on scripture were written, in Britain as well as on the continent. These often merged into treatises of theological debate, usually focused on some passage or passages from scripture.

Much philosophy was also firmly based in Christian doctrine. 'Scolasticism', the dominant philosophy of the period 1100-1500, was essentially based on Aristotelian concepts interpreted in the light of Christian doctrine. Ethics, political theory, epistemology, law, and several areas of natural science were much written about. Among the more eminent British philosophers were the following, all of whom were at Oxford University at some period of their lives:

- Roger Bacon (c. 1214-92), Franciscan friar, philosopher, mathematician and experimental scientist.
- Duns Scotus (c. 1266-1308), Franciscan friar and prolific writer, mainly on Aristotelian concepts.
- William of Ockham (1285-1349), another Franciscan. Wrote on logic, politics and science.

The language of most philosophical writings is replete with specialised vocabulary, much of it based on Aristotle's Greek. It became a highly developed and specialised medium of communication amongst the European philosophical fraternity.

*

Medieval Latin was therefore the principal means of educated written communication throughout Western and much of Central Europe from Roman times until the Renaissance. It was an international language, it was largely free from linguistic change, and anyone who could read it had access to the records, decrees, histories and literatures of most of Europe. For anyone with an interest in

1. Introduction

Medieval Europe it remains an essential tool for the understanding of primary sources of the period.

2

The Anglo-Saxon Period

The period from the arrival in Britain of the Angles and Saxons until
the Norman conquest in 1066 is of particular linguistic interest.
Latin as a language of secular administration did not survive long
after the withdrawal of Roman forces in 410, but the language was
retained within the church, and even during the long and troubled
period of the Germanic incursions into eastern Britain the Celtic-
speaking west retained a thorough grasp of Latin, as can be seen in
the elaborate (if rather obscure) Latin of Gildas, a monk living in
South Wales who wrote about the history of Britain and the sorry
state of the church in his *De Excidio Britonum* (*On the Ruin of the
Britons*), apparently around 540 AD. Augustine's arrival in Kent in
597 began the conversion of the Saxon population to Christianity,
and with it the use of Latin in the Saxon east. The church in the
Celtic west tended to look to Ireland for its leadership, but after the
Synod of Whitby in 664 the church in Britain was essentially united.

Latin was undoubtedly the main written language of the Anglo-
Saxon period, if only because it was the universal language of the
church. However, Anglo-Saxon poetry seems to have been flourishing as a written literature by the early 8th century, and prose
literature soon followed. Bede (c. 673-735) is said to have written in
Anglo-Saxon as well as in Latin, but unfortunately none of his
Anglo-Saxon works survives. From the reign of Alfred (871-99)
literature in Anglo-Saxon flourished, some of it written by Alfred
himself. It is interesting to see that this literature is not restricted
to secular works, such as poetry and the Chronicle, but contains
much of a religious nature, including translations of sections of the
bible. Anglo-Saxon was a literary medium, used by many who were
not priests or monks and who apparently did not know Latin, but
who now had access to the key texts of the church. The Norman
invasion in 1066 certainly retarded the spread of this native literature. It was not until the early 13th century that English (as it can
now be called) again revived as a literary language; and the first

king after the Norman conquest who spoke English as his mother tongue was Henry IV (1399-1413).

The selections which follow are all essentially historical writing, mainly because, other than religious writings, these are the main type of works relevant to this period which survive. Passages from William of Malmesbury (c. 1095-1143) and Matthew Paris (d. 1259) have been included here because of their coverage of the Arthurian period. All other passages were written before 1066.

*

The first few passages focus on the records concerning Arthur. In so far as one can piece together anything truly historical about Arthur, he appears to have been of Celtic origin, perhaps amongst those who were still trying to retain something of the Roman civilisation which was fast disappearing, and to have been a key figure in the resistance against the incoming Germanic groups, as well as being a Christian. The likely dates for his activities seem to be around 485-520, but these dates are far from certain. The following passages illustrate the kind of historical material which survives about Arthur, and also show the problems in trying to put together any kind of historically plausible narrative.

Nennius was a Welsh monk who wrote the *Historia Brittonum*, the earliest manuscript of which is securely dated to 828/9. The work is an odd collection (Nennius himself called it 'Excerpta', Selections) of historical, biographical, genealogical and geographical material, but is nevertheless invaluable because we have so little else from this period. His account of Arthur is in fact the earliest we have; neither Gildas nor Bede mention him by name. What follows is the whole of Nennius' account:

2(a)   In illo tempore Saxones invalescebant in multitudine et crescebant in Britannia. Mortuo autem Hengisto, Octha, filius eius, transivit de sinistrali parte Britanniae ad regnum Cantorum, et de ipso orti sunt reges Cantorum. Tunc Arthur pugnabat contra illos in illis

5   diebus cum regibus Brittonum, sed ipse dux erat bellorum. Primum bellum fuit in ostium fluminis quod dicitur Glein. Secundum et tertium et quartum et quintum super aliud flumen, quod dicitur Dubglas, et est in regione Linnuis. Sextum bellum super flumen quod vocatur Bassas. Septimum fuit bellum in silva Celidonis, id est

10   Cat Coit Celidon. Octavum fuit bellum in castello Guinnion, in quo Arthur portavit imaginem sanctae Mariae perpetuae virginis super

humeros suos, et pagani versi sunt in fugam in illo die, et caedes
magna fuit super illos per virtutem Domini nostri Jesu Christi et
per virtutem sanctae Mariae virginis genitricis eius. Nonum bellum
15   gestum est in urbe Legionis. Decimum gessit bellum in litore fluminis quod vocatur Tribruit. Undecimum factum est bellum in
monte qui dicitur Agned. Duodecimum fuit bellum in monte
Badonis, in quo corruerunt in uno die nongenti sexaginta viri de uno
impetu Arthur; et nemo prostravit eos nisi ipse solus, et in omnibus
20   bellis victor extitit. Et ipsi, dum in omnibus bellis prosternebantur,
auxilium a Germania petebant, et augebantur multipliciter sine
intermissione, et reges a Germania deducebant, ut regnarent super
illos in Brittania usque ad tempus quo Ida regnavit, qui fuit Eobba
filius. Ipse fuit primus rex in Beornica, id est in Berneich.

[Nennius, ch. 56; as in *Arthurian Period Sources*, Vol. 8, *Nennius*,
ed. John Morris, Phillimore 1980, p. 76]

The grammar of the Latin is not difficult (though note that Nennius
leaves the name Arthur as an indeclinable noun; in l.19 he must be
genitive), but identifying Nennius' long list of places where Arthur
fought certainly is difficult. Many attempts have been made to
locate these places, but most remain obscure. The River Glein may
be the River Glen in South Lincolnshire, Linnuis may be Lindsey
(part of Lincolnshire), the 'silva Celidonis' is probably in Scotland,
and the 'urbe Legionis' is either Caerleon in South Wales or Chester
(there was a legionary fortress at both places); the rest are even
more doubtful.

In l.1 (**In illo tempore**) and ll.4-5 (**in illis diebus**) we see the
normal Medieval Latin use of **in** with the ablative to express time
'when', whereas Classical Latin would have used the ablative alone.

*

The *Annales Cambriae* (*The Welsh Annals*) were compiled in Wales
in the 10th century. They are organised on a year-by-year basis (and
hence are strictly 'annals') and cover the years 444 (or 447) to 944,
though the dating system is not 'AD' but a numerical sequence
beginning with 'Year I' in 444 or 447; modern editors have added AD
dates as far as these can be reasonably ascertained. For the earlier
years most entries are very brief. The full entry for the year 72
(apparently 516 AD) is given here as found in the oldest manuscript
(Harleian 3859 in the British Museum); notes below refer to two

later manuscripts (B and C) and illustrate the kinds of variation which occur in manuscript texts.

2(b) [516]: LXXII Annus. Bellum Badonis, in quo [1] Arthur portavit crucem Domini nostri Jesu Christi tribus diebus et tribus noctibus [2] in humeros suos [3], et Britones victores fuerunt.

1. Arthurus, C. Rex Arturus, B.
2. Next three words not in C. In humeris suis, B.
3. Following words read: et victor fuit, C; In illo proelio ceciderunt Colgrinus et Radulphus Anglorum duces, B.

[Rolls Series (see Chapter 8: Resources, for bibliographical details), vol. 20, p. 4]

The Battle of Badon is one the few events that all the Arthurian sources link with a supposedly historical Arthur. However, it seems the author of the *Annales Cambriae* had probably not read Nennius' account reproduced above, because his account of the Battle of Badon contains none of the material from Nennius. And did Arthur really carry 'the cross of our Lord Jesus Christ on his shoulders for three days and three nights'?

In l.2 **tribus diebus et tribus noctibus** is an ablative expressing duration of time ('for three days and three nights'), which in Classical Latin would have been done by an accusative.

*

William of Malmesbury in his *De Gestis Regum Anglorum* has a rather different version, which appears to owe rather more to Nennius, though with modifications:

2(c) Sed, eo [i.e. Vortimer, son of Vortigern, both Celtic kings opposing the Germanic invasions] extincto, Britonum robur emarcuit, spes imminutae retro fluxere; et iam tunc profecto pessum issent, nisi Ambrosius, solus Romanorum superstes, qui post Wortigernum
5 monarcha regni fuit, intumescentes barbaros eximia bellicosi Arturis opera pressisset. Hic est Artur de quo Britonum nugae hodieque delirant; dignus plane quem non fallaces somniarent fabulae, sed veraces praedicarent historiae, quippe qui labantem patriam diu sustinuerit, infractasque civium mentes ad bellum
10 acuerit; postremo, in obsessione Badonici montis, fretus imagine

Dominicae matris, quam armis suis insuerat, nongentos hostium solus adorsus incredibili caede profligarit.

[William of Malmesbury, *De Gestis*, ch. 8; as in Rolls Series, vol. 90A, p. 11]

So William of Malmesbury says Arthur had 'an image of the Lord's mother' stitched onto his 'arms' (probably his corslet or maybe his shield). If we look back to Nennius' account (2(a) ll.10-12), this is pretty well what he says Arthur was wearing *at the battle of Fort Guinnion* (wherever that was). The sources seem to have mixed the battles – or maybe Arthur regularly wore a picture of the Virgin Mary, which is not unlikely as a Christian champion fighting heathen Saxons. Incidentally, William of Malmesbury makes the name Arthur into a *third* declension noun: Artur, -is (see ll.5-6).

The Latin is certainly more complex than in the previous passages. The following notes may help.

In l.3 **fluxere** is an alternative form of **fluxerunt**. **-ere** instead of **-erunt** is a common alternative form of the 3rd person plural of the perfect active in both Classical and Medieval Latin.

The second part of the first sentence (ll.3-6) consists of a past unfulfilled condition with two pluperfect subjunctives, **issent** (a shortened form of **ivissent**, from **ire**, to go) and **pressisset** (from **premere**, to crush); the phrase **pessum ire** means 'to go to ruin' and is good Classical Latin.

In ll.7-8 **dignus** is used with following relative clauses with subjunctives, which are in fact purpose clauses, and a very literal translation would be '... clearly worthy whom false tales might not dream about, but true histories might proclaim'. This is followed by **quippe qui** with two subjunctives, a common Classical construction which means 'seeing that [he] ...'.

In l.12 **adorsus** is the past participle of the deponent verb **adorior**, to attack; therefore **adorsus** means 'having attacked'.

In l.12 **profligarit** is a shortened form of **profligaverit**, the perfect subjunctive of **profligare**; these shortened forms, created in Classical times when the 'v' was pronounced as 'w', and often very lightly, are very common in Medieval Latin.

*

Matthew Paris in his *Chronica Maiora* has a much fuller account of Arthur, amounting to several pages of text. However, even though

Matthew is on the whole a reliable historian (see Chapter 6, preliminary note to passage 6(l) for some details of his career), we know that much of his account of Arthur comes from Geoffrey of Monmouth, and Geoffrey is *not* the most reliable of historians. Geoffrey said that he obtained much of his material on the early history of Britain from a Celtic chronicle given to him by Walter, Archdeacon of Oxford, who had brought it from Brittany, but nobody else ever saw this book and it is quite possible it never existed. Even if it did, it appears from what Geoffrey took from it that much of it was of dubious historical value. So although Matthew Paris has much interesting information purporting to be real history about Arthur and his times, one has to suspend judgement about it. That is not to say that this is all fictional. There may well be a historical foundation for much of what Geoffrey and Matthew record, and Matthew does try to extract the historically probable from Geoffrey's more fanciful stories; but the details remain for the most part unverifiable. The two following excerpts contain Matthew Paris's account of Arthur's battles against the Saxons in Lincolnshire and Scotland, and also the Battle of Badon, whose location continues to be disputed. As we have seen, there are at least independent sources indicating that Arthur did fight in these areas.

2(d) *De victoria Arthuri in monte Colidonis*

Anno gratiae DXVIII. Bonefacius sedit in cathedra Romana duobus annis et diebus septem. Per idem tempus Arthurus, rex Britonum, collecto exercitu grandi, urbem Kaerlindcoit, quae nunc Lincolnia dicitur, petivit, ubi inventis Saxonibus inauditam ex eis stragem
5   fecit; ceciderunt namque ex eis una die sex milia hominum, qui partim fluminibus submersi, partim telis perforati, partim in fugiendo trucidati, vitam miserabiliter finierunt. Arthurus vero fugientes insecutus non cessavit, donec ad nemus Colidonis pervenerunt, ibique ex fuga confluentes Arthuro resistere conati sunt, sese
10   viriliter defendentes; quod Arthurus intuens, iussit arbores circa partem illam nemoris incidi, et truncos ita in circuitu locari, ut egressus eis penitus negaretur; volebat namque eos ibidem diu obsidere, donec omnes inedia interirent. At Saxones, quo vescerentur non habentes, eo pacto petierunt egressum ut saltem nudis
15   corporibus Germaniam petere sinerentur. Tunc Arthurus, quaesito consilio, petitioni eorum adquievit, retinens eorum opes, et spolia, reddendique vectigal obsides, solummodo recessum concessit.

2. The Anglo-Saxon Period

[Matthew Paris, *Chronica Maiora* for the year DXVIII; as in Rolls Series, vol. 57A, pp. 234-5]

Matthew changes the grammar of Arthur's name yet again and makes the name into a *second* declension noun, Arthurus. The name Kaerlindcoit is also interesting. 'Lind' was apparently the pre-Roman native Celtic name for what became Lincoln. The Romans made this into **Lindum** to give it a workable Latin ending, and since a colony of veteran legionaries was established there it became known as 'Lindum Colonia', which accounts for the modern spelling, since the Saxon settlers used the Latin name and not the Celtic name of the town. Matthew (l.3) gives the post-Roman Celtic name, which consists of Lind prefixed with Kaer, which is the Celtic version of the Latin **castra** (camp, legionary fortress, which Lincoln had been, though only for a few years from about 60 to 75) and suffixed with the word 'coit', which means wood or forest (the modern Welsh 'coed'). The story as told here (essentially as in Geoffrey of Monmouth) does at least look historically feasible.

Matthew Paris has a great liking for participles as a way of stringing clauses together, and this also leads him to make frequent use of the ablative absolute. In this passage he has the following ablative absolutes:

    collecto exercitu grandi (l.3)
    inventis Saxonibus (l.4)
    quaesito consilio (ll.15-16)

and there are eleven other participles (present, e.g. **confluentes**, l.9, 'coming together', **intuens**, l.10, 'seeing'; and perfect, e.g. **inauditam**, l.4, 'unheard of, unprecedented', **submersi**, l.6, 'drowned').

In ll.1-2 **duobus annis et diebus septem** is another example of the use of the ablative to express duration of time, where Classical Latin would have used the accusative.

Matthew also shows a very careful use of **donec**. In l.8 it is followed by an indicative (**donec ... pervenerunt**), 'until they [actually] arrived'; but at l.13 it has the subjunctive (**donec ... interirent**), 'until they died ...', here expressing purpose or anticipation. This distinction between the use of the indicative and subjunctive after **donec** (or **dum** or **quoad**) is a standard classical usage.

In l.17 the gerund **reddendi** is genitive dependent on **obsides**; a literal translation would be 'hostages of paying tribute', i.e. hostages to ensure tribute was paid.

2(e)　　　　　　*De admiranda pugna regis Arthuri contra Saxones*

Anno Gratiae DXX. Paenituit Colgrinum, Baldulfum et Cheldricum, Saxones, pactum cum Arthuro fecisse; unde in Britanniam revertentes in Totonesio litore appulerunt, et ad ultimum urbem Badonis obsederunt. Rumore itaque divulgato, Arthurus obsides eorum sus-
5　pendi praecepit; deinde obsidionem petens praecepit omnibus ad arma convolare; ipse lorica indutus galeam simulacro draconis insculptam capiti adaptavit; humeris quoque suis clipeum vocabulo Pridwen appendit, quo imago sanctae Dei genitricis depicta, ipsam ad memoriam eius saepissime revocabat; accinctus etiam Cali-
10　burnio gladio optimo, lancea nomine Rou eius dexteram decoravit. Dein catervis dispositis audacter paganos invasit; ipsi die tota viriliter resistentes, Britones assidue prosternebant. Vergente tandem ad occasum sole, Saxones proximum occupant montem, illum pro castro habituri; at ubi sol posterus diem reduxisset, Arthurus
15　cum exercitu suo montis cacumen ascendit; sed in ascendendo multos suorum amisit, Saxones namque ex alto occurrentes facilius vulnera infligebant. Britanni tamen maxima probitate cacumen montis adepti, hostibus strages acerrimas ingerebant; quibus Saxones pectora praetendentes omni nisu resistere perstiterunt.
20　Cumque multum diei in certando consumpsissent, Arthurus, tandem abstracto Caliburnio gladio, nomen beatae Mariae virginis invocavit, atque cito impetu sese infra densas hostium acies immittens, quemcumque attingebat solo ictu perimebat; nec cessavit impetum facere, donec octingentos quadraginta viros solo gladio
25　interfecit. Ceciderunt ilico Colgrinus et Baldulfus frater eius, et cum eis multa milia barbarorum; at Cheldricus, viso sociorum periculo, cum reliquiis exercitus in fugam conversus est. Iussit itaque rex Cadorem Cornubiae ducem illos insequi, qui postremo, cum nihil tutaminis accessisset, laceratis agminibus Thanet insulam
30　petierunt. Insequitur eos ibidem dux, nec quievit donec, perempto Cheldrico, ceteros in deditionem accepit. Eodem anno Ioannes sedit in cathedra Romana annis duobus.

[Matthew Paris, *Chronica Maiora* for the year 520; as in Rolls Series, vol. 57A, pp. 235-6]

A good story, told in elegant Latin, again essentially from Geoffrey of Monmouth. We see an elaboration of Arthur's armour compared with the earlier sources, though the image of the Virgin Mary remains. The numbers killed by Arthur have varied in the different sources, but they have remained around the 900 mark, though now his magic sword seems to be a dominant feature. In fact all Arthur's weapons now have romantic names, and when a little later in both Geoffrey of Monmouth and Matthew Paris we read that Arthur went on to conquer Ireland, Iceland, Jutland and the Orkneys, all apparently in the year 525, credibility is strained. But it's a good story.

We can again see Matthew's fondness for participles, this time including a future participle, **habituri**, l.14, 'intending to hold ...'.

In this passage there are seven ablative absolutes, at lines 4, 11, 12-13, 21, 26, 29, and 30-1.

A point of vocabulary worth noting is that the noun **obses**, gen. **obsidis**, m/f means 'hostage' (or sometimes 'pledge, security'), whereas the verb **obsideo, obsidere, obsedi, obsessum** means 'to besiege', with the noun **obsessio, -onis**, f., a siege, derived from it. All three are common words in descriptions of medieval warfare, and all are used here in ll.4-5.

*

Before we leave Arthur, it is worth mentioning two passages in Gildas, the monk who wrote his *De Excidio Britonum* c. 540 in South Wales. Though he does not mention Arthur by name, he does mention the Battle of Badon:

2(f)   Ex eo tempore nunc cives, nunc hostes vincebant, ut in ista gente experiretur Dominus solito more praesentem Israelem, utrum diligat eum an non; usque ad annum obsessionis Badonici Montis, novissimaeque ferme de furciferis non minimae stragis, quique
5   quadragesimus quartus (ut novi) orditur annus mense iam uno emenso, qui et meae nativitatis est.

[Gildas 26.1; as in *Arthurian Period Sources*, Vol. 7, Gildas, ed. John Morris, Phillimore 1978, p. 98]

Gildas appears to confirm that the Battle of Badon was the last battle in which the native Britons fought the Germanic invaders, as Nennius also implies. If the Latin of the last two lines means that the Battle of Badon took place 44 years before Gildas was actually writing this, in the year when he was born, then either the battle took place around 500, and not 516 (as in the *Annales Cambriae*) or 520 (as in Matthew Paris), or we have the wrong date at which Gildas wrote this work. The latter seems unlikely, so the evidence seems to favour this earlier date for the Battle of Badon. Even in this short excerpt one can see the rhetorical style of Gildas.

*

The next passage is even more allusive; Gildas is here addressing in condemnatory fashion a local ruler called Cynglas (Cuneglasus):

2(g)   Ut quid in nequitiae tuae volveris vetusta faece et tu ab adolescentiae annis, urse, multorum sessor aurigaque currus receptaculi ursi, Dei contemptor sortisque eius depressor, Cuneglase, Romana lingua lanio fulve?

[Gildas 32.1; John Morris, op. cit., p. 101]

Cynglas was a contemporary of Gildas, and Gildas clearly did not think much of him. But what are the references to 'bears' all about? We know that several Celtic kings took the name of an animal as a title, and it seems Cynglas had the title of 'Bear'. Now the name Arthur also appears to mean 'Bear', from the Celtic root ARTH, which is still the word for bear in modern Welsh. However, Cynglas can hardly be Arthur, who would by this time have been at least in his eighties if he had been alive; and Gildas, later in this same passage, criticises Cynglas for having an affair with his wife's sister (who incidentally was a nun). But Cynglas is called 'the charioteer of the stronghold of the Bear', which may mean that Cynglas was the successor of Arthur and kept the same title. Tenuous, but possible.

In the first line Gildas has used a perfect subjunctive (**volveris**) after **ut quid** (a not uncommon expression for 'why?'). The sense appears to be simply 'Why have you indulged in ...?'

*

The remaining passages are taken from Bede (673-735), who spent most of his life at the monastery at Jarrow on the south bank of the Tyne. His *Historia Ecclesiastica Gentis Anglorum* is only one of some 40 works written by him; the others contain commentaries on scripture, lives of saints, lives of abbots, and even a book on Natural Science. He writes excellent Latin, if a little florid at times.

The following are well known stories from Bede's *Historia*, and they well illustrate his style and his interests. He enjoyed narrative, especially with a few touches of the miraculous or the prophetic. However, Bede's Latin can be difficult, and it might be useful to list a few characteristics of his style before we embark on these passages:

- he likes long sentences, with several 'when ...', 'because ...' 'after ...' clauses, and often with two or more main clauses joined together by 'and', 'but', 'however', and so on; they are best dealt with clause by clause, and in translation they are often best split into two or more sentences in English;
- he often deliberately separates words which grammatically go together. This was a feature of many Classical Latin authors, and Bede has a particular liking for it; it can make sorting out some of his more complex sentences yet more difficult. See the first grammatical note on the next passage;
- he often uses 'connecting relative' clauses, i.e. **qui** clauses which simply link two main clauses together. These are usually best translated by '[And] he/they ...' rather than by a relative clause in English;
- he uses a very wide vocabulary, often deliberately using different words for the same idea to add variety, e.g. the different words for 'coffin' in passages 2(l) and 2(m) (see also the note after passage 2(l));
- he has a liking for rather flowery language, especially when describing religious sentiments. Expect God, saints and miracles to be accompanied by plenty of it.

The texts are taken from B. Colgrave and R.A.B. Mynors, *Bede's Ecclesiastical History*, Oxford 1969, with some slight modifications to spelling and punctuation.

2(h)   *St Gregory and the Angles*

Nec silentio praetereunda opinio quae de beato Gregorio traditione maiorum ad nos usque perlata est, qua videlicet ex causa admonitus tam sedulam erga salutem nostrae gentis curam gesserit. Dicunt quia die quadam cum, advenientibus nuper mercatoribus, multa
5 venalia in forum fuissent conlata, multi ad emendum confluxissent, et ipsum Gregorium inter alios advenisse ac vidisse inter alia pueros venales positos, candidi corporis ac venusti vultus, capillorum quoque forma egregia. Quos cum aspiceret, interrogavit, ut aiunt, de qua regione vel terra essent adlati; dictumque est quia de Brittania
10 insula, cuius incolae talis essent aspectus. Rursus interrogavit ut-

rum idem insulani Christiani, an paganis adhuc erroribus essent
implicati. Dictum est quod essent pagani. At ille, intimo ex corde
longa trahens suspiria, 'Heu, pro dolor!' inquit, 'quod tam lucidi
vultus homines tenebrarum auctor possidet, tantaque gratia fron-
15 tispicii mentem ab interna gratia vacuam gestat!' Rursus ergo
interrogavit quod esset vocabulum gentis illius. Responsum est
quod Angli vocarentur. At ille, 'Bene,' inquit, 'nam et angelicam
habent faciem, et tales angelorum in caelis decet esse coheredes.
Quod habet nomen ipsa provincia de qua isti sunt adlati?' Respon-
20 sum est quia Deiri vocarentur idem provinciales. At ille, 'Bene,'
inquit, 'Deiri, de ira eruti, et ad misericordiam Christi vocati. Rex
provinciae illius quomodo appellatur?' Responsum est quod Aelli
diceretur. At ille adludens ad nomen ait, 'Alleluia! Laudem Dei
Creatoris illis in partibus oportet cantari.'

[Bede, *Hist*. 2.1]

This incident took place in the 580s. Gregory became Pope in 590
and sent Augustine and others to Britain to evangelise the Angles
and Saxons in 597.

In this passage (and in all the others) there are several examples
of Bede's habit of separating words which go closely together in
sense, for instance:
    sedulam ... **curam** (l.3)
    talis ... **aspectus** (l.10)
    paganis ... **erroribus** (l.11)
    angelorum ... **coheredes** (l.18)
In ll.3-8 Bede has a rather complex series of indirect statements,
which he begins with **Dicunt quia** ... followed by two pluperfect
subjunctives, but then at the beginning of line 6 he switches to the
accusative and infinitive construction, ... **ipsum Gregorium** ...
advenisse ac vidisse; actually Bede, as nearly all medieval writers
of Latin, much preferred the **quod** or **quia** construction, and he
reverts to this in lines 9 and 12. From l.13 he introduces direct
speech, using the classical **inquit** each time, which is Bede's habit.

In l.8 is a 'connecting relative', '**Quos** ...' – 'When he saw *them* ...'

Each time Bede uses **interrogavit** (ll.8, 10, 16) he follows it with
the subjunctive, the normal rule for indirect questions in both
Classical and Medieval Latin (though less able writers often forget
and use the indicative).

34

*

The following story of Caedmon is quite long; we shall take it in three parts.

2(i) *Caedmon (I)*

In huius monasterio abbatissae fuit frater quidam divina gratia specialiter insignis, quia carmina religioni et pietati apta facere solebat; ita ut quicquid ex divinis litteris per interpretes disceret, hoc ipse post pusillum verbis poeticis maxima suavitate et compunc-
5 tione compositis, in sua, id est Anglorum lingua proferret. Cuius carminibus multorum saepe animi ad contemptum saeculi, et appetitum sunt vitae caelestis accensi. Et quidem et alii post illum in gente Anglorum religiosa poemata facere tentabant, sed nullus eum aequiperare potuit. Namque ipse non ab hominibus, neque per
10 hominem institutus canendi artem didicit, sed divinitus adiutus gratis canendi donum accepit. Unde nil unquam frivoli et super-vacui poematis facere potuit, sed ea tantummodo quae ad religionem pertinent, religiosam eius linguam decebant. Siquidem in habitu saeculari usque ad tempora provectioris aetatis constitutus
15 nil carminum aliquando didicerat. Unde nonnumquam in convivio, cum esset laetitiae causa decretum ut omnes per ordinem cantare deberent, ille ubi adpropinquare sibi citharam cernebat, surgebat a media caena et egressus ad suam domum repedabat.

[Bede, *Hist.* 4.24]

Bede does not tell the story from the beginning, so to speak, but gives a brief sketch of Caedmon as a monk with poetic powers before telling the story of how he acquired them.

In l.1 **huius** modifies **abbatissae**; this is the famous Hild (or Hilda), who was abbess of Whitby 657-680. She was at Whitby when the great Synod took place in 664. Another example of Bede's liking for the separation of words which are grammatically linked, as is **carmina** ... **apta** in l.2.

In l.5 is another 'connecting relative', '**Cuius** ...' – '... by *his* songs ...'.

In ll.6-7 **sunt** forms a perfect passive with **accensi**, and another **ad** has to be assumed before **appetitum**.

In l.10, **divinitus**, despite its apparently adjectival ending, is an adverb ('divinely, from heaven').

In l.12 **poematis** could be genitive singular of **poema** (the word is of Greek origin) and intended to be read as 'poetry', though the word normally means 'poem'. But Bede most probably intended it as a 2nd declension ablative plural with the sense 'in his poems'.

*

2(j)   *Caedmon (II)*

Quod dum tempore quodam faceret, et relicta domo convivii egressus esset ad stabula iumentorum quorum ei custodia nocte illa erat delegata, ibique hora competenti membra dedisset sopori, adstitit ei quidam per somnium, eumque salutans, ac suo appellans nomine,
5 'Caedmon,' inquit, 'canta mihi aliquid.' At ille respondens, 'Nescio,' inquit, 'cantare; nam et ideo de convivio egressus huc secessi, quia cantare non poteram.' Rursus ille qui cum eo loquebatur, 'Attamen,' ait, 'mihi cantare habes.' 'Quid,' inquit, 'debeo cantare?' At ille, 'Canta,' inquit, 'principium creaturarum.' Quo accepto responso,
10 statim ipse coepit cantare in laudem Dei Conditoris versus, quos nunquam audierat, quorum iste est sensus: 'Nunc laudare debemus auctorem regni caelestis, potentiam Creatoris, et consilium illius, facta Patris gloriae; quomodo ille, cum sit aeternus Deus, omnium miraculorum auctor extitit; qui primo filiis hominum caelum pro
15 culmine tecti, dehinc terram custos humani generis omnipotens creavit.' Hic est sensus, non autem ordo ipse verborum quae dormiens ille canebat. Neque enim possunt carmina, quamvis optime composita, ex alia in aliam linguam ad verbum sine detrimento sui decoris ac dignitatis transferri. Exsurgens autem a somno, cuncta
20 quae dormiens cantaverat memoriter retinuit, et eis mox plura in eundem modum verba Deo digni carminis adiunxit.

[Bede, *Hist.* 4.24 (continued)]

Bede often uses **dum** to mean 'when' as well as 'while'. In ll.1-3 **dum** introduces three subjunctives, but the translation 'while' would be appropriate only for the first.

Competenti in l.3 is a 'faux ami'; it means 'proper, appropriate', not 'competent'.

Ait in l.8 is an alternative to **inquit**, used only with direct speech.

Also in l.8 Bede uses **habere** with an infinitive. This can be used in three ways in Medieval Latin. For instance, the phrase (**aliquid**)

dicere habeo can mean 'I have something to say'; *or* it could mean 'I shall say something', simply substituting for a future (and this is the origin of the future tense in most Romance languages, which use the infinitive with the present tense of the verb 'to have' appended to it); *or* it could mean 'I must say something' (as in French 'J'ai à travailler', 'I have to, must work', linked in meaning with the first option illustrated here). In this case any of the three senses is possible, either 'You have something to sing to me', or 'You will (or perhaps more emphatically 'You shall') sing to me', or 'You must sing to me.'

Near the end of l.8 **At** is here a fairly weak conjunction (as often in Bede); 'but' would not be an appropriate translation here. It is worth noting that Latin uses conjunctions to link sentences in this way rather more often than English does.

Extitit (from **existo**) in l.14 is a common alternative for **esse** ('to be').

In ll.16-19 Bede gives a very clear summary of the problems of translating poetry. His own language was, of course, Anglo-Saxon, but he knew Greek as well as Latin, and so was familiar enough with the problems of translation.

The word order of the last clause (ll.20-1) needs careful attention. **Eis** is 'to these' [he added]; **plura** modifies **verba** ('more [in the same style] words'); **carminis** is dependent on **verba** and **Deo** is ablative with **digni** (in English 'worthy *of*') – '... words of poetry worthy of God'.

We actually possess the Anglo-Saxon words of Caedmon for this hymn, given here in the Northumbrian dialect which is most probably the dialect Caedmon spoke (later manuscripts use other dialects; this became a popular poem and was transcribed into the local dialect of different areas). It is interesting to see how well Bede translated them.

Nu scylun hergan   hefaenricaes Uard,
Metudaes maecti   end His modgidanc,
uerc Uuldurfadur,   sue He uundra gihuaes,
eci Dryctin,   or astelidae.
He aerist scop   aelda barnum
heben til hrofe,   haleg Scepen.
Tha middungeard   moncynnaes Uard,
eci Dryctin,   aefter tiadae
firum foldu,   Frea allmectig.

The following is a fairly literal line-by-line translation:

Now must we praise	the Guardian of heaven,
The might of the Creator	and His purpose,
The works of the Father of Glory,	as He of every wonder,
the eternal Lord,	established the beginning.
He first shaped	for the children of men
heaven for a roof,	the holy Maker.
Then the earth	the Guardian of mankind,
the eternal Lord,	afterwards prepared
a land for men,	the almighty Ruler.

So Bede seems to have done a very good job! Unfortunately this is the only poem which can confidently be ascribed to Caedmon, though others bear his name.

*

2(k) *Caedmon (III)*

Veniensque mane ad vilicum qui sibi praeerat, quid doni percepisset indicavit, atque ad abbatissam perductus, iussus est, multis doctioribus viris praesentibus, indicare somnium et dicere carmen, ut universorum iudicio quid vel unde esset quod referebat probaretur.
5 Visumque est omnibus, caelestem ei a Domino concessam esse gratiam. Exponebantque illi quendam sacrae historiae sive doctrinae sermonem, praecipientes ei, si posset, hunc in modulationem carminis transferre. At ille suscepto negotio abiit, et mane rediens optimo carmine quod iubebatur compositum reddidit. Unde mox
10 abbatissa amplexata gratiam Dei in viro, saecularem illum habitum relinquere, et monachicum suscipere propositum docuit, susceptumque in monasterium cum omnibus suis fratrum cohorti adsociavit, iussitque illum seriem sacrae historiae doceri. At ipse cuncta quae audiendo discere poterat, rememorando secum et quasi mun-
15 dum animal, ruminando, in carmen dulcissimum convertebat, suaviusque resonando, doctores suos vicissim auditores sui faciebat. Canebat autem de creatione mundi, et origine humani generis, et tota Genesis historia, de egressu Israel ex Aegypto et ingressu in terram repromissionis, de aliis plurimis sacrae scripturae historiis,
20 de incarnatione Dominica, passione, resurrectione, et ascensione in caelum, de Spiritus Sanci adventu, et apostolorum doctrina. Item de terrore futuri iudicii, et horrore poenae Gehennalis, ac dulcedine regni caelestis multa carmina faciebat; sed et alia perplura de

25 beneficiis et iudiciis divinis, in quibus cunctis homines ab amore scelerum abstrahere, ad dilectionem vero et sollertiam bonae actionis excitare curabat. Erat enim vir multum religiosus, et regularibus disciplinis humiliter subditus, adversum vero illos qui aliter facere volebant, zelo magni fervoris accensus; unde et pulchro vitam suam fine conclusit.

[Bede, *Hist.* 4.24 (continued)]

The compounds of **fero**, **ferre**, **tuli**, **latum** ('to bring, carry') are very common in all forms of Latin, both with literal meanings associated with movement and with extended, more metaphorical meanings. In this passage there is **referebat** at l.4, which can have the literal meaning of 'bring back', but just as frequently means (as here) 'report, repeat', or even 'mention, refer [to]' – the last, of course, deriving from this usage. There is also **transferre** at l.8 (which also occurred in 2(j) l.19), and again this word can have the literal meaning of 'carry across', but just as often means 'translate' from one language or medium to another (as here); the English is derived from the perfect participle, as one often finds in verbal derivatives.

In l.5 **caelestem** describes **gratiam** – with five words in between; but we are quite used to this by now! In ll.6-7 **quendam** modifies **sermonem** – with four words between.

In ll.14-16 Bede uses four gerunds in the ablative case, **audiendo** (by listening), **rememorando** (by turning over in his mind), **ruminando** (by ruminating; it also has the extended meaning of 'thinking over', as in English), and **resonando** (literally, 'by resounding'; here perhaps 'by repeating').

Mundus is a word to note carefully. Its commonest meaning (at least in Medieval Latin) is 'world', and it has this meaning at l.17 in this passage. But **mundus-a-um** as an adjective means 'clean, neat, tidy', and this is the meaning at ll.14-15. The reference here is to Jewish law, in which ruminant and cloven-footed animals are 'clean'. There is also a verb **mundare** (to clean, tidy) and a noun **munditia** (cleanness, neatness). The noun **mundus** is possibly linked with the root of **mundare** in the sense of 'putting in order'; the Greek word for world, *kosmos*, is likewise linked with the Greek verb *kosmeo*, to adorn, or to arrange.

In l.16 **sui** is not a possessive adjective qualifying **auditores**, which is anyhow accusative, the direct object of **faciebat**, but the genitive of the pronoun **se**, literally [hearers] 'of himself'.

In l.22 **Gehannalis** refers to the Hebrew word Gehenna, which means hell.

Vero (ll.25 and 27) is often difficult to translate accurately. Basically the word is an adverb from **verus** and therefore means 'truly, surely, in fact', but it is much more often used to indicate a contrast, with the meaning 'but, however, though, and in fact', and in this contrastive sense it never comes first in its clause but always follows a word or phrase, as in these cases.

*

Bede wrote a separate *Life of Cuthbert*, which still survives, but the *Ecclesiastical History* also contains many details about Cuthbert's life, death and bodily remains. Cuthbert lived from about 634 to 687, and Bede was therefore 14 years old when Cuthbert died, but there is no evidence that Bede ever met him, although Cuthbert was Bishop of Lindisfarne only 60 miles from Jarrow. The following story is taken from ch. 30 of book IV of his *Ecclesiastical History*, though most of it is also to be found in the *Life of Cuthbert*, chs. 42-3 (see Bede's own note at the end of this account). We shall take it in two parts.

2(1)   *Cuthbert (I)*

Volens autem latius demonstrare divina dispensatio, quanta in gloria vir Domini Cudberct post mortem viveret, cuius ante mortem vita sublimis crebris etiam miraculorum patebat indiciis, transactis sepulturae eius annis undecim, immisit in animo fratrum ut toller-
5   ent ossa illius, quae more mortuorum, consumpto iam et in pul-verem redacto corpore reliquo, sicca invenienda putabant; atque in novo recondita loculo, in eodem quidem loco, sed supra pavimentum dignae venerationis gratia locarent. Quod dum sibi placuisse Ead-bercto antistiti suo referrent, adnuit consilio eorum, iussitque ut die
10 depositionis eius hoc facere meminissent. Fecerunt autem ita; et aperientes sepulcrum, invenerunt corpus totum quasi adhuc viveret integrum, et flexilibus artuum compagibus multo dormienti quam mortuo similius; sed et vestimenta omnia quibus indutum erat, non solum intemerata, verum etiam prisca novitate et claritudine mi-
15 randa parebant. Quod ubi videre fratres, nimio mox timore perculsi, festinaverunt referre antistiti quae invenerant, qui tum forte in remotiore ab ecclesia loco refluis undique pelagi fluctibus cincto, solitarius manebat. In hoc etenim semper Quadragesimae tempus

20 agere, in hoc quadraginta ante Dominicum natale dies in magna
continentiae, orationis et lacrimarum devotione transigere solebat;
in quo etiam venerabilis praedecessor eius Cudberct priusquam
insulam Farne peteret, aliquandiu secretus Domino militabat.

[Bede, *Hist.* 4.30]

In the first four lines the subject is **divina dispensatio** (Divine
Providence); this is still the subject of **immisit in animo** ... in l.4.

Latin has a good range of funerary vocabulary. **Loculus** (literally
'little place') in l.7, **arca** (literally 'box') in the following passage, l.5
and l.18, and **theca** (a Greek word meaning basically a box), also in
the following passage, l.12, are all used to mean 'coffin'.

In l.8 the phrase **sibi placuisse** means literally 'that it pleased
them', but the phrase **mihi placet** ('it pleases me') is used to
indicate 'it is my wish, opinion, view'. The **quod** is a link with the
previous sentence, so this might be translated 'When they reported
to ... that this (**quod**) was what they wanted ...'.

There are again numerous cases in this passage where Bede
separates words which are grammatically linked, e.g.

> **corpus** ... **integrum** ... **similius** (ll.11-13; **similius** is the
> neuter singular of the comparative of **similis** – 'more like')
> **remotiore** ... **loco** ... **cincto** (l.17)
> **in magna** ... **devotione** (ll.19-20)

*

2(m) *Cuthbert (II)*

Adtulerunt autem ei et partem indumentorum quae corpus sanctum
ambierant; quae cum ille et munera gratanter acciperet et miracula
libenter audiret, nam et ipsa indumenta quasi patris adhuc corpori
circumdata miro deosculabatur affectu, 'Nova,' inquit, 'indumenta
5 corpori pro his quae tulistis circumdate, et sic reponite in arca quam
parastis. Scio autem certissime quia non diu vacuus remanebit locus
ille, qui tanta miraculi caelestis gratia sacratus est; et quam beatus
est cui in eo facultatem quiescendi Dominus totius beatitudinis
auctor atque largitor praestare dignabitur.' Haec et huiusmodi
10 plura ubi multis cum lacrimis et magna compunctione antistes
lingua etiam tremente complevit, fecerunt fratres ut iusserat, et
involutum novo amictu corpus novaque in theca reconditum, supra
pavimentum sanctuarii posuerunt. Nec mora, Deo dilectus antistes
Eadberct morbo corruptus est acerbo, ac per dies crescente mul-

15　tumque ingravescente ardore languoris, non multo post, id est
pridie nonas Maias, etiam ipse migravit ad Dominum; cuius corpus
in sepulcro benedicti patris Cudbercti ponentes, adposuerunt desu-
per arcam in qua incorrupta eiusdem patris membra locaverant; in
quo etiam loco signa sanitatum aliquoties facta meritis amborum
20　testimonium ferunt, e quibus aliqua in libro Vitae illius olim
memoriae mandavimus. Sed et in hac Historia quaedam quae nos
nuper audisse contigit, superadicere commodum duximus.

[Bede, *Hist.* 4.30]

The first four lines are a complex construction. The sentence begins
with a main clause '**Adtulerunt** ...', 'They brought to him ...' Then
in l.2 **quae** modifies both **munera** and **miracula**, and the **cum** is
followed by two subjunctives, **acciperet** and **audiret** – 'when he
was thankfully receiving these (**quae**) gifts and listening willingly
to these miracles ...'. Then the clause beginning with **nam** is in-
serted as if in brackets (literally 'for he was kissing the garments
themselves with obvious feeling ...'). This is followed by a further
main clause '... **inquit** ...' – '... he said ...'. Not an easy start – and
the rest is not much easier! Follow the translation very carefully in
this one. There are again many examples of the deliberate separation of words which are grammatically linked, e.g.

　　patris ... **corpori** (l.3)
　　miro ... **affectu** (l.4)
　　tanta ... **gratia** (l.7)
　　morbo ... **acerbo** (l.14)
　　incorrupta ... **membra** (l.18)

In l.6 **parastis** is a shortened form of **paravistis** – 'you have
prepared'.

In l.13 **nec mora** (also **haud mora**) is a common idiomatic
phrase for 'and without delay'.

In l.16 Bede uses the Roman calendar system. The 'Nones' of May
is the 7th of the month, and **pridie** is the day before.

In l.22 **audisse** is a shortened form of **audivisse**.

Also in l.22 Bede uses **ducere** (**duximus**) to mean 'to think,
consider'; this is a frequent use, especially with an accusative adjective such as **commodum**, 'we have thought it fitting, appropriate'.

*

During this period, then, Latin continued to be used in Britain as the language of the church and also for some historical records, though these were always written by churchmen; few outside the church used Latin, and when literacy did spread outside the church, mainly from Alfred's reign onwards, it was more often in Anglo-Saxon than in Latin, as we see in the Anglo-Saxon Chronicle, in the prose secular literature, and in most of the wills, charters and laws. And many churchmen wrote in Anglo-Saxon as well as in Latin. But Latin was never in any danger of falling out of use in Britain during this period. It was the intellectual language not only of the church and of theology but of the culture of western Europe, and was to remain so until the national languages of Europe developed sufficient literary competence to replace it.

Grants, Deeds, and Other Legal and Ecclesiastical Documents

Most city, county and diocesan archives contain numerous examples of grants, deeds and quitclaims associated with land transactions, and also copies of wills and inventories of goods which are often part of the records of such transactions. Financial documents of various kinds survive in manorial records, in local, national and ecclesiastical archives, and also among family records. The language of most of these documents is highly formulaic, and the style and structure is remarkably consistent throughout Britain (and indeed throughout western Europe) and throughout the later Middle Ages. A major sub-category is those documents dealing with church lands and goods, and these contain some specifically ecclesiastical phraseology, as will be seen in several of the passages below. Linguistically (or to be more precise, syntactically) grants, deeds, quitclaims, wills, inventories and accounts are usually uncomplicated and amongst the easier documents in Medieval Latin – though there are exceptions!

The first document has been chosen because it illustrates very well the usual formulas found in grants and deeds, and these we shall analyse in some detail so that the structure of such documents can be seen. This deed comes from the cartulary (the register of deeds) of Selby Abbey (*Cartularium Abbathiae S. Germani de Seleby*, vol. 2, published by the Yorkshire Archaeological Association, Record Series vol. 13, 1892), and dates from around 1250. It refers to a grant of land in Stallingborough near Grimsby. It was brought to my attention because the grant appears to have been made by one of my own ancestors.

3(a)   *Carta Gaufridi de Thorlay*

Sciant presentes et futuri quod ego Gaufridus de Thorlay dedi concessi et hac presenti carta mea confirmavi Sarae filiae meae et heredibus suis quattuor bovatas terrae cum meo mesuagio ad eas

pertinente in territorio de Stalingburg, cum pratis et cum pasturis
5   et cum omnibus aliis aisiamentis infra praedictam villam et extra,
illas scilicet quattuor bovatas terrae cum pertinenciis quas tenui de
Gilberto de Turribus; habendum et tenendum de me et heredibus
meis in feodo et hereditate, libere et solute, quiete et pacifice,
reddendo inde annuatim michi et heredibus sex solidos pro omni
10   servicio, videlicet ad festum Sancti Botulfi tres solidos, et ad festum
Sancti Andreae tres solidos. Praeterea dedi concessi et hac presenti
carta mea confirmavi eidem Sarae et heredibus suis terciam partem
duarum bovatarum terrae in territorio predicto cum omnibus pertinenciis, illam scilicet partem quam Matilda filia Roberti quondam
15   tenuit; habendum et tenendum libere, solute et quiete, absque omni
servicio, salvo forinseco servicio. Et ego et heredes mei warantizabimus totam predictam terram cum omnibus pertinenciis suis
predictae Sarae et heredibus suis versus omnes homines imperpetuum. His testibus: Gaufrido Neuil, Thoma de Turribus, etc.

[Document MXXVI; op. cit., p. 187]

The opening lines in transcription from the original with abbreviations actually read:

> Sc. praes. et fut. quod ego Gaufridus de Thorlay d. c. et h. p. c.
> m. conf. Sarae, filiae meae et her. s. iiijor bovatas terrae ...

From l.11 the same abbreviated forms are used again:
> Praeterea d. c. et h. p. c. m. conf. eidem Sarae et her. s. terciam
> partem ...

And at the end, l.16 ff.:
> Et ego et her. m. war. totam praed. terram cum omn. pert. s.
> praed. Sarae et her. s. versus omnes homines imperpetuum.
> H. t. ...

The rest of the text is written out more or less as transcribed above,
with the abbreviation only of words such as **her.**(-edibus) and
s.(-uis), **habend.**(-um) **et tenend.**(-um). Once one knows what the
formulae are there is little problem in reconstructing the full text.

    l.1: **Sciant presentes et futuri** ... A regular opening formula.
Common variations are:

> **Notum sit omnibus** (OR **tam presentibus quam futuris**)
>   ... (Let it be known to all OR to both present and future)
> **Sciant universi** ... (Let all know ...)
> **Noverint universi** ... (Let all know ...)

This is followed EITHER by

> **quod ego** [name] **dedi concessi et hac presenti carta mea confirmavi** (or similar) …

OR by an accusative and infinitive construction,

> **me** [name] **dedisse concessisse et hac presenti carta mea confirmavisse** [or the shortened form **confirmasse**]

1.2: Then follows a dative to indicate the person who is the recipient of the grant, in this case **Sarae filiae meae et heredibus suis**.

ll.3-7: This is followed by the goods granted in the accusative, here **quattuor bovatas** …, but this will often be extended, as here, by **cum** … There will also often be participial phrases, e.g. **in** … **iacentes**, to indicate where the property is located, and the phrase **cum pertinenciis** is almost obligatory. It is also very common to find a phrase such as **quas tenuit** [name], as here, to indicate the previous owner and thereby to identify the property more securely.

A bovate is an 'oxgang', the amount of land attributed to one ox out of a ploughing team of eight. It was about 13 acres, one eighth of a 'carucate', which was the land a whole team of eight oxen could cope with in a year (around 100 acres).

1.7: **Gilberto de Turribus** is Gilbert of Tours, in France, obviously a Norman lord.

ll.7-8: **habendum et tenendum de me et heredibus meis in feodo et hereditate, libere et solute, quiete et pacifice** … A fairly standard formula with some variations found in the adverbs used. It is worth noting that the word **quiete** frequently has the sense of 'freely', 'with immunity', i.e. 'quit from any claim to ownership by another person' (see introduction to passage 3(g) for the concept of a 'quitclaim'). But **libere et solute** imply the same thing, and the phrase **quiete et pacifice** appears to mean broadly 'without hassle', with **quiete** having its classical meaning of 'quietly'. As often in such formulas, the precise meaning of each word is often difficult to define.

ll.9-10: **reddendo inde annuatim** … The standard formula for what is to be paid annually. **Pro omni servicio** indicates that the rent covers all feudal services attached to the land. Feudal services were progressively converted into cash payments, though this was not always so; see l.16 below.

ll.10-11: **videlicet ad festum** … Payment was regularly in several instalments, nearly always specified by feast days which are fairly equally spaced round the year.

ll.11-16: **Praeterea** ... An additional grant worded in a similar way to what has gone before.

l.12: The phrase **terciam partem** usually means 'a dower of a third part of the estate', and not just 'a third' of whatever follows. Here the whole phrase means 'a third part (dower) consisting of two bovates of land ...'; this interpretation is confirmed by associated deeds in the cartulary.

l.16: **salvo forinseco servicio** makes it clear that the feudal duty (ultimately to the king) to provide for foreign military service is still applicable to the person receiving the property.

ll.16-19: **warantizabimus** ... Often followed by **et defendemus** ... which in this context means 'we shall uphold' (i.e. this agreement), though the conventional translation is simply 'we shall defend'. **Contra omnes homines** is often used instead of **versus** ... There is always an accusative of the property 'guaranteed' and a dative of the person or persons for whom it is guaranteed.

l.19: **His testibus**: the usual phrase to introduce the witnesses to the deed. It is grammatically an ablative absolute, with the witnesses likewise being in the ablative.

*

The next document comes from Mountnessing in Essex (just north of Brentwood) and is dated around 1152. It concerns the grant by a certain Michael Capra of the church of St Giles, Mountnessing, to the Priory of Thoby (here referred to as the church of St Mary and St Leonard), also in Mountnessing, which Michael had himself established a few years before. The document is actually not itself the deed of gift, but a notification to the Dean of St Paul's in London that the gift has been made. Mountnessing is called **Ging'** (for **Ginga** or **Ginges**) in the text. The modern name comes from its ownership by the de Mounteney family – 'Mounteney's Ginga', the first 'G' of **Ginga** being pronounced in Anglo-Saxon as 'y' – one of whose members acted as a witness to this document. The text is transcribed from Hilda E.P. Grieve, *Examples of English Handwriting 1150-1750*, Essex Record Office Publications, No. 21, 1954, Plate XVII.

3(b)   Domino Radulpho Dei gratia decano ecclesie Sancti Pauli Lundon', et Ricardo eiusdem ecclesie archidiacono, et totius ecclesie capitulo, et omnibus Sancte Matris ecclesie fidelibus Michael Capra in Christo salutem. Sciatis me dedisse et concessisse et carta mea

5   confirmasse in perpetuam elemosinam pro anima patris mei et
matris mee et omnium antecessorum meorum Deo et ecclesie Sancte
Marie et Sancti Leonardi de nemore meo in Ging' et fratribus ibidem
Deo servientibus tam futuris quam presentibus ecclesiam Sancti
Egidij de Ging' et omnia eidem ecclesie pertinencia sicut unquam
10   melius pertinuerunt. Scilicet in terris et decimis nemoris et prati et
pomarij, cum omnibus liberalibus consuetudinibus prefate ecclesie
pertinentibus. His testibus: Willelmo eiusdem ecclesie persona qui
hoc concessit, Gileberto ipsius vicario, et Willelmo eiusdem
Michaelis filio et herede qui et hoc concessit, Roberto de Munten',
15   Roberto preposito Hundredj, Ricardo Lepuhier, Jordano fratre eius,
Alwino fabro, Roberto Morel, Jordano Rufo, Ricardo filio Willelmi.

The language of ll.5-9 is typical of ecclesiastical documents. The
phrase **in perpetuam elemosinam** ('in/for perpetual alms'; the
last word variously spelt; it is the Greek word **eleemosyne**, meaning 'mercy' or 'alms') is often found in deeds of gift to churches; the
gift was regarded as a kind of everlasting lump sum donation! **Pro
anima** ... is, of course, very frequent in such documents, with
usually the name of a deceased relative or relatives following – 'for
the soul of ...' Gifts are usually allocated **Deo et ecclesie Sancte/i**
... ('to God and to the church of St ...'), and then **fratribus/parsone**
('to the brothers/parson') with some indication of 'present and future'
(as in this example), to make it clear that the gift was for the benefit
of those holding the office and not for a specific individual.

In l.10 is an example of the use of a comparative (**melius**) in a
clause introduced by **sicut** – 'just as they ever quite properly belonged'. See also passage 4(c), note on l.8.

*

Within ecclesiastical records the presentation of a priest to a living
has some similarities to land records since the priest in effect
became the temporary landowner of the church's property in his
parish. These notices of presentation to a parish are mostly in a
fairly set format, consisting of the name of the priest, then the
person or institution by whom he is being presented (usually the
holder of the benefice), then the statement of admission to the
parish, which is named either here or as a heading to the whole
entry. There follow the details of the parish and the priest's holdings, including a statement of the stipend attached to the parish.
The following example is taken from *Rotuli Hugonis de Welles,*

Episcopi Lincolnensis, AD 1209-35, vol. 3, ed. Rev. F.N. Davis, Canterbury and York Society, 1908, where many of the same kind are to be found.

3(c)   Canewic (xx marcarum). Alanus de Canewic, capellanus, presentatus per dictos Priorem et conventum Hospitalis Lincolnie, ad perpetuam vicariam dicte ecclesie est admissus; et in eadem, etc., que consistit in toto alteragio et in sex acris terre arabilis in campis
5   de Brascebrig, cum quodam tofto proximo ecclesie de Canewic ex parte aquilonari et in quodam alio tofto versus australem partem ecclesie, ad curtillagium vicarii faciendum. Et est vicaria iiij marcarum, et eo amplius. Prior respondebit ut supra.

In l.1 **Canewic** is Canwick, about a mile to the south-east of Lincoln. The figure of 20 marks given in the genitive (a 'genitive of value') after the name is the valuation of the parish property. From his name it appears that Alan was in fact a native of the village.

In l.2 the **Priorem** is the Prior of the Gilbertine priory of St Catherine, about a mile to the south of Lincoln, who also had charge of the Hospital of the Holy Sepulchre (**Hospitalis Lincolnie**) which was located nearby, on what is now South Park. St Catherine's held the patronage of Canwick (see Hugh de Welles, op. cit., vol. 1, p. 199, and *The Victorian History of the Counties of England: Lincolnshire*, vol. 2, London 1906, pp. 188-91).

In l.3, **vicaria** is the office or benefice of a vicar; the vicar himself is a **vicarius** (as in l.7).

In l.3 the **etc.** could imply one of several phrases used in this position in other examples from these same records, the most common of which is (**et in eadem**) **canonice vicarius perpetuus institutus** – '(and) being instituted according to law as perpetual vicar (in the same [church])'.

In l.4 **alteragium** is 'altarage', one of those many medieval words indicating privileges or other sources of income, most of which end in -age (talliage, pannage, carrucage ...). 'Altarage' is offerings made in church for the specific benefit of the priest.

Brascebrig in l.5 is Bracebridge, also to the south of Lincoln, a mile or so to the west of Canwick.

A **toftum** (ll.5 and 6) is a toft or homestead, consisting of the house itself and the plot on which it stands. It is always modest in size.

In ll.7-8 **iiij marcarum** is another genitive of value, giving the value of the living. **Et eo amplius** is literally 'and more than that', the **eo** being an ablative of comparison. The implication is that the living was just a bit more than 4 marks.

The phrase **Prior respondebit** appears to mean that the Prior as patron was responsible to the bishop for this appointment.

*

Another document from Essex, this time from c. 1170 and from the village of Fryerning, just two miles to the north of Ginges (Mountnessing), demonstrates the typical format of a deed of gift. It is the kind of document which offers all kinds of leads into the local history of the area, and these are no more than touched on in the notes which follow. The person granting the land is in this case a woman – not by any means exceptional, since many women owned property, mainly in the form of their dower from a deceased husband. Rents paid in pepper are also by no means uncommon. Pepper was an expensive commodity which was imported from South Asia, mainly by Genoese merchants. The text is transcribed from Hilda E.P. Grieve, op. cit., Plate XVIII.

3(d)   Notum sit tam presentibus quam futuris quod ego Margareta de Munfichet concessi et dedi Fulconi v. acras terre quas tenuit Godefridus le Fuchel et alias v. quas tenuit Rogerus filius Aldive in villa mea de Ginges pro servitio suo, tenendum de me et meis heredibus,
5   ipse et heredes sui, annuatim reddendo unam libram piperis in vigilia Sancti Johannis Baptiste pro omni servitio, salvo servitio regis. Et hanc predictam libram piperis reddet ecclesie beati Johannis de Ginges. His testibus: Warino de Bassingeburne, Alexandro fratre eius, Willelmo capellano de Ginges, Serlone capellano de
10   Ginges, Rogero de Trepalawe, Warino de Barentune, Eustachio fratre eius et Ricardo fratre eius, Johanne filio Eustachij, Willelmo de Thalamo.

In l.2 the phrase **concessi et dedi** does not necessarily (in fact does not usually) imply actually 'giving', but rather letting for payment and for services rendered, as here.

In ll.2-3 the use of the phrase **quas tenuit** is a very common way of defining which lands are meant.

In l.3 **Aldive** is more likely to be masculine than feminine, 'of Aldiva'. The name could, of course, be feminine from its ending; if it *is* a woman, then presumably she was a widow (or maybe unmarried), but it is rare not to have the father's name mentioned.

In ll.6-7 **salvo servitio regis** is the kind of ablative absolute phrase often found to make it clear that, although the payment of rent absolves the lessees from service to the lord, service to the king is *not* excluded, and the king could therefore still call upon the lessees to carry out military service as a feudal right.

Willelmo capellano de Ginges mentioned in l.9 might just be the same person as mentioned in 3(b) l.12.

Bassingbourn, Thriplow and Barrington are three small villages to the south-west of Cambridge; presumably Margaret de Munfichet had connections in this area.

*

The next document concerns the estate of Marbury in Cheshire, about three miles north of Whitchurch. The name Marbury means 'lake-fort'; the estate was located beside Big Mere. The history of the estate was that it had been granted, with much other land in Cheshire, by William the Conqueror to the Vernon family from Vernon in Normandy (on the Seine between Rouen and Paris). They in turn had granted Marbury to Ranulph the Norman, whose son Richard inherited the estate some time in the first half of the 12th century. The charter below, dating from around 1170, records the sale of the Marbury estate by Richard to his brother William for a payment of three and a half marks and an annual 'rent' of four barbed arrows (a token replacement for military service to Richard and his heirs, though *not* for the feudal duty to the lord; see ll.10-13). The payment of three and a half marks was distributed across three court sessions, in the Cheshire County Court, the baronial court of the Vernons, and the local court of the Wapentake of Halton, to ensure that the transaction was recorded in all courts with an interest in the transaction (though Halton is well to the north, near Runcorn; perhaps William had connections there). The text is transcribed from J. Barrett and D. Iredale, *Discovering Old Handwriting*, Shire Publications 1995, p. 122ff.

3(e) Notum sit omnibus tam presentibus quam futuris quod ego Ricardus de Merebira dedi et concessi Willelmo fratri meo de Merebiria et hac mea presenti carta confirmavi totam terram de Merebira cum omnibus pertinenciis suis in bosco in plano in pratis in pascuis in
5   molendinis in vivariis et in omnibus aliis locis ad eandem villam pertinentibus liberam et quietam et solutam a me et heredibus meis sibi et heredibus suis tenendam et habendam in feodum et heredi-

tatem inperpetuum, reddendo mihi et heredibus meis ipse et heredes sui annuatim ad pasca quatuor sagittas barbatas pro omni
10   servicio mihi et heredibus meis pertinente. Ita quidem quod predictus Willelmus frater meus iddem servicium facere debet domino
Gwarino de Vornon quod egomet feci domino meo vel pater meus
ante me fecit dominis suis. Hoc autem feci consensu et concessu
domini Gwarini de Vornon et heredorum meorum. Et depono a me
15   et heredibus meis omne ius meum de tera predicta Willelmo fratri
meo predicto et heredibus suis inperpetuum pro tribus marcis et
dimidia, quas Willelmus frater meus predictus dedit mihi, partem
coram omni comitatu Cestrie et partem in curia domini mei Gwarini
de Vornon et partem coram Wapentach de Hatheltona. Teste Lidul-
20   pho de Twamlawe, Hamone de Borthintona, Gileberto filio Nigelli,
Roberto de Stochal, Radulpho capellano, Ricardo de Vornon, Raer de
Stanthurn, Gileberto de Bostoc, et omni comitatu Cestrie.

There are some aberrant spellings in this charter (as in many): in
ll.2-3 **Merebira/Merebiria**; in l.9 **quatuor** (as commonly for **quattuor**); l.11 **iddem** for **idem**; l.15 **tera** for **terra**. There is also a
grammatical error: **heredorum** for **heredum** in l.14. Abbreviations in the manuscript often make it difficult to check what spelling
the writer was envisaging, but those listed are clear enough in this
particular charter.

In ll.7-8 the phrase **in feodum et hereditatem** indicates that
the land is to be held 'in fee' (i.e. with the condition of military
service on behalf of the lord) as well as hereditarily; ll.10-13 make
this absolutely clear.

The witnesses in ll.19-22 are all from manors in the Crewe area.
The reference to 'all the county of Chester' is to the dignitaries who
will have been present at the County Court.

*

The following deed of land exchange, dating to about 1212, concerns
land at Takeley (three miles east of Bishop's Stortford) and the
abbey at Colchester. From the tenor of the deed it would appear that
the exchange was favourable to the abbey, since it is referred to as
a gift for the salvation of the soul of king John and of the soul of
William de Hautville, the donor (ll.15-18). The text is transcribed
from Hilda E.P. Grieve, op. cit., Plate XIX.

3(f)   Sciant presentes et futuri quod ego Willelmus de Hauuville filius

Willelmi concessi et dedi et presenti carta confirmavi ecclesie Sancti
Johannis Baptiste de Colecestr' et Abbati et monachis eiusdem loci
Helyam filium Gileberti et totum tenementum suum in Takeleia,
5 scilicet masuagium ipsius et tres cruftas terre que iacent inter
predictum masuagium et terram ecclesie de Takeleia et unam acram que iacet inter Le Wardbroc et inter terram Ernoldi Berard, et
unam acram pasture que iacet inter terram Ernoldi et terram
Hardwini, et totum campum de dominio meo qui vocatur Newenhale
10 cum omnibus suis pertinentiis in Takeleia preter molendinum in
eodem campo situm in puram et perpetuam elemosinam, et hec
prenominata tenementa dedi prefatis Abbati et monachis de Cole-
cester in escambium quater viginti acrarum terre quas Willelmus
pater meus prius eisdem donaverat in parco suo de Takeleia in
15 puram et perpetuam elemosinam. Hanc autem donationem feci pro
salute anime domini Regis Johannis et antecessorum et successorum suorum et pro salute anime mee et omnium antecesssorum
et heredum meorum. Et ego et heredes mei warantizabimus prefatis
ecclesie Sancti Johannis et Abbati et monachis Colecestr' prenomi-
20 nata tenementa in puram et perpetuam elemosinam quietam ab
omni seculari servitio et exactione contra omnes homines et feminas. His testibus: Gaufrido filio Petri Comite Esex, Albrico de Ver
Comite Oxon, Willelmo filio Fulconis, Roberto de Cantelu, Rogero
de la Dune, Radulfo de Berners, Magistro Roberto de Cantia,
25 Willelmo de Haya, Alexandro filio Oseberni, Ricardo filio Pagani,
Willelmo de Takeleia, Nicholao filio Gerardi, Nigello de Hauekes-
tun, Ricardo filio Radulfi, Ricardo de Bumsted, Laurentio de
Takeleia, Reymundo de Selford, Rogero Testard, Roberto de Cam-
pes, Rogero de Teya, et multis aliis.

The syntax of the deed is quite simple, despite the rather lengthy
opening sentence.

In l.5 a **crufta** (also **crofta**; and either of these versions may be
neuter, **cruftum**, **croftum**) is a croft or smallholding, usually an
acre or two of arable land attached to a dwelling, as here.

In l.13 the phrase **quater viginti** ('four times twenty', i.e. eighty)
is, of course, taken from the French usage. There was a perfectly
good Latin word **octoginta**.

In l.20 the word **quietam** should strictly be **quieta** (agreeing
with **tenementa** rather than with **elemosinam**).

The witnesses are a mixture of Norman French and English
names. Those whose provenance is an English place-name come
from villages in Essex or Cambridgeshire. William de Hautville

obviously had influential friends – the earls of Essex and Oxfordshire are both in the list of witnesses.

*

'Quitclaims' are deeds by which a person gives up a claim to a property or a rent. They are usually either associated with a deal in which property is exchanged, or they are the result of litigation and the deed is a final statement of the relinquishing of rights. Because they deal with property and rents the vocabulary of quitclaims is very similar to that used in deeds of gift or purchase, though some specific formulas are also used. The following example comes from the cartulary of Lanercost Priory near Brampton in Cumbria, a priory of Augustinian canons. The cartulary itself has an interesting history. It was lost after being used in a court case in Carlisle in 1826, and was only rediscovered in 1982 by Bruce Jones, the Cumbria County Archivist, in the papers of the family of one of the lawyers involved in the case. It was as well that the lawyer concerned had held onto the cartulary (he had done so for good legal reasons, incidentally), since Naworth Castle, the home of the Earls of Carlisle where the cartulary had previously been held, was largely destroyed in a fire in 1844, and it had been assumed that the cartulary had been lost in this fire. This document is dated about 1255. The full circumstances are not clear, but the canons certainly had had some difficulty in establishing their claims to some of their properties around this period. The land in question here is called 'Cumquenecath', which was a few miles to the north-east of Lanercost in the valley of the King Water, though the name has unfortunately not survived to modern times. The text is transcribed from *The Lanercost Cartulary*, ed. John M. Todd, Surtees Society vol. CCIII and Cumberland and Westmorland Antiquarian and Archaeological Society Record Series vol. XI, 1997, document 67, p. 117.

3(g) Carta Agnetis filie Willelmi filii Jonette de Karliolo de quietaclamatione de Cumquenecath.

Omnibus Christi fidelibus ad quos presens scriptum pervenerit, Agnes filia Willelmi filii Jonette de Karliolo salutem in Domino.
5   Noverit universitas vestra me, pro salute anime mee et patris et matris mee et omnium antecessorum meorum, concessisse et pro me et heredibus meis inperpetuum quietumclamasse, priori et conventu de Lanercost, totum jus et clameum quod habui vel ego sive

heredes mei aliquo tempore habere poterimus in Cumquenecath
10 cum omnibus pertinenciis suis, ita scilicet quod nec ego nec heredes
mei in predicta Cumquenecath cum suis pertinenciis aliquod jus vel
clameum in posterum exigere poterimus vel vendicare. Et si quod
habui, vel aliquis heredum meorum aliquo tempore habere poterit,
illud tactis sacrosanctis evangeliis omnino abjuravi. In cuius rei
15 testimonium sigillum meum huic scripto apposui. Hiis testibus:
dominis Roberto de Mulecaster, Johanne de Irreby, Ada de Bas-
tenthwayt, Radulfo de Pockelinton tunc vicecomite Cumbrie, Patricio de Wluesby, Matheo clerico, Jakelino de Karliolo, Johanne de
Burton clerico, Walteri filio Warini, Roberto de Carwyndelaue, et
20 multis aliis.

In ll.1-2 the word for 'quitclaim' is (in the nominative) **quietacla-matio**, and both parts of the word decline, so that the accusative, for instance, is **quietamclamationem**. The verb is similarly a compound (see l.7), with the first part acting as an adjective and agreeing with the object quitclaimed.

In l.5 the phrase **noverit universitas vestra** (literally 'let your totality know') is a variation on the commoner **noverint universi**.

The whole of ll.5-14 contains the regular formulas of a quitclaim, in particular **me ... quietumclamasse ... totum jus et clameum quod habui vel ego sive heredes mei aliquo tempore habere poterimus ... ita scilicet quod nec ego nec heredes mei in ... aliquod jus vel clameum in posterum exigere poterimus vel vendicare** (or **vindicare**). **Et si quod habui, vel aliquis here-dum meorum aliquo tempore habere poterit, illud ... abjuravi**.

In the list of witnesses (ll.15-20) Muncaster, Ireby, Bas-senthwaite, Ouseby, Burton (probably Burton-in-Kendal) and Carwinley are all in Cumbria; Pocklington, the home of Radulf, Sheriff of Cumbria, is about 14 miles east of York.

*

The following grant of land comes from the parish records of Little Waltham in Essex, three miles north of Chelmsford. The date is around 1275. It has a particularly detailed definition of the land to be transferred, and is also noteworthy for the clause excluding the purchaser from transferring the land at any future date to any religious bodies. The deal consists of a one-off payment and also a

small annual payment for 'services', etc. The text is transcribed from
Hilda E.P. Grieve, op. cit., Plate I.

3(h)   Sciant presentes et futurj quod ego Willelmus de la Grave de Parva
Waltham concessi dedi et hac mea presenti carta confirmavi
Willelmo Russel mercatori de Chelmarford pro homagio et servicio
suo, et pro viginti et quatuor solidis sterlingorum quos mihi dedit in
5   gersumam, duas acras terre mee cum omnibus suis pertinenciis in
Parva Waltham, iacentes in quadam crofta que vocatur Langecroft
sicut sepibus et fossatis includitur, inter terram Johannis de Belsted
que vocatur la Reden ex una parte et venellam ducentem de regali
chemino ad gravam Galfridi de Belsted ex altera, unde unum capud
10   abutat se super curtillagium dicti Johannis et aliud capud super
messuagium meum, habendum et tenendum dicto Willelmo et
heredibus suis vel suis assignatis vel eorum heredibus de me et
heredibus meis vel meis assignatis, et quandocumque et quibus-
cumque dictas duas acras terre cum suis pertinentiis dare, vendere,
15   legare, invadiare vel aliquo modo assignare voluerit, exceptis viris
religiosis et Judeis, libere quiete bene et in pace, iure et hereditarie
imperpetuum, reddendo inde annuatim mihi et heredibus meis vel
meis assignatis ipse et heredes sui vel sui assignati octo denarios ad
duos anni terminos, videlicet ad Pascha quatuor denarios et ad
20   festum sancti Michaelis quatuor denarios, pro omnibus secularibus
serviciis, consuetudinibus, sectis curiarum et omnibus secularibus
demandis, salvo servicio domini regis quando evenerit, ad plus et ad
minus unum quaterantem. Et ego dictus Willelmus et heredes mei
vel mei assignati warantizabimus, defendemus, et acquietabimus
25   dictas duas acras terre cum suis pertinenciis dicto Willelmo et
heredibus suis vel suis assignatis vel eorum heredibus sicut predictum est per prenominatum servicium contra omnes homines et
feminas imperpetuum. Et ut hec mea concessio donacio et mea
confirmacio rata et stabilis imperpetuum perseveret huic presenti
30   carte sigillum meum apposui. Hiis testibus: Roberto de Haylesden,
Rogero de Wymbis, Galfrido de Belsted, Ricardo Koc, Sawal de
Springfeud, Ricardo de Munchanesy, Stephano le Franceis, et aliis.

The typically long opening sentence is not in fact complicated in its
syntax. Some punctuation has been added here to give help in
separating the clauses (as in most of the texts in this collection). It
is perhaps an opportune point to add a warning about the various
stops and dashes to be found in many manuscripts. Until the
15th-16th centuries such punctuation is hardly a help to a modern

reader since it is rarely systematic; at best it divides the text into coherent phrases, but often it is used in such an unsystematic way as to be quite misleading.

In l.4 **sterlingorum** means 'of silver pennies'. The word appears to derive from the Anglo-Saxon **steorra**, 'star', which was often depicted on these pennies.

In l.5 is the word **gersuma**, which here means no more than 'payment', though it often has the more specialised meaning of 'merchet', i.e. the fine paid by a tenant to a lord on the marriage of a daughter of the tenant. The argument for this practice presumably was that the lord was in effect losing a working member of the tenant's family, all of whom did feudal service for the lord.

In ll.8-9 the words **venellam** and **chemino** are from the French **venelle** and **chemin**.

In ll.9 and 10 the word **capud** (more correctly **caput**) is here used to mean 'headland', the edge of a field where the plough turns.

In l.15 **invadiare** does not mean 'to invade' but 'to mortgage'.

In l.21 **sectis curiarum** means 'attendances at the courts'. See passage 3(o), note on ll.3-4 for additional details of this feudal duty.

In l.24 the verb **acquietare** needs a little explanation. It is usually translated simply as 'to acquit', but its use in documents of this kind is not in the sense of 'to free from a charge', but 'to declare quit', i.e. to guarantee that the donor or vendor no longer lays any claim to the property in question. It is, of course, a word often found in quitclaims, though it was not actually used in the example quoted above (passage 3(g)).

The witnesses in ll.30-2 all seem to come from Essex – as one might expect for a transaction of just two acres.

*

Melrose Abbey in the south of Scotland was founded in 1136. It was a Cistercian foundation, and one of the largest monastic houses in Britain. The abbey acquired much land in the south of Scotland, mainly through gifts from a succession of Scottish kings. The following charter is from 1315 and records the gift to the abbey by king Robert I of his estate of Lessuden in the old county of Roxburghshire.

3(i)   Robertus Dei gracia rex Scottorum omnibus probis hominibus tocius terre sue tam clericis quam laicis salutem. Sciatis nos pro salute anime nostre et pro salute animarum omnium antecessorum et

successorum nostrorum regum Scocie dedisse concessisse et hac
5   presenti carta nostra confirmasse Deo et ecclesie beate Marie de
Melros' abbati et monachis ibidem Deo servientibus et in perpetuum
servituris totam terram nostram et tenementum de Leshidwyne
cum pertinenciis. Tenendam et habendam dictis abbati et monachis
et eorum successoribus in perpetuum in liberam puram et per-
10   petuam elemosinam per omnes rectas metas et divisas suas cum
serviciis liberetenencium et nativis hominibus dicte terre debitis et
consuetis tempore bone memorie domini Alexandri regis Scocie
predecessoris nostri ultimo defuncti et domine Marie regine Scocie
matris sue et cum omnibus aliis libertatibus commoditatibus pis-
15   cariis molendinis asiamentis et iustis pertinenciis suis tam nominatis quam non nominatis adeo libere et quiete plenarie et honorifice
sicut aliqua elemosina in regno Scocie liberius seu quiecius plenius
seu honorificencius tenetur aut possidetur, salvis nobis tantum
oracionum suffragiis devotarum. In cuius rei testimonium presenti
20   carte nostre sigillum nostrum precepimus apponi. Testibus: venerabilibus patribus Willelmo et Roberto Dei gratia Sancti Andree et
Glasguensi episcopis, Edwardo de Brus' comite de Carryc' et domino
Galwydie fratre nostro, Thoma Ranulphi comite Moravie nepote
nostro, Patricio comite Marchie, Jacobo domino de Duglas, et
25   Roberto de Keth marescallo nostro. Apud Are primo die Maii anno
regni nostri decimo.

[*Regesta Regum Scottorum*, vol. VI, David II, 1324-71, Edinburgh
1982, Document 65]

In ll.2-7 there are the religious formulaic phrases which have been
noted in 3(b) above.

In l.11 the word **nativus** (often a noun, though here an adjective
with **homo**) does not mean 'native' but 'a villein, serf ', i.e. a man
bound to his lord's land by various forms of service to the lord. This
is the commonest use of the word. The word is here contrasted with
liberetenencium – 'of freeholders', who either had no such duty of
service or made a cash payment instead of such duty.

In ll.17-18 we again have the use of comparative adverbs in a
comparative clause beginning with **sicut**.

In l.25 **Are** is Ayr; Robert was holding a great council at Ayr from
late April to early May 1315.

*

59

Now to Essex again. The following charter comes from Harlow and was written in 1324. John de Stanton was rector of Harlow, and he acquired various lands and rents to endow the Chantry of St Petronilla in his parish church. This charter records the gift by a certain William of Mashbury (about 12 miles due east of Harlow, and 5 miles north-west of Chelmsford) of rents paid to him by John, son of Stephen, for land at Great Parndon (now part of Harlow). The chantry is not in fact mentioned in this charter; other documents make the purpose of this grant clear. The text is transcribed from Hilda E.P. Grieve, op. cit., Plate II.

3(j)   Sciant presentes et futuri quod ego Willelmus de Massceberij de
comitatu Essex' dedi concessi et hac presenti carta mea confirmavi
Magistro Johanni de Stantone clerico tres solidos annui redditus
percipiendos annuatim ad duos anni terminos per equales porciones
5   ad festum Sancti Michaelis et ad Pascha de Johanne filio Stephani
de Perrys pro duodecim acris terre arabilis et duabus acris prati
quas de me tenuit in villa de Magna Perndon iacentibus in campo
vocato Wedhey in dicta villa inter Perndon' Wode ex una parte et
terram Walteri Coci ex altera. Et abbuttat unum caput super Farn-
10   hel, et aliud caput super viam communem que ducit de Ryhel versus
Waltham. Habendum et tenendum predictos tres solidos cum
homagijs wardis esscahetis releuijs maritagijs et omnibus alijs ad
dictum redditum pertinentibus dicto Magistro Johanni de Stantone
heredibus et assignatis suis de capitali domino feodi illius per
15   servicia de iure inde debita et consueta. Et ego predictus Willelmus
de Massceberi heredes mei et assignati predictos tres solidos annui
redditus cum homagijs wardis esscahetis releuijs maritagijs et omnibus alijs ad dictum redditum pertinentibus dicto Magistro Johanni de Stantone heredibus et assignatis suis contra omnes gentes
20   warantizabimus imperpetuum. In cuius rei testimonium huic presenti carte sigillum meum apposui. Hijs testibus: Thoma de Cann,
Gileberto ate Chambr', Galfrido Maulle, Jacobo de Weld', Johanne
Campyon et alijs. Datum apud Herl' nono die Aprilis anno regni
Regis Edwardi filij Regis Edwardi septimo decimo.

In ll.11-15 it is made clear that the transfer of rent also carries with it the transfer of all feudal responsibilities to the lord which are associated with the land. These might be defined as follows:

> **Homagium**: a general term for feudal homage to the lord;
>
> **Warda** (or **wardum**): guardianship (by the lord) of the prop-
> erty in the case of there being no immediate heir;

3. Grants, Deeds, and Other Legal and Ecclesiastical Documents

Esscaheta (variously spelled): escheat, i.e. the power of the lord to reclaim property when there is no heir;

Relevium: payment by an heir to the lord on taking over a property;

Maritagium: the lord's right to give a female dependant of a tenant in marriage.

*

Most wills in Latin are just as formulaic as the preceding documents; very few depart from the simple framework which is illustrated below, though of course the degree of detail does vary considerably. This will comes from Northumberland and is dated 1358. Sir William Felton is known from other sources as a prominent citizen of the region. He owned large estates in Northumberland, and in 1336 he is recorded as the constable of Roxburgh Castle and the sheriff of the county of Roxburghshire. Felton is a small village on the A1 (though now bypassed) nine miles south of Alnwick, and Edlingham is an even smaller village eight miles south-west of Alnwick, four miles from Rothbury.

3(k)   *Testamentum Willelmi Felton Militis*

In Dei nomine, Amen. Ego Willelmus de Felton miles sanae memoriae et compos mentis, die lunae proxime ante festum Nativitatis Beatae Mariae Virginis Anno Domini Millesimo CCC quinquagesimo octavo, condo testamentum meum in hunc modum. In
5   primis do et lego animam meam Deo omnipotenti et Beatae Mariae et omnibus sanctis, et corpus meum ad sepeliendum in Ecclesia beati Johannis Baptistae de Edlyngeham. Item pro oblacione xl.s. Item pro lumine circa corpus meum in die sepulturae meae c. solidos. Item do et lego Isabellae uxori meae quinque discas argenti
10 et unum calicem argenti. Item do et lego Domino Petro Vicario de Edlyngeham xx.s. Item do et lego totum residuum bonorum meorum mobilium et immobilium et omnia michi debita per quoscunque Domino Willielmo filio meo, debitis meis plenarie solutis. Et ad haec fideliter exequenda et adimplenda hos executores meos ordino, facio
15 et constituo, predictum Dominum Willielmum de Felton filium meum et heredem, Isabellam uxorem meam, et predictum Dominum Petrum Vicarium Ecclesiae de Edlyngeham. His testibus: Willielmo Clerk, Willielmo Zole, ac Willielmo de Crokisdon et aliis.

[From *Wills and Inventories illustrative of the History, Manners, Language, Statistics, etc. of the Northern Counties of England from the 11th c. onwards*, Part 1, London, J.B. Nichols and Son, Surtees Society 1834, p. 29]

l.1: **In Dei nomine, Amen** – the regular opening phrase of a will.

In ll.1-2 the phrase **sanae memoriae et compos mentis** is a frequent formula, though often replaced, if the testator is already ill, by the phrase **compos mentis licet eger in corpore** – 'sound in mind though sick in body'.

The date is usually given according to the ecclesiastical calendar (as here, ll.2-3), at least until the 15th century when the day of the month became the usual system. The Nativity of the BVM is 8th September.

Condo testamentum meum in hunc modum (l.4) is the standard formula.

Then follows normally the care of the soul (ll.4-6), usually in the words as given here or some slight variation, followed by the arrangements for the burial of the body (ll.6-7), again usually in the kind of formula found here, with only slight variations. If the spouse has already died it is common to find a phrase such as **iuxta Elizabetham, nuper uxorem meam** – 'next to Elizabeth, my late wife'.

Then follows the list of bequests, each usually preceded by the word **item** – 'likewise'. **Do et lego** (or either word individually) is the usual term for 'I bequeath' (as here in ll.5,9,10,11). Often these are preceded by the arrangements for the paying of debts, in a phrase such as **lego et volo quod omnia debita mea de bonis meis persolvantur** – 'I bequeath and desire that all my debts be paid from my goods', though in this example the debts are covered in the ablative absolute phrase **debitis meis plenarie solutis** (l.13), which is also common.

In l.7 **pro oblacione** appears to be a general offering to the church, though the word **oblacio/oblatio** often refers specifically to the offering of bread and wine at the eucharist.

In ll.8-9 William does seem to be paying rather a lot for the light around his body at his burial. Some detailed rite seems to be implied.

In ll.9-10 Isabella, wife of William, does not seem to be benefiting too generously from this will – five silver dishes and a silver chalice. It could be that separate provision had already been made in a deed of gift for her to receive the normal dower of one third of her husband's estate as long as she lived (or for her to dispose of as she wished).

One often finds contingency clauses (there are none in this example) to cover the situation if a beneficiary to the will dies without heirs. The usual phrase is **Et si contingat quod dictus ... obierit sine heredibus [de proprio corpore legitime procreatis], tunc do et lego** ... – 'And if it should happen that the said ... shall die without heirs [legitimately procreated from his own body], then I bequeath ...'.

The final bequest in ll.11-13 is again a fairly standard formula – **Item do et lego totum residuum ... per quoscunque**, often with the ablative absolute **debitis meis plenarie solutis** appended, as here.

In ll.13-17 is the designation of executors. An alternative formula is **Huius testamenti mei executores meos ordino, facio et constituo** ....

In l.18 Crokisdon is presumably a local estate; there is no village of that name now in the area.

*

For such a wealthy person as Sir William Felton the above will is remarkably short. Many wills, as one might expect, are far more detailed. The following is a very small part of the much longer will of Lady Margaret de Eure of Whitton Castle near Rothbury in Northumberland. She was widowed in 1362 and then lived for the rest of her life in Newcastle, where she died in 1378, apparently not long after she made this will.

3(l)   *Testamentum Dominae Margaretae de Eure relictae*
Johannis de Eure Militis

... Item Elizot., ancillae meae, unum coopertorium de rubio et glauco, unum par linthiaminum, item j. banker. Item eidem j. gowne
5   furr. cum nigro; item eidem x.s. Item Margaret Eglyston unum coopertorium, cum tapite pudrato cum vynys et grapys. Item j. canevas, j. par lintheaminum, ij. blanketts, ij. mappas, ij. manutergia, j. capucium bene furratum, aliud capucium furratum cum purydmenev. Item Radulpho de Lumley j. coopertium cum iiij. tapetis
10   pudratis cum papejoys. Item Roberto Heron j. lectum integrum de opere parisiensi ...

[Source as for 3(k), no. XXXI, p. 35]

In l.1 **relicta** is the common word in legal documents for 'widow'. She was, as the heading says, the widow of Sir John de Eure.

In l.3 **coopertorium** here means 'coverlet'. The word can mean a cover of any sort, from a roof to a lid on a box, but in the context of furnishings it means the cover for a bed.

In ll.3-4, **de rubio et glauco** is strange Latin, since these terms do not normally have nominal forms, but the sense is clear enough.

In l.4, the word **par** means 'pair', a common usage especially in lists of this sort. **Linthiamen** is a linen sheet (spelled **lintheamen** in l.7), and a 'banker' is a bench cover. The writer did not know of a Latin equivalent, so, as often happens in wills and inventories, he simply wrote the English word, on this occasion without any attempt to give it a Latin termination; and there are several other examples in this passage of the same practice. Incidentally, words used in this way with no attempt to make them look like Latin do not occur in Latham's *Medieval Latin Word-list* or in the *Dictionary of Medieval Latin from British Sources* (see Chapter 8 for bibliographical details); one has to try to find them in the *Oxford Dictionary*.

In l.5 **furr.** is for **furratus**, an English word, but this time with a Latin termination, though the writer has avoided the issue of gender of an un-Latinised word **gowne** by using a sign of abbreviation.

In l.6 the word **pudrato** strictly means 'powdered', but in describing cloths it means 'spangled' or more generally 'decorated'.

In ll.8-9 **purydmenev.** (with a stop to indicate an abbreviation) is clearly not a Latin word, but neither does it appear in the *Oxford Dictionary*. From the context it seems to indicate either a kind of fur or possibly a colour. It may be a mistranscription; if not, it is a very rare word.

In l.10 **papejoys** are parrots. The word is the same as 'popinjays', and comes from Arabic via Spanish. The Latin was usually **papagallus**, or some similar spelling, but the writer apparently did not know this form. Parrots, vines and grapes were favourite motifs for medieval tapestries, as can be seen from many surviving examples.

*

Inventories show many of the characteristics of the last passage. They are, of course, essentially lists of goods and other possessions, and the main difficulty is usually one of vocabulary. Latham's *Medieval Latin Word-list* is a great help, but it cannot be expected to contain every word to be found in inventories, in which the compilers frequently used local words for objects, with or without a Latin ending. The following example does not present too many such problems and was written by a fairly competent Latinist. The date was 1472, but no place of origin is given. It was probably Northumberland.

3(m) *John Pykeryng*

Inventarium omnium bonorum mobilium et immobilium Domini Johannis Pykeryng, capellani, nuper defuncti, appreciatum per iiii viros decentes et discretos, quorum nomina sunt haec: Ricardus Patason, Henricus Coniers, Johannes Tranome, Johannes Wylkyn-
5 son; qui quidem Johannes Pykeryng obiit x die mensis Octobris Anno Domini Millesimo cccc.lxxii.

AULA. In primis, nec in aula nec in cameris aliquid invenitur ad valorem 1d, exceptis solummodo vestibus quotidie indutus fuerat; quod dictum est omnia intrinseca, videlicet ollae, patellae, disci,
10 linei panni et lanei, et cetera ornamenta ablata fuerunt per nequissimam mulierem.

IN STABULO. Una equa cum pullo ad valorem x.s. Alia equa viij.s. Unus equus v.s.

IN HORRIO. xxiiij. quartaria frumenti pr. j. qu. iij.s iiij.d. xx. quarter.
15 avenae pr. unius qu. xx.d. Pisa x. quarter. pr. j. qu. xx.d. Fenum xvj.s.

IN AGRO. Sex bovatae bladi pr. unius bovatae x.s. Unum plaustrum x.s.

CATALLA. Sex boves liiij.s. Quinque buculi et sex iuvencae pr. unius
20 iiij.s. ij.d. Quatuor vacae cum vitulis pr. unius ix.s. xxiij. oves pr. unius xij.d. vj. porci vj.s viij.d.

Summa totalis: xix.l vj.s viij.d.

[Source as for 3(k), no. LXVI, pp. 96-7]

ll.7-11 tell a sorry tale. It would appear that the writer knew who the **nequissima mulier** (1.10-11) was, but he is not saying.

    In l.8 the writer (or possibly the transcriber) has omitted **quibus** after **vestibus** ('the clothes *in which* ...'). The phrase **quod dictum est** is also rather vague grammatically, though the writer clearly intends 'which is to say ...'.

Pr. j. qu. in l.14 and subsequent lines is an abbreviated from of **pretium unius quorum** – 'the price of one of which'. **Unius** is sometimes written in full.

The total given in l.22 is incorrect, according to my calculation, and no simple change will account for the discrepancy. Either there is an error (possibly more than one) in the transcription, or in the original arithmetic.

*

Financial records of various sorts survive in national, county and ecclesiastical archives, from the Pipe Rolls (the annual accounts of sheriffs with the British Exchequer, county by county, from 1131 to 1831) to very simple family household accounts. These latter often contain no more than a few words in each line to identify the item of expenditure or income, and they present few syntactical problems. They *do* often present palaeographical and lexical problems, but the handbooks and dictionaries listed in Chapter 8 will usually resolve these. The Pipe Rolls are a different matter, and the precise meaning of the specialised vocabulary and of the records themselves is a complex study. They are not strictly accounts in the sense of balanced lists of income and expenditure, but rather lists of the sheriff's financial transactions. The earlier ones, such as the example below, are not even divided into financial categories as the later rolls were, and this presents considerable problems of interpretation. The following extract from the Pipe Rolls for Oxfordshire for 1161-2 (the 8th year of Henry II) illustrates the nature of earlier examples of these records:

3(n) *Oxenefordscira*

Manesser Arsic reddit compotum de firma de Oxenefordscira.

In thesauro £76 13s 6d blanc. in ii. talliis.

In elemosina constituta militibus de Templo i. marcam.

Et in liberatione constituta infirmis tredecim £19 15s 5d et eisdem

5   65s ad pannos.

Et in donis abbati de Oseneia 9s 5d; et canonicis de Sancta Frideswida 25s pro consuetudine feriae

Et eisdem 17s 7d de novo dono.

Et in liberatione constituta Willelmo filio Baldewini 102s 6d per
10   breve Regis

Et in terris datis Engelgero de Bohun £20 blanc. in Blochesham; et
eidem in villa Ricardi de Luci £20 numero.

Et Comiti Flandriae £76 blanc. in Betona, cum 100s de Wicha. Et
Hugoni de Plugeno £42 10s blanc. in Hedendona. Et abbatissae
15   de Godesto 100s blanc. in eadem villa. Et in eadem villa Henrico
de Oxenford 50s blanc.

Et Gilleberto Angevino £10 numero in Besentona. Et in eadem villa
abbatissae de Godesto 100s numero.

... et in operatione domorum infirmorum de Oxeneford 60s. Et ad
20   prata falcanda et fenum parandum et conducendum ad Wudestoc
60s.

[From Stubbs, *Select Charters from the Beginning to 1307*, 9th ed.,
Oxford 1913, repr. 1951, pp. 158-9 with omissions]

Firma (l.1) is the term used in the Pipe Rolls for the taxes of various
kinds administered by the sheriffs from each county.

In l.2 the word **blanc.** (regularly so abbreviated) means
'blanched', i.e. money which has been assayed, or tested as genuine.
The procedure was that a sample of one pound weight of silver
coinage was melted down and tested for purity. Counterfeiting was
clearly a problem!

Also in l.2, the word **tallia** refers to the wooden tallies on which
accounts were kept. In 1834 thousands of these tallies were foolishly
burned in the furnaces of the House of Lords, which started the
blaze which destroyed the old Parliament buildings.

In l.3 the alms were probably paid to the house of the Knights
Templar in Cowley, on the south-east side of Oxford.

The use of **in** at the beginning of l.3 illustrates its use to introduce
nearly all items of income or expenditure. 'With regard to ...', 'in
respect of ...' is a rather clumsy translation, but simply 'in ...' would
be misleading.

In l.6 **Oseneia** is Osney abbey, on the west side of Oxford. The
abbey of St Frideswide (ll.6-7) was on the site of the present Christ
Church Cathedral.

In l.11 **Blochesham** is Bloxham, about four miles south of Ban-
bury. Of the other names mentioned here **Betona** (l.13) is possibly
Barton on the east side of Oxford, and **Hedendona** (l.14) is Headington, also on the east side of Oxford. **Godesto** (ll.15 and 18) is
Godstow nunnery on the west side of the city (there are still substan-

tial ruins standing). **Wicha** (l.13) and **Besentona** (l.17) are more doubtful.

In ll.17 and 18 **numero** refers to 'unblanched' (i.e. untested) money; it had been counted and tallied, but not assayed.

Wudestoc in l.20 is Woodstock, about seven miles north-west of Oxford.

*

This final extract is from a manorial survey at Thaxted in Essex, carried out about 1395. Again the records here are not strictly accounts, but they include a list of the potential income from each holding. The columns to the right indicate the payments due each quarter, which were traditionally at Christmas, Easter, the Nativity of St John the Baptist (24th June), and Michaelmas (29th September), though there were variations – see e.g. passage 3(a), ll.9-11. In this example the first item is transcribed in full, with square brackets indicating letters omitted and usually shown in the manuscript as one of the many signs of abbreviation. Items after this are given as a simple transcription of the manuscript form with stops indicating where the manuscript has a sign of abbreviation (or a stop!); the ampersand (a long curl in the manuscript, for **et**) is transcribed &. The translation at the end of the book is given in full for each item.

3(o)	Thomas Tewe ten[et] vj. acr[as] pastur[e] [et] facit sect[am] co[mmun]em [et]				
5	r[eddit] p[er] annu[m]				j.d
	Idem Joh.es Benge ten. unam grouettam nup. Rog.i atte Welde & r. p. annu.		j.d.ob.		j.d.ob
10	Will.s Yerdele ten. unu. mes. & unam acr. t.re	iiij.d	iiij.d	iiij.d	iiij.d
	Joh.es Proude ten. iiij acr. t.re de ten. James quod quid.m ten. deb.				
15	sect. co.em & r. p. annu.	iiij.d	iiij.d	iiij.d	iiij.d

Henr. Boyton ten. un. mes. & xxx acr. t.re p.ti & pasture & deb. sectam co.em & r.	xv.s		xv.s	
20 Idem Henr. ten. dj. virg. t.re de ten. quondam Goldsmith & deb. sect. co.em & fac. iij cariag. blad. & feni recap. de 25 d.no iiij.d.ob. vel dab. d.no vj.d & r. p. annu.	xx.d.q	xx.d.q	xx.d.q	xx.d.q
Will.s Symond ten. iij acr. t.re & r. p. annu.	iiij.d.ob j cap[onem]	iiij.d.ob	iiij.d.ob	iiij.d.ob
30 Thomas Maij ten. vj acr. t.re & unam p.prest. & r.	iiij.d.q	iiij.d.q	iiij.d.q	iiij.d.q
Walt.us Ewayn ten. vj acr. t.re & j pec. p.ti & r.	ij.d.q	ij.d.q	ij.d.q	ij.d.q
Joh.es Herry Bocher 35 ten. j acr. t.re & r.	j.d	j.d	j.d	j.d
Joh.es Thrower Joh.es Dod tenent una. acr. t.re & r. p. annu.	j.d	j.d	j.d	j.d

[From Hilda E.P. Grieve, op. cit., Plate XXI]

At first the abbreviations look formidable, but they are mainly standardised forms of commonly used words, and after a little practice they present few problems. **j** is consistently used for the numeral '1', or for the last item in any number, as was normal practice. The translation will help on the few forms not found either in the first item or in the following notes.

In ll.3-4 **facit sectam communem** (lit. 'does common suit') refers to the duty to attend the manor court, usually held about every three weeks. All villeins were under this obligation, and so too were many free tenants. Absence usually resulted in a fine. With this duty went other forms of service to the lord, not fully specified in this particular document (though see ll.23-6 and the note below);

some manors had full lists of all such obligations, called 'custumals', though in others they were a matter of tradition. These duties varied considerably, and manors had their own particular customs of service. As a general rule villeins held their land under the obligation of service to the lord, whereas free tenants paid a rent in money, but gradually the distinction was eroded. In practice, by the 14th century and even earlier, many tenants held some land as villeins and some as free tenants, since it was usually the *land* that determined whether the tenure was villein or free, as the wording of ll.14-15 clearly shows. Often, at least by the time of this document, the villeinage resulted in a lower rent. In this case Thomas paid only 1d per year for his 6 acres of pasture. A convenient summary of manorial practices is to found in Denis Stuart, *Manorial Records*, Phillimore 1992, pp. 1-4.

In l.9 **ob.** is for **obolus**, 'a halfpenny'. The word is from the Greek for a small coin worth one-sixth of a drachma. A farthing was **quarta**, seen as **q.** in ll.26, 31 and 33.

In ll.13-14 **ten.** is for **tenementum** in the appropriate case. The same usage is found in l.21.

In l.20 **dj. virg.** is for **dimidiam virgatam**, 'half a virgate' (about 15 acres).

In ll.23-6 the service performed by Henry for this particular piece of land is specified in detail. It is interesting to note that the conversion into a cash payment is also given as an option.

In l.29 William Symond also has to give the lord a capon at Christmas!

In l.31 **p.prest.** is for **purpresturam**, frequently found in court records as the offence of 'encroachment', usually onto public property (see passage 5(a) for several examples of this). Here the meaning is 'the *right* of encroachment', presumably granted by the lord for encroachment onto some specific piece of land.

In l.34 **Bocher** is more likely to be his profession ('butcher') than an additional name.

From accounts like this one can get a fair idea of the rents for land at this period, allowing for the different quality of the land and for the value of the **secta communis** and the associated feudal duties.

*

A brief note finally about parish records. Many of these have been transcribed and published by local historical societies and are available in county and other record offices. Latin was often used well into the 17th century (I found one set still in Latin up to 1680), though many records were kept in English from the middle of the 16th century; it obviously depended on the skill or taste of the local priest or parish clerk. The Latin is mostly quite minimal. Birth records usually have only **filius/filia** (often simply **fil.**) in Latin, with the father's name in a Latin genitive form if the writer knew it. Burial records usually have **uxor**, **relicta**, or **filia** with the genitive of the husband or father in the case of women, and sometimes **infans** added in the case of a small child; ages are rarely given. Marriage records usually have only one word in Latin – **et** to link the couple! Occasionally one finds a brief comment if the circumstances are in any way exceptional, but the Latin is rarely taxing.

4

Charters

The charters which follow are, with the exception of 4(a), royal charters. Most have been taken from Stubbs' *Select Charters from the Beginning to 1307*, 9th ed., Oxford 1913, repr. 1951. They have been chosen because they are fairly representative of this kind of document and because they illustrate the kind of local circumstances which are a part of every such charter. Indeed some knowledge of the local circumstances is usually essential to the understanding of the text of a charter, because these are frequently referred to in such documents but are rarely explained in any detail; it was assumed those concerned would know all the necessary background.

Most royal charters open with a royal greeting. In its fuller form this is often expressed along the following lines:

Henricus Dei gratia Rex Anglorum omnibus episcopis, justitiariis, vicecomitibus, baronibus et omnibus fidelibus suis salutem. [Henry by the grace of God King of the English to all the bishops, justices, earls, barons, and all his faithful [subjects] [gives] greetings.] But the greeting is regularly shortened either by the use of **etc** (e.g. **Henricus Dei gratia etc omnibus episcopis etc salutem**) or by the kind of formula found in 4(j) – **Rex Archiepiscopis et ceteris salutem**.

The structure of the greeting, whether long or short, is fairly standard – the king and his title in the nominative followed by a list of the addressees in the dative, and finally **salutem**. The verb (**dicit**, **dat** or **mittit**) is rarely expressed.

The sentence after this is frequently in the form usually found in grants and deeds – **Sciatis** or **Noverint omnes** or a similar phrase, followed by **quod** or an accusative and infinitive construction, as described at the beginning of Chapter 3. Other phrases commonly found in grants and deeds may follow, such as **habendum et tenendum**, and phrases indicating the location of lands granted by the charter. They also often end with a list of witnesses, as in grants and deeds (**Testibus** ...). However, charters are far more varied than grants and deeds and are hence frequently more difficult as far as the Latin is concerned; though they can also be rather repetitive, as example 4(j) shows.

*

The first charter we shall deal with was granted by Archbishop Thurstan of York to the town of Beverley about 1130. The charter illustrates the power of the Archbishop, who in this charter grants to Beverley all (or most) of the privileges which the king (Henry I) had granted to York, though he does in fact make it clear that he does this only through the power bestowed on him by the king. The charter is also important because it indicates the privileges granted by the king himself to the city of York, and these are not extant in any other form.

4(a) Turstinus, Dei gratia Eboracensis Archiepiscopus, cunctis Christi fidelibus tam praesentibus quam futuris salutem et Dei benedictionem et suam.

    Notum sit vobis me dedisse et concessisse, et consilio capituli
5 Eboracensis et Beverlacensis et consilio meorum baronum mea carta confirmasse, hominibus de Beverlaco omnes libertates eisdem legibus quibus illi de Eboraco habent in sua civitate. Praeterea non lateat vos quod dominus Henricus rex noster nobis concessit potestatem faciendi hoc de bona voluntate sua, et sua carta confirmavit
10 statuta nostra et leges nostras iuxta formam legum burgensium de Eboraco, salva dignitate et honore Dei et Sancti Johannis et nostri et canonicorum, ut ita scilicet honorem eleemosynarum praedecessorum suorum exaltaret et promoveret cum omnibus his liberis consuetudinibus.

15 Volo ut burgenses mei de Beverlaco habeant suam hans-hus, quam eis do, et concedo ut ibi sua statuta pertractent ad honorem Dei et Sancti Johannis et canonicorum et ad totius villatus emendationem, eadem libertatis lege sicut illi de Eboraco habent in sua hans-hus. Concedo etiam eis thelonium in perpetuum pro viii. mar-
20 cis annuatim; praeterquam in tribus festis in quibus theloneum ad nos et ad canonicos spectat, in festo scilicet Sancti Johannis Confessoris in Maio, et in festo Tranlationis Sancti Johannis, et in Nativitate Sancti Johannis Baptistae; in his vero tribus festis omnes burgenses de Beverlaco ab omni teloneo liberos et quietos dimisi.
25 Hujus etiam cartae testimonio eisdem burgensibus liberos introitus

et exitus concessi in villa et extra villam, in plano et bosco et
marisco, in viis et in semitis, et ceteris convenientiis, excepto in
pratis et bladis, sicut unquam melius liberius et largius aliquis
possit concedere et confirmare; et sciatis quod sint liberi et quieti ab
30 omni telonio per totam schiram Eboraci sicut illi de Eboraco. Et volo
ut quicunque hoc disfecerit, anathema sit, sicut ipsius ecclesiae
Sancti Johannis asserit consuetudo et sicut statutum est in ecclesia
Sancti Johannis.

Hii sunt testes: Galfridus Murdac, Nigellus Fossard, Alanus de
35 Perci, Walterus Espec, Eustachius filius Johannis, Tomas praeposi-
tus, Turstinus archidiaconus, Herebertus canonicus, Willelmus
filius Tole, Willelmus Baiocensis; coram tota familia archiepiscopi,
clericis et laicis, in Eboraco.

[Stubbs, op. cit., pp. 131-2]

We have the usual mixture of ways of indicating indirect statement.
In ll.4-6 there is the formulaic use of **notum sit** with the accusative
and infinitive; in ll.7-9 there is **non lateat** ... **quod** followed by
indicatives **concessit** ... **confirmavit**; and in l.29 there is **sciatis
quod** with a subjunctive **sint**.

In l.11 **Sancti Johannis** is St John of Beverley, who was Bishop
of Hexham (AD 685), then of York (705); he retired to a monastery
near Beverley in 718 and died in 721. He ordained Bede as deacon
(691) and as priest (702). Bede has an account of his ministry and
miracles (Bede, *Hist.* 5.2-6; also 5.24). He appears again in ll.17, 22
and 32-3. The feast of the Translation of St John of Beverley (l.22)
is 25 October.

The **hans-hus** in ll.15 and 19 is a Guildhall, for the local merchants' guilds. The power of the guilds is well illustrated here (as in
most borough charters); it is to the members of the guilds that
concessions are granted.

In l.20 **praeterquam** here means 'moreover', 'in addition' (like
praeterea); the word can mean 'except', but often the idea is one of
an added fact rather than an exception. In this case the archbishop
is adding that the burghers of Beverley are also being freed from
the taxes due to him and his canons. Incidentally the spelling of
thelonium/theloneum is very variable; **tol**, **thol**, **thol**, **tholl**,
teloneum, **theloneum** are just some of the variants.

In the names of witnesses in ll.34ff. we see the usual system of
latinising first names but leaving surnames undeclined. In the

use of **filius** we see the origin of many English surnames ending in -son.

*

This next text is a charter of Stephen drafted in 1136. When Stephen came to the throne in 1135 after the barons had refused to accept Maud, Henry I's only surviving offspring, he was anxious to ensure the support of the church in his somewhat insecure constitutional position. This doubtless explains the emphasis, in the opening sentence, of his acceptance by the church authorities. The actual provisions of the charter are mainly based on those already agreed (with some reluctance) by Henry I, but Stephen was keen to assure the church that the privileges they had gained under Henry would be fully maintained.

4(b)   *Carta Stephani Regis de libertatibus Ecclesiae*
               Anglicanae et regni

Ego Stephanus Dei gratia assensu cleri et populi in regem Anglorum electus, et a Willelmo Cantuariensi archiepiscopo et sanctae Romanae ecclesiae legato consecratus, et ab Innocentio sanctae Romanae sedis pontifice confirmatus, respectu et amore Dei sanc-
5 tam ecclesiam liberam esse concedo et debitam reverentiam illi confirmo.

Nihil me in ecclesia vel rebus ecclesiasticis simoniace acturum vel permissurum esse promitto. Ecclesiasticarum personarum et omnium clericorum et rerum eorum justitiam et potestatem et
10 distributionem honorum ecclesiasticorum in manu episcoporum esse perhibeo et confirmo. Dignitates ecclesiarum privilegiis earum confirmatas, et consuetudines earum antiquo tenore habitas, inviolate manere statuo et concedo. Omnes ecclesiarum possessiones et tenuras quas die illa habuerunt qua Willelmus rex avus meus fuit
15 vivus et mortuus, sine omni calumniantium reclamatione, eis liberas et absolutas esse concedo. Si quid vero de habitis vel possessis ante mortem ejusdem regis, quibus modo careat ecclesia, deinceps repetierit, indulgentiae et dispensationi meae, vel restituendum vel discutiendum, reservo. Quaecunque vero post mortem ipsius regis
20 liberalitate regum vel largitione principum, oblatione vel comparatione, vel qualibet transmutatione fidelium eis collata sunt, confirmo. Pacem et justitiam me in omnibus facturum, et pro posse meo conservaturum eis promitto.

Forestas quas Willelmus avus meus et Willelmus avunculus
25   meus instituerunt et habuerunt mihi reservo. Ceteras omnes, quas
rex Henricus superaddidit, ecclesiis et regno quietas reddo et concedo.

Si quis episcopus vel abbas vel alia ecclesiastica persona ante
mortem suam rationabiliter sua distribuerit vel distribuenda
30   statuerit, firmum manere concedo. Si vero morte praeoccupatus
fuerit, pro salute animae ejus ecclesiae consilio eadem fiat distribu-
tio. Dum vero sedes propriis pastoribus vacuae fuerint, ipsas et
earum possessiones omnes in manu et custodia clericorum vel
proborum hominum ejusdem ecclesiae committam, donec pastor
35   canonice substituatur.

Omnes exactiones et injustitias et mescheningas, sive per vice-
comites vel per alios quoslibet male inductas, funditus exstirpo.

Bonas leges et antiquas et justas consuetudines, in murdris et
placitis et aliis causis, observabo, et observari praecipio et constituo.
40   Haec omnia concedo et confirmo salva regia et justa dignitate mea.

Testibus W. Cantuariensi archiepiscopo, etc.

Apud Oxenforde, anno ab Incarnatione Domini MoCoXXXoVIo,
set regni mei primo.

[Stubbs, op. cit., pp. 143-4]

The charter contains a considerable number of legal 'doublets',
where the same thing (or very nearly) is expressed in two words or
phrases. Some of these became quite standard, such as **perhibeo et
confirmo** (l.11), **statuo et concedo** (l.13), **liberas et absolutas**
(ll.15-16). It is often not easy to establish whether there *is* a real
difference in the two (or sometimes more) expressions, or whether
they have become purely formulaic.

The word **consuetudo** (l.12) is worth noting. It can mean 'custom' in the sense of an accepted practice, usually legal in some sense,
or it can mean 'customary due/tax'.

In ll.14-15 occurs the rather curious phrase **die illa** ... **qua** ...
fuit vivus et mortuus, a fairly common way of indicating 'on the
day that ... died'.

In l.19 the verb **discutire** can mean 'to discuss', but it also means
'to investigate'. The literal meaning is 'to shake apart', and hence 'to
sort out the details'.

In l.22 **posse** is used as a noun ('power'); the phrase **pro posse
meo** means 'as far as I am able'.

In ll.29-32 **distribuerit** ... **statuerit** ... **fuerit** ... **fuerint** are all future perfects (though **fuerint** in l.32 hardly seems appropriate in the future perfect). Latin was always fairly fussy about the distinction between the simple future ('he will [buy]') and the future perfect ('he will have [bought]'), the latter indicating an action which *will have* taken place by a certain time. The Romance languages still tend to preserve this distinction. In some circumstances it is difficult to decide whether a future perfect or a perfect subjunctive is intended, since the two have the same endings except in the 1st person singular (**-ero** for the future perfect and **-erim** for the perfect subjunctive). In fact the future perfect is the commoner of the two, and in practice there is little problem since the translation 'have/has ...', will usually be adequate for both anyway, although for the Latin future perfect an English present is often a more natural translation.

ll.24-35 give some indication of the difficulties which the church had faced under William II and in the early years of Henry I, and which had been to a large extent removed by the insistence of Anselm, archbishop of Canterbury 1093-1109.

*

The Charter of Henry II to Lincoln was issued about 1157, in the early years of Henry's reign. His intention to restore good government after the feuding of Stephen's reign is evident from the wording of the opening sections of this charter, as of many others drafted at this time; Stephen's name is pointedly omitted (Henry II was grandson of Henry I and son of Maud, who had continued to oppose Stephen for much of his reign), and the one William referred to is, of course, William I and not William II.

4(c) Henricus Dei gratia, etc., episcopo Lincolniensi, justitiariis, vice-comitibus, baronibus, ministris et omnibus fidelibus suis Francis et Anglis Lincolniae salutem. Sciatis me concessisse civibus meis Lincolniae omnes libertates et consuetudines et leges suas quas
5 habuerunt tempore Eduardi et Willelmi et Henrici regum Angliae, et gildam suam mercatoriam de hominibus civitatis et de aliis mercatoribus comitatus, sicut illam habuerunt tempore praedictorum antecessorum nostrorum regum Angliae melius et liberius. Et omnes homines qui infra quatuor divisas civitatis manent et
10 mercatum deducunt, sint ad geldas et consuetudines et assisas civitatis sicut melius fuerunt tempore Eduardi Willelmi et Henrici regum Angliae. Concedo etiam eis quod si aliquis emerit aliquam

terram infra civitatem de burgagio Lincolniae, et eam tenuerit per annum et unum diem sine calumnia, et ille qui eam emerit possit
15 monstrare quod calumniator exstiterit in regione Angliae infra annum et non calumniatus est eam, extunc ut in antea bene et in pace teneat eam et sine placito. Confirmo etiam eis quod si aliquis manserit in civitate Lincolniae per annum et unum diem sine calumnia alicujus calumniatoris, et dederit consuetudines, et cives
20 poterint monstrare per leges et consuetudines civitatis quod calumniator exstiterit in regione Angliae et non calumniatus est eum, extunc ut in antea remaneat in pace, in civitate mea Lincolnia, sicut civis meus. Testibus Ph. episcopo Baioc., Ern. episcopo Lexov., Toma Cancellario, Comite Regin., Ric. de Humes Constabulario, H. de
25 Essexa Constabulario. Apud Notingeham.

[Stubbs, op. cit., pp. 197-8]

In l.8 there is a very common usage of comparative adverbs (ending in **-ius**) in a clause of comparison (**sicut** ...). This is not a Classical Latin usage, nor is it from English or French, and it is difficult to see why it developed specifically in this type of clause. The literal meaning is 'as they had it better and more freely in the time of our aforesaid predecessors the kings of England', but the sense is no more than 'fully and freely', or perhaps 'quite fully and freely', which is a nuance sometimes conveyed by the comparative. The usage is found again in l.11, though in l.16 **bene** is used in a similar context.

In ll.12-15 **emerit** ... **tenuerit** ... **emerit** ... **exstiterit** are all future perfects. Another series of future perfects occurs in ll.18-21 – **manserit** ... **dederit** ... **poterint** ... **exstiterit**. See note on 4(b) ll.29-32.

In l.14 the word **calumnia** means 'claim', i.e. a claim to the land in question. The word can also mean 'accusation' or 'charge' in a court case, or more generally 'a challenge', usually in a legal context. The classical meaning was 'a *false* accusation' (hence the English 'calumny'), but the sense of falseness or injustice was not necessarily implied in Medieval Latin usage. The general sense of the next few lines is that if none of the people who might possibly have any right to object had actually done so within a year and a day, then the purchaser of the land or the newly arrived citizen of Lincoln could feel secure.

*

79

The Charter of Henry II to Nottingham is probably also from 1157 or thereabouts. It contains rather more local detail than the Lincoln Charter, though there is also much 'common law' contained in both in very similar wording, and most charters have this kind of material with slight variants in the conditions which apply locally.

4(d)   Henricus, Rex Angliae, etc. Sciatis me concessisse et hac carta mea confirmasse burgensibus de Notingeham omnes illas liberas consuetudines quas habuerunt tempore Henrici avi nostri; scilicet tol et theam et infangenetheof et telonia a Thermotestona usque ad New-

5   arc, et de omnibus Trentam transeuntibus, ita plenarie ut in burgo de Notingeham, et ex alia parte a duito ultra Rampestunam usque ad aquam de Radeford in Nort. Homines etiam de Notingehamscira et de Derbescira venire debent ad burgum de Notingeham die Veneris et Sabbati cum quadrigis et summagiis suis; nec aliquis

10   infra decem leucas in circuitu de Notingeham tinctos pannos operari debet, nisi in burgo de Notingeham. Et si aliquis, undecunque sit, in burgo de Notingeham manserit anno uno et die uno, tempore pacis, absque calumnia, nullus postea nisi rex in eum ius habebit. Et quicunque burgensium terram vicini sui emerit et possederit per

15   annum integrum et diem unum absque calumnia parentum vendentis, si in Anglia fuerint, postea eam quiete possidebit. Neque praeposito burgi de Notingeham aliquem burgensium calumnianti respondeatur nisi alius fuerit accusator in causa. Et quicunque in burgo manserit, cujuscunque feodi sit, reddere debet simul cum

20   burgensibus talliagia et defectus burgi adimplere. Omnes etiam qui ad forum de Notingeham venerint, a vespere diei Veneris usque ad vesperam Sabbati, non namientur nisi pro firma regis. Et iter de Trenta liberum esse debet navigantibus quantum pertica una obtinebit ex utraque parte fili aquae. Quare volo et praecipio quod

25   praedicti burgenses praedictas consuetudines habeant et teneant bene et in pace, libere et quiete, et honorifice et plenarie et integre, sicut habuerunt tempore regis Henrici avi mei.

[Stubbs, op. cit., p. 198]

There are quite a lot of technical legal terms in this charter. The following brief definitions give the basic meaning of the words, but in many cases a complex legal concept lay behind the term:

     tol (l.3):the right to exact a toll on strangers bringing goods to the market.

     theam (l.4): the right to compel a person found in possession

of stolen property to name the person from whom he
received it.

infangenetheof (l.4): the right to punish anyone caught thiev-
ing within the borough.

telonia (l.4): usually assumed to be an alternative for **tol**,
though, if the drafter of this charter is presumed to know
what he was talking about, then it must be some other
kind of tax.

talliagium (l.20): a tax, usually specifically one imposed at
will by the lord on his vassals.

defectus (l.20): a default or deficit, or more generally a debt.

namiare (l.22): to distrain, i.e. to seize someone's goods in
payment of debt.

firma (l.22): any fixed payment such as an annual tax or a
lease; refers here to the annual tax to the king paid by
every borough.

The area defined in ll.4-7 covers a long swathe of territory each
side of the Trent, from Newark to Thurmaston (now a part of the city
of Leicester) on the south-east side and from Rampton (7 miles south
of Gainsborough) to Radford (now within the city of Nottingham) on
the north-west side – about 50 miles long by 10 miles wide.

In l.7 **Nort** is not a standard Latin word. The classical Latin word
was **septentrionalis**.

In ll.8-9 **die Veneris** means 'Friday' (see also l.21). Classical
Latin did not have words for the seven-day week; medieval Latin
made them up on the model of the vernacular languages, and thus
created **dies Solis** (or more usually **Dominica**), **Lunae, Martis,
Mercurii, Jovis, Veneris, Saturni** (or more usually **Sabbati**).

In ll.16-18 **Neque ... respondeatur** is an impersonal passive
subjunctive meaning literally 'let it not be replied', i.e. 'let no answer
be given'. The verb is here used in the legal sense of answering to a
charge in court. **Praeposito burgi** in ll.16-17 is the reeve of the
borough, here in the dative, and **calumnianti** is a present participle
agreeing with him. A fairly literal translation of this rather complex
sentence would be: 'Let no answer be given to the reeve of the
borough of Nottingham charging any of the citizens (burghers)
unless there shall be (future perfect in Latin) another accuser in the
case'; in other words, the reeve could not of his own accord bring a
charge against a burgher, but could only act if a formal accusation
was made by a third party.

In ll.21-2 **a vespere ... ad vesperam** shows the variable declension of this word. In fact it can be 1st declension **vespera** (f), or 2nd

declension **vesper-i** (m, of the **-er** group, retaining the **-e-**), or 3rd
declension **vesper-is** (m).

In ll.22-4 the statement that the course of the Trent is 'free' (i.e.
of any tolls) for one perch (5.5 yards) each side of the river refers to
the tow-path and landing areas within the borough boundaries.

*

The Great Charter of Liberties, or Magna Carta, of 1215, was issued
by king John after the barons had presented their demands in the
'Articles of the Barons'. The barons' demands were incorporated into
the Magna Carta, frequently in virtually the same words as written
in the 'Articles of the Barons'; in fact the text of the Magna Carta
was produced at Runnymede only a few days after John accepted
the barons' demands on 15th June. Magna Carta covered the freedom of the church (this was an addition to the barons' demands),
rights of inheritance, general principles of justice, ownership of
property, freedom of movement, and crucially the powers of the king
himself.

In the following texts the relevant sections of the 'Articles of the
Barons' is given first, followed by the clauses of the Magna Carta on
the same topic. The first texts are on the rights of widows:

4(e)   *'Articles of the Barons', sections 4 and 17*

Ne vidua det aliquid pro dote sua vel maritagio post decessum
mariti sui, sed maneat in domo sua per xl. dies post mortem ipsius,
et infra terminum illum assignetur ei dos; et maritagium statim
habeat et haereditatem suam.

5   Ne viduae distringantur ad se maritandum, dum voluerint sine
marito vivere; ita tamen quod securitatem facient quod non mari-
tabunt se sine assensu regis, si de rege teneant, vel dominorum
suorum de quibus tenent.

[Stubbs, op. cit., pp. 286-7]

The present subjunctives (**ne ... det ... maneat ... assignetur ...
habeat; ne ... distringantur**) are 3rd person commands – 'Let not
a widow give ...'

Inevitably there are some legal and technical terms:
dos, dotis, f. (l.1): not (at least at this period) a dowry in the
    sense of property given by the bride's father on her mar-

82

riage, but a dower or jointure, which was the widow's share of the lands of her deceased husband (a third if the husband held the land freehold).

maritagium (l.1): the word has two meanings: (i) the right of a lord to bestow a feudal dependant in marriage; (ii) the money or property which a wife brings to her husband, i.e. the dowry. In this case it is clearly the second meaning which is intended.

distringere (l.5): here in the sense 'to compel'. The word implies the seizure of possessions in case of default.

securitas (l.6): a pledge or guarantee.

tenere (ll.7-8): here as often used in the technical sense of holding property with feudal obligations to a lord.

4(f)   *Magna Carta, sections 7 and 8*

Vidua post mortem mariti sui statim et sine difficultate habeat maritagium et haereditatem suam, nec aliquid det pro dote sua vel pro maritagio suo vel haereditate sua, quam haereditatem maritus suus et ipsa tenuerint die obitus ipsius mariti, et maneat in domo
5   mariti sui per quadraginta dies post mortem ipsius, infra quos assignetur ei dos sua.

Nulla vidua distringatur ad se maritandum dum voluerit vivere sine marito, ita tamen quod securitatem faciat quod se non maritabit sine assensu nostro, si de nobis tenuerit, vel sine assensu
10 domini sui de quo tenuerit, si de alio tenuerit.

[Stubbs, op. cit., p. 294]

The lawyers have clearly dressed the text up a bit, but the demands of the barons have been fully met.

The freedom of movement for merchants and others was demanded by the barons and John agreed to this, with some interesting refinements:

4(g)   *'Articles of the Barons', sections 31 and 33*

Quod mercatores habeant salvum ire et venire ad emendum vel vendendum, sine omnibus malis toltis per antiquas et rectas consuetudines.

Ut liceat unicuique exire de regno et redire, salva fide domini

5   regis, nisi tempore werrae per aliquod breve tempus propter communem utilitatem regni.

[Stubbs, op. cit., p. 288]

In l.1 the phrase **habeant salvum** means literally 'they may have [it] safe', 'it' being the infinitives **ire et venire**, i.e. 'merchants should have safe passage in going and coming to buy or to sell'.

In l.2 **tolta** is a tax of any sort.

In l.5 the word **werra** is from the Norman French **werre**, which derives from the Old High German **werra**, to quarrel. The later French word **guerre** comes from the Norman French, and it is interesting to note that in the Magna Carta version the Latinised form is **gwerra** (see below, l.5 onwards), which reflected the contemporary French pronunciation. There is, of course, a perfectly good Latin word, **bellum**.

4(h)   *Magna Carta, sections 41-2*

Omnes mercatores habeant salvum et securum exire de Anglia, et venire in Angliam, et morari et ire per Angliam, tam per terram quam per aquam, ad emendum et vendendum, sine omnibus malis toltis, per antiquas et rectas consuetudines, praeterquam in tem-
5   pore gwerrae, et si sint de terra contra nos gwerrina; et si tales inveniantur in terra nostra in principio gwerrae, attachientur sine dampno corporum et rerum, donec sciatur a nobis vel capitali justiciario nostro quomodo mercatores terrae nostrae tractentur, qui tunc invenientur in terra contra nos gwerrina; et si nostri salvi sint
10   ibi, alii salvi sint in terra nostra.

     Liceat unicuique de cetero exire de regno nostro et redire salvo et secure per terram et per aquam, salva fide nostra, nisi tempore gwerrae per aliquod breve tempus, propter communem utilitatem regni, exceptis imprisonatis et utlagatis secundum legem regni, et
15   gente de terra contra nos gwerrina, et mercatoribus de quibus fiat sicut praedictum est.

[Stubbs, op. cit., pp. 297-8]

We see again the lawyers refinements to the Barons' text, but also considerable additions to cover the situation in time of war.

In l.6 is the legal term **attachiare**, meaning to seize a person or,

84

more usually, property by legal process ('to attach' in the legal sense).

In l.11 **de cetero** is a common way of expressing 'moreover', 'in addition'.

In l.14 **utlagatis** are outlaws, from the Old English **utlaga**. In Medieval Latin there are several words created from **utlaga**: **utlagus/utlagatus** (an outlaw), **utlagare** (to outlaw), and **utlagia** (outlawry).

*

The following short charter comes from Scotland. There are no differences in the style of the document from the ones above, in that the same formulaic phrases are used, and this was so throughout most of western Europe, with only minor regional variations. In this charter there is an interesting problem of date:

4(i)   *Charter granted by Alexander, King of Scots, to Elgin*

Alexander Dei gracia Rex Scottorum omnibus probis hominibus totius terrae sue salutem. Sciatis nos concessisse et hac carta nostra confirmasse burgensibus nostris de Elgyn ut ipsi ad melioracionem burgi nostri de Elgyn habeant in eodem burgo gildam suam merca-
5   tricem adeo liberam sicut aliquis burgorum nostrorum in toto regno nostro gildam suam habet liberiorem. Testibus Alano hostiario, Reginaldo le Chen camerario, Hugone de Abbirnyth, Willelmo et Bernardo de Monte Alto, Alexandro de Moravia, et Willelmo Byset. Apud Elgyn, vicesimo octavo die Novembris, anno regni nostri
10   vicesimo.

                                                              Anno 1234

[Transcribed from J. Barrett and D. Iredale, op. cit., p. 128ff.]

In the manuscript it is clear that the date of 1234 was added in a different hand from the rest of the text, probably in the 18th century. The problem is that the charter does not make it clear which Alexander granted it. Alexander II and Alexander III both ruled for more than twenty years, and so either would be possible from the statement that the charter was drafted in the twentieth year of the reign. Alexander II ruled from 1214 to 1249, and some helpful later antiquarian has assumed that the charter is from his reign and added the date of 1234. But it happens that the date of Reginald le

Chen's chancellorship (who is one of the witnesses) is known from other sources, and it was very short – from 1267 to 1269. The charter must therefore be from the reign of Alexander III, who ruled from 1249 to 1286; his twentieth year was 1268, in the middle of Reginald's short chancellorship, and this must be the date of the charter.

*

In 1283 Edward I completed the conquest of Wales, and in 1301 he made his son (later Edward II) Prince of Wales. The charter in which the declaration was made was issued at Nettleham in Lincolnshire (where Edward's court happened to be staying at the time) on 7 February 1301. It is a rather rambling and repetitive document, but of special interest because of its details about the settlement of affairs in Wales and of the establishment of the first Prince of Wales. The full text is given, if only to show how repetitive such documents can be!

4(j)   *Pro Edwardo filio Regis*

Rex Archiepiscopis et ceteris salutem. Sciatis nos dedisse, concessisse et hac carta mea confirmasse Edwardo filio nostro karissimo omnes terras nostras Northwallie, Angleseye et de Hope cum omnibus terris et tenementis nostris infra quatuor cantreda existentibus
5   et etiam omnes terras nostras Westwallie et Southwallie, videlicet comitatibus de Kermerdyn et de Kaerdigan castra et manoria de Hauerford et de Buelt, omnes terras et tenementa que fuerunt Resi ap Mereduk et que sunt in manu nostra per forisfactum ipsius Resi, una cum omnibus aliis terris et tenementis nostris in partibus illis
10   in manu nostra die confectionis presentis carte existentibus, exceptis castro et villa de Monte Gomeri cum pertinenciis que karissime consorti nostre Margarete Regine Anglie assignavimus in dotem. Dedimus etiam et concessimus eidem filio nostro totum comitatum nostrum Cestrie, una cum maneriis nostris de Maclesfeld et de
15   Overton ac tota terra nostra de Meilor Seisnek cum omnibus suis pertinenciis, habendum et tenendum, cum castris villis maneriis libertatibus consuetudinibus homagiis serviciis redditibus feodis militum advocationibus ecclesiarum escaetis mineris wrecco maris et omnibus aliis ad terras et tenementa supradicta pertinentibus,
20   quocunque nomine censeantur, prefato filio nostro et heredibus suis Regibus Anglie imperpetuum, adeo integre et plenarie sicut nos terras et tenementa illa cum omnibus suis pertinenciis tenuimus,

86

salvis prefate consorti nostre castro et villa de Monte Gomeri cum
pertinenciis que ei assignavimus in dotem ut predictum est; faci-
25   endo nobis pro comitatibus et terris et tenementis supradictis tale
servicium quale invenietur nos fecisse celebris memorie domino
Henrico quondam Regi Anglie patri nostro pro comitatibus et can-
tredis predictis dum ea tenuimus ex concessione eiusdem patris
nostri. Quare volumus et firmiter precipimus quod predictus filius
30   noster et heredes sui Reges Anglie imperpetuum habeant et teneant
omnes predictas terras tenementa cum comitatibus predictis, una
cum castris villis maneriis libertatibus consuetudinibus homagiis
serviciis redditibus feodis militum advocationibus ecclesiarum escaetis mineris wrecco maris et omnibus aliis ad terram et tenementa
35   supradicta pertinentibus quocunque nomine censeantur, adeo integre et plenarie sicut nos terras et tenementa illa cum omnibus suis
pertinenciis tenuimus, salvis prefate consorti mee castro et villa de
Monte Gomeri cum pertinenciis que ei assignavimus in dotem,
faciendo nobis pro comitatibus et terris et tenementis supradictis
40   tale servicium quale invenietur nos fecisse celebris memorie domino
Henrico quondam Regi Anglie patri nostro pro comitatibus et can-
tredis predictis dum ea tenuimus ex concessione eiusdem patris
nostri sicut predictum est. Hiis testibus venerabilibus patribus R.
Cantuar. Archiepiscopo, J. Lincoln., S. Sarum, J. Norwyc, W.
45   Coventr. et Lycheff. et J. Karliolen. Episcopis; Johanne de Warenne
comite Surr., Rogero le Bigod Norf. et marescallo Anglie, Radulfo de
Montehermer Gloucestr. et Hereford, Guidon de Bello Campo Warr.,
et Ricardo Arundell comitibus; Johanne de Britannia, Reginaldo de
Grey, Johanne de Sancto, Johanne de Hastings, et aliis. Datum per
50   manum nostram apud Netleham vij. die februar.

[Transcribed from Public Record Office, London, Document
C53/87/36]

Despite the long sentences the grammar of the Latin is not complex.
The writer has an odd liking for the letter 'k', even in a purely Latin
word **karissimus** (l.2 and 11).

In l.4 a **cantredum** is an administrative division or region (a
'cantred'). The word comes from the Welsh **cant** (hundred) and **tref**
(town).

The use of **dotem** in l.12, for example, is as noted in passage 4(e)
l.1.

The word **escaeta** (l.18 and 33-4) is 'escheat' (from Old French

eschoir, from the Latin **excadere**, to fall out), the reversion of a property to the lord when the feudal tenant has no heirs.

A copy of the letters sent by Edward to the various guardians of the properties granted to his son has also survived:

4(k)   Rex dilecto et fideli suo Philippo Abhowel custodi castri ville et terre de Buelt salutem. Cum per cartam nostram dederimus et concesserimus Edwardo filio nostro karissimo castrum villam et terras predicta cum omnibus suis pertinenciis habendum et tenendum sibi
5   et heredibus suis regibus Anglie imperpetuum prout in carta predicta plenarie continetur, vobis mandamus quod prefato filio nostro castrum villam et terram cum suis pertinenciis quibuscunque sine dilatione liberetis habenda et tenenda iuxta formam carte predicte, testibus ut supra.
10   Consimiles littere diriguntur Willelmo Chykum custodi castri et ville de Aberconewey, Johanni de Haueringg [sic], custodi castri de Beaumareys et terre de Angleseye, Thome de Makelesfeld custodi maneriorum de Makelesfeld et de Overton cum pertinenciis et terre de Mailor Seisnek, et Waltero Hachit custodi castri et ville de
15   Hauerford, testibus ut supra.

[Transcribed from same document as 4(j)]

In ll.2-3 **dederimus** and **concesserimus** are perfect subjunctives after **cum**, meaning 'since ...'

In l.4 **habendum et tenendum** should strictly be **habenda et tenenda** (neuter plural), since the two words should agree with the mixed gender list of **castrum villam et terras**. The writer correctly wrote **predicta**, but then forgot to change the regular formula of **habendum et tenendum**. This occurs so frequently as to be regarded as a standard (if non-classical) usage.

*

These examples give the flavour of royal charters and related documents. The Latin is frequently rather repetitive and hedged about with legal cautions, and, as we have seen, often contains a fair amount of specialised legal vocabulary. However, it is invariably carefully drafted and grammatically accurate, even though one is often faced with long rambling sentences with little help from the sparse punctuation. It is essential to identify the clausal structure of such material and then to deal with each clause or phrase as a unit. Main verbs and participles are usually the key elements in this framework. Lists of various sorts are also important parts of the charter structure, and the beginning and end of these are usually fairly easy to identify. An analytical approach of this sort will usually give at least the main structures of any charter. To get all the details right often requires a lot of checking in dictionaries and other reference works – even for those who know Latin well!

5

Court Rolls

Court rolls are usually to be found in county, borough or city archives, and also in ecclesiastical records since ecclesiastical courts were a feature of the medieval scene. During the post-conquest period there were several different layers in the civil judicial system, and there were considerable changes between the 11th and 17th centuries during which Latin was used for all court records. In brief, until the fourteenth century most local cases were tried in manorial or baronial courts, but from 1362 these were replaced by courts of Justices of the Peace in each borough. There were at the highest level 'crown courts' of various sorts, under the direct authority of the king. The ecclesiastical courts were usually under the authority of the bishops, though in some cases they were administered by local monasteries (until they were dissolved in 1536-9).

The content of court rolls is, as one might expect, very varied since all manner of cases were dealt with, particularly in the local courts. The Latin legal vocabulary can be very daunting, and often translations do no more than give an English version which itself is no more helpful in defining what the words actually mean. The following short list of some very frequently occurring terms may be found helpful:

affido, -are: to declare on oath.
amerciamentum: amercement, fine.
amercio, -are: to fine.
assisa, assisum, assisia, assissium (and various other spellings): a difficult word! (i) assessment, tax; (ii) statute, regulation; (iii) action, claim; (iv) (mainly in Scotland) a court.
attachiamentum: 'attachment', i.e. seizure of a person's goods in payment, usually of a fine and usually carried out by a bailiff.
attachio, -are: to 'attach', i.e. to seize a person's goods (see also **distringo** and **namio**); also 'to arrest' a person.
breve, -is, n.: a writ.

calum(p)nia: (i) accusation, charge; (ii) claim (NB the word rarely means 'calumny').

camera: ecclesiastical court.

compurgator: a supporter in court (see also **manus**).

curia: court.

dam(p)num: loss, damage; in pl. damages, compensation.

deforcio, -are: to 'deforce', i.e. to prevent a person from possessing what is rightfully theirs – a common accusation!

distringo, -ere, -inxi, -ictum (and various derivatives): to 'distrain', i.e. to seize a person's goods in payment (like **attachiare** and **namio**).

divisa, divisum: (i) a boundary; (ii) a court or court-day.

emenda, amenda, emendatio: fine, compensation.

emendo, -are: to pay a fine or compensation (*not* 'to fine'). The word also means 'to correct, improve'.

finis, -is, m.: payment of a legal due, often 'final payment' to settle a lawsuit (NB not normally 'fine' in a punitive sense).

gravamen, -inis, n.: (i) injury; (ii) accusation.

indentatus: 'indented', i.e. cut with an irregular zigzag edge. Two copies of a document were often cut this way so that the shape of the cut was evidence that the two were in fact copies of the same thing.

insulto, -are: the regular word for 'to *assault*'.

loquela: court action.

manus, -us, f.: 'hand', but often found in the odd phrase '**cum ... manu**' with a numeral between the two words and meaning 'with ... supporters or compurgators'.

misericordia: lit. 'mercy', but in court records usually found in the phrase **in misericordia**, lit. 'in mercy', i.e. at the mercy of the court and therefore 'to be fined'.

namium: distraint, goods distrained (see **distringo** and **attachio**).

namio, -are: to distrain. Any distinction that may have existed between **namiare**, **attachiare**, and **distringere** seems to have been lost.

nocumentum: harm, damage, annoyance.

petens, -ntis: plaintiff (see also **querens**).

plegagium: pledge, security.

plegius: (i) surety, one who stands bail; (ii) bail.

presento, -are: to show, state in court. The usual word for 'to present a case' – **presentant quod** ... 'they present/state that ...'.

purprestura (also **perprestura**, **proprestura**): (i) illegal encroachment, usually onto public land; (ii) can also mean *the right* to encroach by agreement onto such land (see note on text 3(o), l.31).

querens, -ntis: lit. 'complainant', plaintiff (see also **petens**).

secta: (i) a case in court; (ii) the feudal duty to attend a manorial court (see note on text 3(o), ll.3-4); (iii) a body of witnesses produced in court.

tenens, -ntis: (i) a tenant; (ii) a defendant in court.

Numerous formulaic phrases will be found in the 17th century Quarter Session records in 5(d)(i)-(viii) below. Most of these are typical of all such records of the 17th century, when a style developed which was rather different from earlier court records.

*

The first example comes from Great Waltham in Essex (about three miles north of Chelmsford and a mile from Little Waltham – see 3(h)), and is a manor court roll from 1318. The court was the manor court of Walter de Mandeville, Lord of the Manor of Chatham Hall in Great Waltham. The text is transcribed from Hilda E.P. Grieve, *Examples of English Handwriting 1150-1750*, Essex Record Office Publications, No. 21, 1954, Plate XX.

5(a)   Visus Franciplegii ibidem die et anno supradictis.

Communis finis Omnes capitales plegii dant de communi fine
v.s' j.d' v.s' j.d'

Omnes capitales plegii presentant quod
5 Willelmus Heynon fecit purpresturam fodiendo
terram in quadam venella que ducit de domo
misericordia Johannis Coci versus planistriam de Chatham,
iij.d' ideo in misericordia, per plegium Johannis Cook
et Johannis Lytle.

10 Item presentant quod Willelmus Mot fecit
purpresturam ponendo fimum in communi
misericordia strata ad nocumentum domini et vicinorum.
iij.d' Ideo ipse in misericordia.

Item presentant quod Robertus Leuelif fecit
15 purpesturam cum j. muro obstupando quemdam
cursum aque ad nocumentum vicinorum, ideo
ipse in misericordia, per plegium Johannis

	misericordia vj.d'	Cok et Willelmi Heynon. Et preceptum est ammovere dictum murum.
20		Et postea dictus Robertus fecit finem ut possit dictus murus stare in pace quia non stat ad magnum nocumentum, per plegium
	finis ij.s'	predictorum Johannis Cook et Willelmi Heynon.
25		Item presentant quod Robertus Leuelif fecit purpresturam ponendo fimum in communi strata ad nocumentum vicinorum, ideo ipse in
	misericordia iij.d'	misericordia, per plegium Johannis Cok et Willelmi Heynon.
30		Item presentant quod Thomas Randolf fecit purpresturam cum quadam haya iuxta
	misericordia ij.d'	Colkeslane ad nocumentum Jacobi de la Hyde et aliorum, ideo ipse in misericordia, per plegium Ade Rat et Ricardi Hwytbred. Et preceptum est
	preceptum est	ammovere dictam purpresturam.
35	preceptum est	Item presentant quod dominus deberet mundare fossatum iuxta venellam sub Curia sua per quod via vicina tempore iemali est omnino submersa ad nocumentum vicinorum.
40	misericordia iij.d'	Item presentant quod Ricardus filius Ricardi Hwytbred fecit defaltam, ideo ipse in misericordia.

In most court rolls abbreviations are taken to their limit, mainly because the language is so repetitive. In this document, for instance, the following abbreviations are used throughout (with or without signs to indicate an abbreviation):

> **cois**: communis
> **fin**: finis
> **ps**: presentant
> **qd**: quod
> **mia**: misericordia
> **it/itm**: item
> **plm**: plegium
> **p**: preceptum
> **dcus**: dictus
> **Johis**: Johannis
> **Ric**: Ricardus (or any other case)

Wills: Willelmus

Most case endings are omitted, usually with the customary bar over the final vowel. All this can make the reading of court rolls a tricky business, made worse by the fact that individual clerks developed their own styles and abbreviations. But the fact that the material *is* so repetitive means that after a page or two one gets used to the individual idiosyncrasies of the clerk. Even so, spellings can be disconcertingly varied (as in the name 'Cook' in this example – **Coci, Cook, Cok**). Also many clerks had a restricted Latin vocabulary, and were very prone to slipping in English words with Latin endings.

The layout of this document is typical of most court rolls well into the 17th century. Down the left-hand margin (sometimes the right-hand margin is used) the clerk kept a running record of all fines, payments, and court orders. The amounts to be paid were usually totalled at the end of the record for each session. This layout obviously enabled the clerk to refer quickly to previous court decisions, and also to keep the accounts straight.

In l.1 the word **frankiplegium** is 'frankpledge', a system in which a group of tithe-payers formed a mutual suretyship and were responsible for one another's tithe payments, and also for any fines. The recipients of the tithe liked the system, and it also offered a measure of protection to individuals in time of hardship. This explains the first item, which is the joint payment of the tithing group. This also illustrates the use of the word **finis**, which can mean a payment of any legal due, and is in this document clearly distinguished from **misericordia**, which means 'fine' in a punitive sense.

In l.7 **planistriam de Chatham** refers to Chatham Green, a village about two miles to the north-east of Great Waltham.

Gerunds crop up frequently in court rolls, explaining how a person has actually committed the offence. In this example there is **fodiendo** ('by digging') in l.5, **ponendo** ('by putting') in l.11, **obstupando** ('by blocking') in l.15, and **ponendo** again in l.25.

In l.37 **per quod** is odd Latin. It doubtless represents the Middle English expression 'for that' (meaning 'because'). It is interesting to note that the lord is given an instruction in his own court.

Because the communities covered by these local courts were quite small, one finds the same names occurring frequently – often for the same offences!

*

95

The following short excerpt comes from a manor court roll from Antingham, three miles north-west of North Walsham in Norfolk and is dated to September 1438. It concerns a certain Richard Jonyour who was accused of neglecting the upkeep of his house (**messuagium**). Richard was a villein, and the maintenance of the house was apparently part of his duty as a villein. The case was brought on behalf of the lord of the manor of Antingham, who was the Lady Joan Witchingham of Witchingham Magna. The clerk of the court found himself switching gender from **domini** ('of the lord', l.5) to **domine** ('of the lady') in l.12. The text is transcribed from J. Barrett and D. Iredale, *Discovering Old Handwriting*, Shire Publications 1995, p. 140ff.

5(b) Capitulum: Curia ibidem tenta die mercurii proxima post festum
Exaltacionis Sancte Crucis anno regni regis Henrici sexti xvijmo.

<table>
<tr><td></td><td>Capitulum: Iuratores ex officio presentant quod</td></tr>
<tr><td></td><td>Ricardus Ionyour graviter vastavit messuagium</td></tr>
<tr><td>5</td><td>suum de villenagio domini in Antyngham ita</td></tr>
<tr><td></td><td>quod sunt in periculo cadere pro defectu tecture,</td></tr>
<tr><td></td><td>daubure, et carpentarie. Ideo in misericordia. Et</td></tr>
<tr><td>Misericordia</td><td>preceptum est ei dictum messuagium bene et</td></tr>
<tr><td>vj.d'</td><td>sufficienter reperare citra proximam Curiam</td></tr>
<tr><td>10</td><td>sub pena vj.s' viij.d'. Et quia impotens est</td></tr>
<tr><td></td><td>dictum tenementum reperare ut dicitur, ideo</td></tr>
<tr><td></td><td>preceptum est seisire in manum domine, et</td></tr>
<tr><td></td><td>cetera.</td></tr>
</table>

In the manuscript the word **Capitulum** in ll.1 and 3 is written simply as a rather ornate capital C. Often it is written as a large and decorated reverse capital P (for the abbreviation Cp).

The feast of the Exaltation of the Holy Cross (ll.1-2) is on 14 September, but since this can be any day of the week the actual date of the Wednesday after this would have to be calculated – if anyone is sufficiently interested!

In l.6 **sunt** should be **est**, referring to **messuagium**.

The last sentence, beginning with **Et** ... at l.10, may have been added at the next court session, when it became clear that Richard was unable to carry out the necessary work on the messuage.

*

5. Court Rolls

The ecclesiastical courts dealt with cases which in some way involved the church. These included cases concerning the duties and rights of the clergy and often their misdemeanours, but also cases which in any way touched on marital law – and there were plenty of these, mostly concerning the dissolution of marriages. But morality in its many forms was also seen as the rightful domain of the ecclesiastical courts, and perhaps inevitably sexual morality, or rather the lack of it, features fairly prominently in many ecclesiastical court records.

The following extracts come from the *Act Books of the Ecclesiastical Court of Whalley*, published by the Chetham Society, Manchester, vol. 44 (New Series), 1901. Whalley Abbey was a Cistercian house, about eight miles west of Burnley in Lancashire. The abbey owned considerable amounts of land in the area, and hence the abbot became in effect a feudal lord. By the time of the following record, which is dated 10 May 1532, these powers were still reflected to some extent in the fact that it was the abbot and not the diocesan bishop who was responsible for the ecclesiastical court in Whalley. The session recorded here was in fact held in Whalley parish church, which is only a few hundred metres from the abbey.

Just four years after this court was held the abbey joined the Pilgrimage of Grace in opposition to Henry VIII's plans for the dissolution of many smaller monasteries, and was dissolved in March 1537 after the execution of its abbot. Its ruins are now partly in the grounds of the Blackburn Diocese Conference Centre and partly in the grounds of a Roman Catholic church.

5(c)   Officium contra Johannem Cronkshay. Notatur quod carnaliter cognovisset Emmotam, uxorem Ricardi Cronkshay, et ipse etiam maritatus et consanguineus dicto Ricardo Cronkshay in secundo et secundo gradibus consanguinitatis et affinitatis. Comparuit vir. Et
5   continuatur in diem Jovis ut supra, et postea comparuit mulier, et moniti sunt ad interessendum die Jovis proximo post festum Penticostes.

... Agnes Marsden de Bollande impregnata est ex illicito coitu per quendam Jacobum Cutler manentem extra jurisdiccionem. Com-
10   paruit mulier et fatetur articulum. Et jurata est de peragendo penitencias sibi factas, etc. Et iniunctum est sibi quod circuat ecclesiam parochialem de Chyppeyne uno die processionaliter et penetensialiter cum candela ceria in manu sua precij unius jd. Et

97

15 similiter uno die circa capellam Sancti Michaelis infra castallum de
Clederoy citra festum Marie Magdalene.

[op. cit., p. 149]

The situation described in ll.2-4 appears to be that John Cronkshay is the son of Richard, since the 'second degree of consanguinity' is the relationship of son to father. The 'second degree of affinity' is the relationship of son to the father's wife. Apparently the situation here described in such ecclesiastically technical language is that John Cronkshay had been having an affair with his father's (presumably young) wife, Emmota.

The sequence of events in ll.4-5 is not entirely clear. It seems that the case had been considered at an earlier session of the court and had been adjourned to this session (**die Jovis ut supra** must refer to the date of this session as given at the beginning of the record), but exactly what is meant by **postea** is unclear. Since the case was not actually completed at this session, it seems that Emmota did not appear actually at the session, but presented herself, perhaps to the clerk of the court, after the session, and she and John Cronkshay were instructed to appear at the court on the Thursday after Pentecost, presumably the next session of the court which would be a few weeks after this one on 10 May.

In l.6 is a non-classical gerund, **interessendum**, formed from the infinitive of the verb **interesse**, 'to be present at', 'to attend'.

In l.8 **Bollande** is the area of the Forest of Bowland. From the references later to **Chyppeyne** (l.12; this is Chipping, about 10 miles north-east of Preston) and **Clederoy** (l.15; Clitheroe, three miles north of Whalley) it seems likely (though the record does not make this clear) that Agnes came from the parish of Chipping and lived on the estates of Clitheroe Castle. This would account for her two acts of penance in these two places. The church at Chipping has a list of the incumbents and records George Wolfet as the rector from 1531 to 1554; his part in all this is not recorded. The Chapel of St Michael in the castle at Clitheroe has long since disappeared, though its position can be traced from 17th century plans.

The penance described in ll.11-15 seems to be about the going rate for such moral lapses in the court at Whalley; there are more such cases in the records and they all receive similar treatment. The specification of a penny candle with 'one' written both as a word **unius** and as the numeral **j** shows the working of a legal mind.

In l.15 the feast of Mary Magdalene is on 22 July, so Agnes had some ten weeks in which to carry out her penance. Naming the feast of Mary Magdalene as the terminal date may have seemed appropriate to the church hierarchy.

*

The following Quarter Sessions records come from Kendal in the former county of Westmorland. These records are from 1694-5, and such documents are amongst the last to be regularly written in Latin; from 1733 Quarter Sessions used English for their records. These examples from Kendal are written in a clear hand though with numerous abbreviations (both standard and non-standard) by a clerk who had a fair command of Latin. They are therefore fairly typical of such records since most clerks to the courts did have a fairly good knowledge of the Latin needed for court purposes – and they did use many abbreviations. In this case the clerk has recorded in the left-hand margin the name of the accused as a quick reference guide to aid future consultation of his records.

These examples were taken at random from the Kendal Quarter Sessions records. They are transcribed from a double-page spread of the records for the Christmas sessions 1694 which were actually held in January 1695 (Westmorland Quarter Sessions, Order Book WQ/0/1, held in the Cumbria Record Office at Kendal). Nationally these Quarter Sessions courts were held at four specified times in the year: within a week of Epiphany (6 January); within the week of Mid-Lent in March; between Pentecost and St John the Baptist in June; and within eight days of Michaelmas (29 October). The court's decision in these cases is not given in these records; presumably it was recorded in the session papers, but these have not survived for this period.

In this transcription the abbreviations of the original have been written out in full, but the first text is repeated in the original abbreviated version to illustrate the kind of abbreviations regularly found in this type of document.

5(d)   Christmas [written Xtmas] 1694

(i)   Juratores pro domino Rege super sacramentum
                             suum presentant quod Lancelot Lancaster de
                             Ambleside in comitatu predicto, yeoman,
                             tricesimo die October anno regni Regis

5	Lancaster	Gullielmi et nuper Regine Marie Anglie etc.
	Lancelot	sexto vi et armis apud Ambleside in comitatu
		predicto aliquam ovem matricem cujusdam
		Thoma Ellis precij quinque solidorum ibidem
		nuper inventam existentem felonice cepit,
10		furatus est et asportavit et alia enormia etc. ad
		grave dampnum etc. et contra pacem etc.

Testibus: George Fisher

Thomas Dixon

Thomas Ellis

15   Jurati

Transcribed with original abbreviations (any superscript mark is indicated by a . in the position of the mark):

> Jur. pro d.no Rege sup. sacrm. suu. p.ntant
> quod Lancelot Lancaster de Ambleside in com.
> predict. yeom. tricesimo die October anno regni
> Rg. Gul. & nup. Regin. Mar. Angl. &c. sexto vi
> & armis apud Ambleside in com. p.dict. .l.m.
> ovem matricem cujusdm. Thoma Ellis p.cij
> quinq. solid. ibm. nuper invent. existen. felonice
> cepit furat. est et asportavit et al. enormia &c.
> ad gra.e dampnu. &c. & contra pac. &c.

The first line is a set formula which appears in every record at this period.

In l.5 **nuper** ('recently', or of a person 'late') is used here of Queen Mary who had died on 28 December 1694, only a few days before this 'Christmas' session was held.

In l.7 an **ovis matrix** is 'a ewe'. The term has good classical precedents.

As will be seen from later examples, the last two lines contain set formulas which are frequently repeated.

(ii)		Juratores pro domino Rege super sacramentum
		suum presentant quod Georgius Browne de
		Troutbeck in comitatu Westmorlandia
	Brown	generosus decimo die Junij anno regni domini
5	George	Regis Gullielmi et nuper domine Regine Marie
		Anglie etc. sexto vi et armis clausuram
		cuiusdam Rowlandi Cookson vocatam

Hindwick Mosse apud Troutbeck in comitatu
predicto fregit et intravit et diversas
10   quantitates canabie (anglice 'hemp'), videlicet
quinque carrectates canabij in clausuram
predictam ejecit (anglice 'did lay') ad grave
dampnum ipsius Rowlandi et contra pacem
domini Regis nunc etc.
15   Teste: Rowland Cookson
                          Juratus

In ll.10-11 the writer has used both feminine and neuter forms of the word **canabia/um**. Both do occur elsewhere. The word is, of course, now used for the botanical name for hemp (*Cannabis sativa*); though the stuff referred to here is the material that ropes and canvas are made of and not the stuff for smoking!

In l.12 **ejecit** appears to mean 'dumped' (rather than the 'did lay' of the text), but exactly what George Brown was doing dumping five cartloads of hemp (perhaps old rope or canvas?) in Rowland Cookson's close is not at all clear.

In l.14 the words implied after the **nunc** are something like 'sole monarch of England etc.' after the death of his wife, the queen.

(iii)

Juratores pro domino Rege super sacramentum
suum presentant quod cum quidam Georgius
Browne generosus et omnes illi quorum statum
ipse habet a tempore cuius contraria memoria
5 hominum non existit diu et legitime
possessionatus fuisset et adhuc possessionatus
existit de et in uno antiquo turbatorio (anglice 'a
peat moss') in quodam loco vocato Hindwick in
Troutbeck in comitatu predicto, et nulle persone
10 quicunque aliquas turbas in eodem sine licentia

Hoggart   ipsius Georgij effodebant, quidam Robert
Robert   Hoggart de Applethwaite in comitatu predicto,
et Mariam yeoman, et Maria uxor eius vicesimo die Junij
uxor   anno regni Regis Gullielmi nuper Regine Marie
15 Anglie etc. sexto vi et armis in turbatorium
predictum intraverunt et diversas carrectates
turbarum anglice 'peats' effodebant et
abcarriaverunt, ad grave dampnum ipsius
Georgij et contra pacem etc.

20   Teste: George Browne generosus
Juratus

The **cum** clause which begins in l.2 goes on until l.11, though after **fuisset** in l.6 the writer has forgotten that subjunctives are required.

The sense of **et omnes illi** ... **habet** in ll.3-4 appears to be that the turbary was available not only to George Brown but also to those who worked on the estate which he owned – but not to any others without George Brown's permission. It is, to say the least, expressed in a somewhat laborious fashion.

This is the same George Brown who, ten days before this event, was dumping hemp in Rowland Cookson's close (see 5(d)(ii)). It seems from this case that Rowland Cookson's close must have been adjacent to George Brown's land. But the story continues ...

(iv)   Juratores pro domino Rege super sacramentum
suum presentant quod cum quidam Georgius
Browne generosus et omnes illi quorum statum
ipse habet a tempore cuius contraria memoria
5   hominum non existit, diu et legitime
possessionatus fuisset, et adhuc possessionatus
existit de et in uno antiquo turbatorio (anglice 'a
peat moss') in quodam loco vocato Hindwick in
Troutbeck in comitatu predicto, et nulle persone
10   quicunque aliquas turbas in eodem sine licentia
      Cookson   ipsius Georgij effodebant, quidam Rowland
      Rowland   Cookson de Applethwaite in comitatu predicto,
      Birkett   et John Birkett de eodem decimo septimo die
      John   Octobri anno regni Regis Gullielmi et nuper
15   Regine Marie Anglie etc. sexto vi et armis in
turbatorium predictum intraverunt et diversas
carrectates turbarum anglice 'peats' effodebant
ad grave dampnum ipsius Georgij et contra
pacem etc.
20   Teste: George Browne
Juratus

The wording is, of course, virtually as for (iii) above; I have retained it mainly to show how formulaic these records usually are! But this time it is Rowland Cookson, with an accomplice John Birkett, who has been accused of stealing turves. We discover that Rowland

Cookson comes from Applethwaite, which is just across the beck from Troutbeck village. One detects something of a local feud going on here.

(v)		Juratores pro domino Rege super sacramentum
		suum presentant quod Thomas Jackson de
		Storth in comitatu predicto yeoman et Thomas
	Jackson	Burrow de Beetham in comitatu predicto
5	Thomas	yeoman secundo die Januarij anno regni domini
	Burrow	Regis Willelmi Dei gratia Anglie Scotie Francie
	Thomas	et Hibernie fidei defensor etc. sexto vi et armis
		apud Storth predictum in comitatu predicto
		aliquam ovem matricem cuiusdam Thoma
10		Burrow senioris ceperunt et asportaverunt et
		alia enormia ei intulerunt ad grave dampnum
		ipsius Thoma et contra pacem dicti domini
		Regis coronam et dignitatem suam etc.

	Testibus:	Ellias Johnson
15		Thomas Burrow
		Richard Fell

In ll.6-7 **Scotie Francie et Hibernie** explains the **Anglie etc** of the earlier examples. The writer has now dropped the reference to Queen Mary since the offence recorded took place in January 1695, after the death of the queen on 28 December 1694.

In ll.12-13 there is a longer version of the formula **contra pacem** ....

Beetham is on the A6 about nine miles south of Kendal, and Storth is a mile west of Beetham. Thomas Burrow senior in ll.9-10 is presumably the father of the Thomas Burrow in ll.3-4; these were small communities!

(vi)		Juratores pro domino Rege super sacramentum
		suum presentant quod Margaret Straker uxor
		Johannis Straker de Kirkby Kendal in comitatu
		predicto undecimo die Januarij anno regni
5		domini Regis Willelmi nunc Anglie etc. sexto
		apud Stainton in comitatu predicto machinans
		et false maliciose intendens quendam
		Richardum Holme ad tunc et ibidem in
		infamiam cum vicinis suis inducere et ipsum
10		Richardum in bono nomine suo pergravare de
		ipso Richardo ad tunc et ibidem in presentia et

Straker	audientia quamplurium ligeorum et fidelium
Margaret	subditorum dicti domini Regis haec falsa ficta
	verba scandulosa et oprobriosa anglicana
15	sequentia dixit propalavit et publicavit videlicet:
	Thou (ipsum predictum Richardum innuendo)
	has my trunck (ipsam predictam Margaret
	innuendo) and is an unworthy man for not
	bringing it out before this. Racione dictionis et
20	propalaceonis dictorum verborum et
	scandulosorum ipse predictus Richardus Holme
	in bono nomine suo valde deterioratus est ad
	grave dampnum ipsius Richardi et contra
	pacem etc.

25	Testibus:	Thomas Swanson
		Katherine Swanson
		Mary Jackson
		Jurati

In ll.6-15 is a long formula for slander cases of this kind (see (viii) below for a similar case). The substance of the case, at least as recorded in ll.16-19, hardly seems to merit the wording of the formula! Stainton is a hamlet about five miles south of Kendal; there cannot have been many neighbours.

In ll.16 and 18 **innuendo** should strictly be a present participle and not a gerund, but this extended use of the gerund was common in Medieval Latin in all but the more grammatically aware historians. It was doubtless this particular use of **innuendo**, which is commonly found, that gave rise to the use of the word as a noun in English.

In l.19 **racione** is the regular spelling in Medieval Latin of **ratione**.

(vii)		Juratores pro domino Rege super sacramentum
	Towanson	suum presentant quod Nicholas Towanson de
	Nicholas	Docker in comitatu predicto yeoman, Willelmus
	Towanson	Towanson de eodem in comitatu predicto
5	Will.	yeoman et Johannes Towanson de eodem in
	Towanson	comitatu predicto yeoman vicensimo secundo
	John	die Decembris anno regni Regis Gullielmi et
		nuper Regine Marie Anglie etc. sexto sepes et
		portas messuagij ipsius Nicholai generosi de
10		New Hutton in comitatu predicto vocati

Woodheads appertas permiserunt (Anglice
suffered to lye open) racione sepes et portas
apperiendi in messuagio predicto abierunt et
effugerunt inde bona et catalla ipsius Nicholai
15   et super comunam vocatam Docker Comon
transgressi sunt (Anglice did trespass) et
herbam et gramina comfregerunt et
consumpserunt ac predictus Willelmus et
Johannes bona et catalla predicta a predicto
20   messuagio ipsius Nicholai usque comunam
vocatam Docker Comon chasiaverunt ad grave
dampnum Bryani Wykman et contra pacem etc.
            Testibus: James Mallinson
                         Bryan Wykman
25   Jurati

The reference to the queen now reappears since the offence recorded
took place before her death.

New Hutton is about three miles to the east of Kendal, and
Docker is to the north of New Hutton.

The 'goods and chattels' of ll.14 and 19 are the various animals
held in Nicholas' paddock. It was winter and therefore he would
have had his livestock penned up near the farm. **Catalla** frequently
has the meaning 'cattle'. It would appear that the cattle crossed the
land of Bryan Wykeman on their trip to Docker Common, as did the
Townsons in their pursuit.

(viii)   Juratores pro domino Rege super sacramentum
                           suum presentant quod Peter Collinson de
      Collinson   Kirkby Lonsdale in comitatu predicto yeoman
        Peter   vicensimo die Decembris anno regni domini
5   Regis Willelmi et nuper domine Regine Marie
                           Anglie etc. sexto apud Kirkby Lonsdale
                           predictum in comitatu predicto machinans et
                           false et maliciose intendens quendam Robertum
                           Dineley ad tunc et ibidem in infamiam cum
10   vicinis suis inducere et ipsum Robertum in bono
                           nomine suo pergravare de ipso Roberto ad tunc
                           et ibidem in presentia et audientia
                           quamplurium ligeorum et fidelium subditorum
                           dicti domini Regis et domine Regine hec falsa
15   ficta verba scandulosa et

oprobriosa Anglicana sequentia dixit et
propálavit et publicavit videlicet: I (ipsum
predictum Peterum innuendo) want my mare,
and thou (ipsum predictum Robertum
20   innuendo) has stolen her. Racione dictionis et
propalaceonis dictorum verborum et
scandulosorum ipse predictus Robertus in bono
nomine suo valde deterioratus est ad grave
dampnum ipsius Roberti et contra pacem etc.
25   Teste: Robert Dineley

ll.1-17 are very similar to the formula used in (vi) above, except that the queen appears in the formula because the offence happened before her death.

Presumably ll.17-20 are only a very brief summary of what was actually said!

The only witness recorded is Robert Dineley himself; normally in these slander cases there are several neighbours who heard the slander.

*

Court records like these from the 17th and early 18th centuries survive in considerable quantity in most local record offices. Though the formulaic expressions do vary a little from area to area, the above sample gives a fair idea of the kind of language to be found. As one can see from these examples, a knowledge of the local geography and of the local customs (in these latter cases particularly of local farming practices) is essential to follow the details of the cases recorded.

6

Domesday Book; Historians after 1066

The Domesday Book is a unique record of the condition of England in 1086, twenty years after the Norman Conquest. Since it is more akin to history than to any other type of record, it is included in this section, though it is, of course, very different in style from the historians who were to follow.

Robert of Hereford, under the year 1086, has this to say about the compilation of the Domesday Book:

6(a)　Hic est annus XXmus Willelmi, regis Anglorum, quo jubente hoc anno totius Angliae facta est descriptio in agris singularum provinciarum, in possessionibus singulorum procerum, in agris eorum, in mansionibus, in hominibus tam servis quam liberis, tam in teguria
5　tantum habitantibus, quam in domos et agros possidentibus, in carrucis, in equis et ceteris animalibus, in servitio et censu totius terrae omnium. Alii inquisitores post alios, et ignoti ad ignotas mittebantur provincias, ut alii aliorum descriptionem reprehenderent et regi eos reos constituerent. Et vexata est terra multis cladibus
10　ex congregatione regalis pecuniae procedentibus.

[Stubbs' *Select Charters from the Beginning to 1307*, 9th ed. Oxford 1913, repr. 1951, p. 95]

In ll.7-8 **Alii ... alios ... alii aliorum** illustrates a common idiomatic use of **alius** (usually in the plural). When paired in this way the first means 'some' and the second 'others', though often a more idiomatic translation into English is preferable. In this case Robert of Hereford has also paired **ignoti ad agnotas** in a similar way.

Robert was no admirer of the early Norman kings, and he saw the Domesday Book as no more than a method of suppression – which indeed it was, no matter how interesting it may be today as a record of the times. Robert of Hereford is a sobering reminder of the original purposes of this unique document; and the very name

'Domesday Book' was a title given to it by the suppressed English peasantry.

Domesday Book contains a detailed inventory of land ownership, households, those who worked the land, livestock, mills – in fact of anything that was or could be taxed. But it also contains for each county an account of the 'customs' (**consuetudines**), in essence the legal system and the taxation practices prevailing in that county. Because it was compiled before the Norman administration had permeated the country (it was, of course, compiled to achieve just that permeation), Domesday Book provides for the most part a picture of the administration of the country as it was under the English administration immediately before the Norman Conquest.

The language of the Domesday Book is inevitably repetitive and focused upon land and property ownership, and it contains its own particular jargon to describe such matters succinctly. The following list explains some of the more common terms.

animal otiosum: an animal not used for draught, mainly used of cows and oxen.

bordarius: a bordar, one who held usually a cottage and a few acres and was in the personal service of the lord of the manor. In effect bordars were labourers, either for the lord or for villeins in the same vill. **Cotarius** ('cottager') appears to be of similar status.

bos, bovis m.f.: an ox or a cow, but also used as an indication of land area – **terra uni bovi** means land enough to keep one ox.

carruca: a plough (an important piece of equipment and therefore a useful guide to wealth, but also used as a rough measure of land – as much as a plough could cope with in a season).

cotarius: see **bordarius**.

defendere se: not 'to defend oneself', but in Domesday 'to be assessed'.

forisfactura: penalty, forfeit.

geldo, -are: to pay tax (**geldum** or **gelda**).

hida: a 'hide' of land, sufficient land for one family. Later this became fixed at 120 acres (which is what it usually is in Domesday). Counties and townships were rated for taxation at an arbitrary number of hides, which did not necessarily represent their true acreage.

molendinum: a mill, always listed where found because of its importance to the rural economy.

ora: usually an eighth of a mark, twenty pence, though sometimes a tenth of a mark, sixteen pence.

recedo, -ere, recessi, recessum: to leave, especially of the right to leave land owned by the lord of the manor (usually in a negative phrase, to indicate that a person could *not* leave the manor because of their feudal duty to the lord).

socha: the power of legal jurisdiction ('soc') granted by the king to individual lords, who therefore held their own courts.

sochemannus: a man who is in the soc of a lord.

villanus: a villein, i.e. one who lives in a vill (village, township), usually implying one who is free (i.e. not a slave) but who owes feudal service to the lord of the manor.

virga, virgata: a virgate of land, a quarter of a hide, and therefore about thirty acres. The normal holding of a villein.

The following is a section from the 'Customs of Chester'. As for all counties in the survey as given in the version known as the Exchequer Domesday Book, there is a brief account of its taxable wealth 'at the time of King Edward' (i.e. Edward the Confessor), followed by a summary of its laws.

6(b) Civitas de Cestre tempore Regis Edwardi geldabat pro l. hidis. Tres hidae et dimidia quae sunt extra civitatem, hoc est, una hida et dimidia ultra pontem, et ii. hidae in Neutone et Redeclive et in burgo episcopi, hae geldabant cum civitate.

5 Tempore Regis Edwardi erant in ipsa civitate cccc. et xxxi. domus geldantes. Et praeter has habebat episcopus lvi. domus geldantes. Tunc reddebat haec civitas x. markas argenti et dimidiam. Duae partes erant regis et tertia comitis. Et hae leges erant ibi:

Pax data manu regis vel suo brevi vel per suum legatum, si ab 10 aliquo fuisset infracta, inde rex c. solidos habebat. Quod si ipsa pax regis iussu ejus a comite data fuisset infracta, de centum solidis qui pro hoc dabantur tertium denarium comes habebat. Si vero a praeposito regis aut ministro comitis eadem pax data infringeretur, per xl. solidos emendabatur, et comitis erat tertius denarius.

15 Si quis liber homo regis pacem datam infringens in domo hominem occidisset, terra ejus et pecunia tota regis erat, et ipse utlagh fiebat. Hoc idem habebat comes de suo tantum homine hanc forisfacturam faciente. Cuilibet autem utlagh nullus poterat reddere pacem nisi per regem ...

20 Vidua si alicui se non legitime commiscebat xx. solidos emendabat; puella vero x. solidos pro simili causa.

Qui in civitate terram alterius saisibat et non poterat diratioci-

nare suam esse, xl. solidos emendabat. Similiter et ille qui clamorem inde faciebat, si suam esse debere non posset diratioci-
25 nare ...

Qui ad terminum quod debebat gablum non reddebat, x. solidis emendabat.

Si ignis civitatem comburebat, de cuius domo exibat emendabat per iii. oras denariorum, et suo propinquiori vicino dabat ii. solidos.
30 Omnium harum forisfacturarum ii. partes erant regis et tertia comitis.

[Stubbs, op. cit., pp. 103-4, with omissions]

The use of the imperfect tense (e.g. l.1 **geldabat**, l.4 **geldabant**) is common throughout the Domesday Book to indicate the situation as it was when the recorders visited, or as it was 'in the time of King Edward'.

In ll.16 and 18 **utlagh** is used in an indeclinable form. In l.16 the word is clearly nominative, and in l.18 it is (not quite so clearly) dative, with **cuilibet**.

iii. oras in l.29 is 60 pence (see notes on 6(c) for details of the monetary system).

*

The following description of Pampisford, about seven miles south of Cambridge, is taken not from the Domesday Book itself but from the *Inquisitio Comitatus Cantabrigiensis*, which gives copies of the original returns for Cambridgeshire town by town, whereas the final Domesday Book organised this material under land owners (short extracts based on this *Inquisitio* follow in passage 6(d)). The original returns do not survive for other counties (except to some extent for the south-west counties in the Exon Domesday), which is a pity since they are clearly more detailed than the final version. But this return illustrates the general style and vocabulary of the Domesday Book while being rather fuller in its phraseology.

6(c) Pampeswrda pro v. hidis et xxii. acris se defendit tempore Regis Aedwardi et modo. De his v. hidis et xxii. acris tenet Abbas de Ely duas hidas et tres virgas et dimidiam. Sex carrucis est ibi terra. Una hida et una virga et dimidia et duae carrucae in dominio. Quatuor
5 carrucae villanis; duodecim villani, quinque bordarii, tres servi; unum molendinum de viginti solidis; pratum unius carrucae. Tredecim animalia otiosa; quater viginti et quindecim oves, viginti tres

110

porci. Inter totum valet et valuit septem libras. Haec terra jacet et jacuit in ecclesia Sanctae Etheldredae de Eli.

10 Et de his v. hidis et xxii. acris tenet Radulfus de Scamnis et Radulfus Brito unam hidam et viginti duas acras de Comite Alano. Duabus carrucis et duobus bobus est ibi terra. Una carruca in dominio et altera carruca villanis. Duo villani, duo bordarii; duae acrae et dimidia prati. Quatuor animalia otiosa; septem et viginti et 15 decem oves; triginta novem porci. Inter totum valet triginta solidos; et aliquando recepit decem solidos et tempore Regis Edwardi triginta solidos. Hanc terram tenuit Almarus homo Eddivae. Potuit dare et vendere cui voluit tempore Edwardi Regis. Sed socham habuit Eddiva.

20 Et de his v. hidis et xxii. acris tenet Radulfus de Scannis de Picito vicecomite de feudo regis tres virgas. Unius carrucae est ibi terra, et est carruca; duae acrae prati et dimidia. Haec terra valet decem solidos et valuit. Hanc terram tenuit Edricus homo Alurici Child. Potuit dare terram suam cui voluit tempore Regis Edwardi.

25 Et de his v. hidis et xxii. acris tenet Hardewinus de abbate decem acras. Uni bovi est terra; duodecim denarios valet et valuit. Hanc terram tenet Suellingus, et tenuit tempore Regis Edwardi, nec potuit recedere. Et in ipsa villa tenet Picotus quinque acras de Eudone Dapifero; sex denarios valet et valuit. Hanc terram tenuit 30 Burro de Alurico Camp; potuit recedere cum voluit. In eadem villa tenet Hardewinus dimidiam virgam de feudo regis; duobus bobus est terra. Haec terra valet et valuit quatuor oras. Duo sochemanni tenuerunt hanc terram, homines Regis Edwardi, et invenerunt inwardos; potuerunt recedere. Et in eadem villa tenet quidam pres- 35 byter dimidiam virgatam de Judeta comitissa; duobus bobus est terra. Hanc terram tenuit unus sochemannus, homo comitis Gurdi; non potuit recedere.

[Stubbs, op. cit., pp. 102-3]

In l.34 **inwardos** means 'watchmen', i.e. men employed to look after the land on behalf of the 'tenants in socage'.

The monetary system used in the Domesday records, and indeed for several centuries afterwards, seems unnecessarily complicated. **Libra** (pound), **solidus** (shilling), and **denarius** (penny) is, of course, the system which continued in use until 1971, though often (and this practice continued) pence and shillings were not converted into the next higher denomination (so one gets **xl. solidi**, for example). But in addition to this, and often happily mingled with it, is the

111

system of marks, one mark (**marca, marcha, marka**) being two thirds of a pound (13s.4d), and ores, one ore (**ora**) being an eighth of a mark (twenty pence, though sometimes, even more confusingly, sixteen pence, which is a tenth of a mark).

It is an interesting exercise in dealing with the Domesday records to check the totals of land for each area against the various subsections as listed. In this case the total land is given as five hides and twenty-two acres. It is useful for calculational purposes to convert all figures into acres, so this is $(120 \times 5) + 22 = 622$ acres. The subdivisions are given as follows:

Abbot of Ely, two hides three and a half virgates,

$$(120 \times 2) + (30 \times 3.5) = 345 \text{ acres}$$

Radulf de Scammnis and Radulf Brito, one hide and twenty-two acres,

$$120 + 22 \qquad = 142 \text{ acres}$$

Radulf de Scamnis (from Picotus, the sheriff), three virgates,

$$30 \times 3 \qquad = 90 \text{ acres}$$

Hardewinus (from the abbot) $\qquad = 10$ acres

Picotus (from Eudo the Steward) $\qquad = 5$ acres

Hardewinus (from the king's fief), half a virgate,

$$30 \times 0.5 \qquad = 15 \text{ acres}$$

A certain priest (from the countess Judith), half a virgate,

$$30 \times 0.5 \qquad = 15 \text{ acres}$$

Total: 622 acres

– which does at least prove that we have used the same system of units as the recorders were using!

Throughout this passage, and in most cases in the Domesday Book itself, there is a careful record of who actually holds each parcel of land, and not simply who owns it. Presumably it was the holder who was responsible for paying the tax.

The Latin is mainly uncomplicated, with few subordinate clauses. There are often variations in spelling, as can be seen here with **Aedwardus/Edwardus**, **Scamnis/Scannis**, and **Ely/Eli**.

In l.4 (and often elsewhere) the verb 'to be' is omitted.

In l.7 is a nice indication that the writer spoke French – **quater viginti et quindecim** is the French quatre-vingt-quinze. The normal Latin would have been **nonaginta quinque**.

In l.8 (and regularly elsewhere) the phrase **valet et valuit** means that the value is now (a certain amount) and was the same under Edward.

In ll.14-15 **septem et viginti et decem** is a strange way of saying thirty-seven. Perhaps the recorder had in mind two, or even three groups of sheep.

*

And now we can see what the compiler of the Domesday Book itself made of this information. The information presented in 6(c) is in fact scattered in several places in the Domesday account of Cambridgeshire, and interestingly not all the information gathered in the *Inquisitio Comitatus Cantabrigiensis* is actually used in the Domesday Book. This is how the sections about the holdings of the abbot of Ely and those of Hardwin appear in the actual text of Domesday, with a stop used to indicate any abbreviation and '&' used for the mark for **et**, which appears in the text rather like a figure 7. Numerals are also followed by a stop (as in the original text). A colon (:) is used to indicate the end of a sentence. With the help of the translation, where all additions in the English are clearly marked by enclosure in square brackets, it should not prove too difficult to decipher this abbreviated text. It is an interesting exercise to compare this Domesday version with the *Inquisitio* version above.

6(d)   *Terra Abbatie de Elyg*

... In Pampesuuorde ten. isd. abb. ii. hid. & iii. virg. & dim.: T.ra e. vi. car.: In d.nio i. hida & i. virg. & dim. & ibi sunt ii. car.: Ibi xii. vill.i & v. bord. cu. iiii. car.: Ibi iii. servi & un. molin. de xx sol.: P.tu. i. car.: Val. & valuit sep. vii. lib.: H. t.ra jacuit & jacet in d.nio eccl.ae
5   de Ely:
     ... In ead. villa ten. Hardwin de abb.e x. ac.s: T.ra i. bov.: Val. xii. den.: Hanc t.ra. tenuit Suellinc de abb.e sed non potuit recedere:

[Text transcribed from *Domesday Book*, general editor John Morris, vol. 18 (Cambridgeshire) ed. Alexander Rumble, Phillimore 1981, sections v.18 and 19]

In the heading the word **abbatie** is genitive of **abbatia**, and means the office of abbot, the 'abbacy'.

In l.4 the clerk has written 'seven' both as **sep.** and as **vii**.

The whole text is in effect written in a kind of shorthand, but it is highly systematic. Where a case ending is important for the grammar or the sense, then it is indicated, as in **d.nio** (ll.2 and 4) and **eccl.ae** (l.4). Words of infrequent occurrence, such as in the final phrase in l.7, are written out in full. With only very rare exceptions it is possible to reconstruct a full version of the text without any ambiguity.

*

The writing of history was a common activity in the monasteries of Britain. It is indeed upon these historians that most of the history of the period from the Norman Conquest to the dissolution of the monasteries has been constructed. Many of these monastic historians were very capable writers, both in their capacity as historians and as Latinists. Though they were not always entirely detached observers, not least since the church was so often involved in the politics of the time, they were for the most part intelligent historians who tried to record events without undue bias.

As far as their Latin is concerned, we are dealing with a much more refined style than is to be found in the typical deed or even royal charter. Amongst British forerunners Bede was very much a model to be followed, but in fact there was by this time a huge quantity of historical prose writing in existence across Europe and British historians were part of a much wider literary genre than anything purely British. Their language and style was truly international. But it is certainly more difficult than deeds and charters.

The first excerpt comes from William of Malmesbury's *Gesta Regum Anglorum*, written around 1120-40. William was a monk and librarian at Malmesbury Abbey in Wiltshire, a Benedictine foundation established by Aldhelm in 970. He appears to have been of Norman origin, probably from the Norman nobility. He did not have much respect for Saxons, as the following passage shows:

6(e)   Verumtamen litterarum et religionis studia aetate procedente obsoleverant, non paucis ante adventum Normannorum annis. Clerici litteratura tumultuaria contenti vix sacramentorum verba balbutiebant; stupori erat et miraculo ceteris qui grammaticam nosset.
5   Monachi, subtilibus indumentis et indifferenti genere ciborum, regulam ludificabant. Optimates, gulae et veneri dediti, ecclesiam more Christiano mane non adibant; sed in cubiculo et inter uxorios amplexus matutinarum sollemnia et missarum a festinante presbytero auribus tantum libabant. Vulgus in medio expositum praeda

10   erat potentioribus, ut, vel eorum substantiis exhaustis vel etiam corporibus in longinquas terras distractis, acervos thesaurorum congererent.

    Ad summam, tunc erant Angli vestibus ad medium genu expediti, crines tonsi, barbas rasi, armillis aureis bracchia onerati, picturatis
15   stigmatibus cutem insignati; in cibis urgentes crapulam, in potibus irritantes vomicam.

[William of Malmesbury, *Gesta Regum Anglorum* 3.245; as in Rolls Series, vol. 90B, pp. 304-5]

The style is elegant with some rhetorical touches. The vocabulary is erudite and even at times deliberately striking. William of Malmesbury was certainly quite a stylist. How accurate a picture he is giving here of Saxon England just before the Norman Conquest is a matter for some debate.

    In l.3 **tumultuaria** implies something done in a hurry and not done very well. 'Tumultuous' in English does not get the sense at all. William is obviously contrasting this kind of inferior writing with good, solid theological works!

    In l.4 there are two 'predicative datives' (**stupori** ... **miraculo**) – literally 'it was for amazement and a miracle'. The **qui** is here used as a subject pronoun – 'anyone who ...'.

    In l.5 **indifferenti** does not mean 'indifferent' in the modern English sense, but 'showing no discrimination'. The implication is, of course, that the monks were not observing the proper dietary rules.

    crines ... **barbas** ... **bracchia** in l.14 are accusatives of respect (literally 'cropped with respect to their hair ...').

    In ll.14-15 **picturatis stigmatibus** refers to the practice of tattooing.

    In l.16 **vomica** is not 'vomit' but 'ulcer', if William is using the word correctly, and he probably is.

*

William's view of Normans is, as one might expect, rather more favourable, though not entirely uncritical. Again the style is quite elaborate.

6(f)   Porro Normanni, ut de eis quoque dicamus, erant tunc et sunt adhuc vestibus ad invidiam culti, cibis citra ullam nimietatem delicati;

gens militiae assueta et sine bello paene vivere nescia; in hostem
impigre procurrere, et ubi vires non successissent non minus dolo et
5 pecunia corrumpere. Domi ingentia, ut dixi, aedificia moderatos
sumptus moliri, paribus invidere, superiores praetergredi velle,
subiectos sibi ab alienis tutari; dominis fideles, moxque levi offensa
infideles. Cum fato ponderare perfidiam, cum nummo mutare sen-
tentiam. Ceterum, omnium gentium benignissimi advenas aequali
10 secum honore colunt; matrimonia quoque cum subditis iungunt;
religionis normam, usquequaque in Anglia emortuam, adventu suo
suscitarunt; videas ubique in villis ecclesias, in vicis et urbibus
monasteria, novo aedificandi genere consurgere, recenti ritu patriam florere, ita ut sibi periisse diem quisque opulentus existimet
15 quem non aliqua praeclara magnificentia illustret.

[William of Malmesbury, *Gesta Regum Anglorum*, 3.246; as in Rolls
Series, vol. 90B, p. 306]

In ll.4-8 William uses a series of infinitives as main verbs – **procurrere** ... **corrumpere** ... **moliri** ... **invidere** ... **velle** ... **tutari** ...
ponderare ... **mutare**. The grammatical term for this usage is the
'Historic Infinitive'. Classical writers used it mainly for graphic
descriptions of events such as battles; William uses it rather more
freely.

In l.12 **videas** is a potential subjunctive – 'you can/may see ...'.

In l.12 **villis** probably means 'towns' rather than 'estates, manors'; and **vicis** means 'villages' rather than 'streets'. It is an
interesting study to follow the development of the meanings of
words for different kinds and sizes of settlements, not only in Latin
but in most languages.

In l.13 the **novo aedificandi genere** is, of course, the Norman
style of architecture.

In l.13 **recenti ritu** means something like 'with fresh observance'. **Recens** means 'fresh' as well as 'recent', and **ritus** means
'observance' in a general sense as well as the more concrete 'rite'.

*

The Latin is rather easier when William is recounting actual events,
such as in the following excerpt from his *Historia Novella* in which
he describes the accession of Stephen:

6(g) Ille [Stephanus] ubi a Londiniensibus et Wintoniensibus in regem

exceptus est, etiam Rogerum Salesberiensem episcopum et
Willelmum de Ponte Arcus, custodes thesaurorum regalium, ad se
transduxit. Ne tamen veritas celetur posteris, omnes ejus conatus
5   irriti fuissent nisi Henricus frater ejus Wintoniensis episcopus, qui
modo apostolicae sedis legatus est in Anglia, placidum ei commodasset assensum, spe scilicet captus amplissima quod Stephanus avi
sui Willelmi in regni moderamine mores servaret praecipueque in
ecclesiastici vigoris disciplina. Quapropter districto sacramento,
10   quod a Stephano Willelmus Cantuariensis archiepiscopus exegit de
libertate reddenda ecclesiae et conservanda, episcopus Wintoniensis se mediatorem et vadem apposuit. ... Coronatus est ergo in
regem Angliae Stephanus XIo kalendas Januarii, Dominica, tribus
episcopis praesentibus, archiepiscopo, Wintoniensi, Salisberiensi,
15   nullis abbatibus, paucissimis optimatibus, XXaIIa die post exces-
sum avunculi, anno Dominici Incarnationis MoCoXXXoVo.

[William of Malmesbury, *Historia Novella*, 1.460; as in Rolls Series,
vol. 90B, p. 538; also in Stubbs, op. cit., p. 136]

The grammar here is mainly classical, as one expects from William
of Malmesbury, with a negative clause of purpose (l.4, **ne ... celetur
...**), an unfilled past condition with two pluperfect subjunctives
(ll.5-7, ... **fuissent nisi ... commodasset** [for **commodavisset**]),
an ablative absolute (l.9, **districto sacramento**), and two gerun-
dives (ll.10-11, ... **de libertate reddenda ... conservanda**),
though in ll.7-9 classical Latin would have used an accusative and
future infinitive (after the idea of 'hoping') instead of **quod** with a
subjunctive. It is interesting to note, though, that Cicero would not
have fully understood around a dozen words in this short passage.

*

In the *Gesta Regum Anglorum* William does occasionally depart
from the strict business of his title and give us an insight into the
events and people in his monastery at Malmesbury. The passage
below concerns a certain Eilmer, who was a monk at Malmesbury
some years before William arrived there, but his fame had certainly
outlived him.

6(h)   Non multo post, cometes stella, ut ferunt, mutationes regnorum
praetendens, longos et flammeos crines per inane ducens apparuit;
unde pulchre quidam nostri monasterii monachus, Eilmerus nom-

117

ine, viso coruscantis astri terrore conquiniscens, 'Venisti,' inquit,
5   'venisti, multis matribus lugende; dudum est quod te vidi, sed nunc
multo terribiliorem te intueor, patriae hujus excidium vibrantem.'
Is erat litteris, quantum ad id temporis, imbutus, aevo maturus,
immanem audaciam prima juventute conatus, nam pennas
manibus et pedibus haud scio qua innexuerat arte, ut Daedali more
10   volaret, fabulam pro vero amplexus, collectaque e summo turris
aura, spatio stadii et plus volavit; sed venti et turbinis violentia,
simul et temerarii facti conscientia, tremulus cecidit, perpetuo post
haec debilis et crura effractus. Ipse ferebat causam ruinae quod
caudam in posteriori parte oblitus fuerit.

[William of Malmesbury, *Gesta Regum Anglorum*, 2.225; as in Rolls
Series, vol. 90A, pp. 276-7]

So we have two stories about Eilmer. The first is that he commented
on the appearance of a comet, not strange in itself, but he claimed
to have seen it *before*. Just before the passage quoted here William
had reported the death of King Henry of France, and this occurred
in 1060. The only reported comet 'not long after' 1060 is Halley's
Comet which appeared in 1065-6. If Eilmer was, as William says, 'of
mature age', then he could indeed have seen the previous appearance of Halley's Comet in 989, though actually another comet is
recorded in 1006. Which one Eilmer had seen depends on how
'mature' he was and how accurate was his observation of the comet.
    But of equal scientific interest is the report of Eilmer's flight.
William came to Malmesbury around 1100 or soon after and it is
very likely that there were some monks still in the abbey then who
remembered Eilmer as an old man, so we can put some confidence
in William's account. It appears that Eilmer managed to fly from the
top of a tower (presumably the abbey tower, though not the present
one, which is early Norman) for a 'stade', which usually means
around an eighth to a tenth of a mile. Unfortunately he landed badly
and damaged his legs for life. Eilmer was at the time a very young
man, so the date of this event was probably between 1000 and 1020,
depending on which comet one believes he had previously seen.
Despite his injury Eilmer's achievement was considerable. What
might he have done if he *had* fixed a tail on?
    In l.5 **multis matribus lugende** is a gerundive phrase, meaning
literally 'to be mourned by many mothers'. **Multis matribus** is
dative of agent, usual with a gerund of obligation, and the gerund

itself is in the vocative case, agreeing with the subject of **venisti** – 'you', i.e. the comet.

There are several examples here of William's range of vocabulary, and even of the odd obscure word: there are only five instances of the use of **conquiniscere** (l.4) quoted in Lewis and Short's *Latin Dictionary*, and three of these are from grammarians explaining what it means – 'to cower'.

*

The Latin is not too complex in the following account by William Fitzstephen of the murder of Thomas Becket in Canterbury Cathedral in 1170. William Fitzstephen was a monk at Canterbury in Becket's time, and he was an eye-witness to the murder. The account comes from his *Vita Sancti Thomae*.

6(i) Quidam eum plano ense caedebat inter scapulas, dicens, 'Fuge, mortuus es.' Ille immotus perstitit, et cervicem praebens se Domino commendebat; et sanctos episcopos martyres in ore habebat, beatum Dionysium et sanctum Aelfegum Cantuariensem. Aliqui dicen-
5   tes, 'Captus es, venies nobiscum', iniectis manibus eum ab ecclesia extrahere volebant. Ille respondens, 'Nusquam ibo; hic facietis quod facere vultis, et quod vobis praeceptum est,' quod poterat renitebatur, et monachi eum retinebant. Cum quibus et magister Edwardus Grim, qui et primum a Willelmo de Traci in caput eius vibratum
10   gladii ictum bracchio obiecto excepit; eodemque ictu et archiepiscopus in capite inclinato et ipse in bracchio graviter sunt vulnerati....

Archiepiscopus a capite cruorem defluentem bracchio detergens et videns, gratias Deo agebat, dicens, 'In manus tuas, Domine,
15   commendo spiritum meum.' Datur in caput eius ictus secundus, quo et ille in faciem concidit, positis primo genibus, coniunctis et extensis ad Deum manibus, secus aram quae ibi erat sancti Benedicti. Et curam habuit vel gratiam ut honeste caderet, pallio suo coopertus usque ad talos, quasi adoraturus et oraturus. Super dextram cecidit,
20   ad dextram Dei iturus.

[William Fitzstephen, *Vita Sancti Thomae*, 140-1; as in Rolls Series, vol. 67C, p. 141]

In ll.3-4 **beatum Dionysium et sanctum Aelfegum Cantuariensem** have particular significance. St Denis is the patron saint of

France and a martyr, and though Thomas was born in London his parents were Norman and he studied theology in Paris; he regarded himself as essentially French. St Alphege was Archbishop of Canterbury and was killed by the Danes in 1012.

In l.8 **retinebant** is a good example of the 'conative' use of the imperfect, in the sense of 'they tried to hold him back'.

Also in l.8, after **cum quibus** the verb 'to be' (**erat**) is to be understood.

In ll.9-10 the whole phrase **primum ... vibratum ... ictum** is the object of **excepit**.

In l.17 the word **secus** means 'near'. In classical Latin it meant 'otherwise', but it was occasionally used in the sense of 'near', though this was apparently a colloquial usage. But by the time Jerome wrote the Vulgate this latter meaning was the regular usage, and the word remained common in this meaning thereafter; though it is occasionally found in the old classical meaning of 'otherwise'.

*

Henry of Huntingdon died about 1155 and his *Historia Anglorum* ends in 1154, presumably just before his death. He was therefore a contemporary of King Stephen, and his work is an important source for the history of Stephen's reign. But his accuracy is sometimes questionable, and in the following excerpt we have the opportunity to compare Henry's account of what Stephen agreed to do at Oxford in 1136 with the actual Charter of Stephen, the official version which we have dealt with earlier as document 4(b).

6(j) Inde perrexit rex Stephanus apud Oxeneforde, ubi recordatus est et confirmavit pacta quae Deo et populo et sanctae Ecclesiae concesserat in die coronationis suae; quae sunt haec: primo vovit quod defunctis episcopis nunquam retineret ecclesias in manu sua, sed
5 statim electioni canonicae consentiens episcopis eas investiret. Secundo vovit quod nullius clerici vel laici silvas in manu sua retineret, sicut rex Henicus fecerat, qui singulis annis implacitaverat eos, si vel venationem cepissent in silvis propriis, vel si eas ad necessitates suas exstirparent vel diminuerent ... Tertio vovit
10 quod Denegeldum, id est duos solidos ad hidam, quos antecessores sui accipere solebant singulis annis, in aeternum condonaret. Haec principaliter Deo vovit et alia, sed nihil horum tenuit.

[Henry of Huntingdon 8.3; as in Rolls Series, vol. 74, p. 258; also Stubbs, op. cit., p. 137]

The first two 'vows' are very brief summaries of the provisions of the Charter of Stephen, and they hardly give adequately the flavour of the actual Charter. The third 'vow', about the Danegeld, does not occur in the Charter at all. Probably Henry of Huntingdon had not actually seen the Charter, but was going on the hearsay and vague accounts which did the rounds of ecclesiastical circles. Whether Stephen ever promised to give up the Danegeld seems very doubtful; he certainly never did so, and his successor Henry II continued to collect it.

In ll.1-3 the **pacta** referred to are the statements made by Stephen in his Coronation Charter in 1135. This Charter still survives and is little more than an assertion by Stephen that he will observe 'good laws and customs'.

ll.6-9 on the ownership of forests is a poor summary of the Charter of 1136. What Stephen actually agreed to was that the forests which Henry I had added to the royal domain would be returned to their owners as they had stood in the reign of William II (see document 4(b), ll.24-7). The question of the royal rights in forests was to be a long-standing bone of contention.

*

William of Newburgh (Newburgh was a small house of Augustinian canons a few miles to the south of the Cistercian abbey of Rievaulx in North Yorkshire) was commissioned in 1196 by Ernald, abbot of Rievaulx, to write a history of England from the Norman Conquest to his own day. The result was the *Historia Rerum Anglicarum*, a very capable work in which William of Newburgh concentrated on the period through which he had himself lived, the reigns of Stephen and Henry II. The work as we have it is clearly unfinished, presumably because William died in 1198.

In the following excerpt William of Newburgh describes the chaotic situation which developed early in Stephen's reign.

6(k)   Et primo quidem videbatur regnum Angliae scissum esse in duo, quibusdam regi, quibusdam imperatrici faventibus, non quod vel rex vel imperatrix suae parti potenter imperaret, sed quod suorum bellicis quisque studiis pro tempore niteretur. Neuter enim in suos
5   imperiose agere et disciplinae vigorem exercere poterat, sed uterque

suos, ne a se deficerent, nihil negando mulcebant. Sane inter partes
.... diu multumque certatum est, alternante fortuna. Processu vero
temporis, inter eas jam saepius fortunae infidelitatem expertas
remissiores motus esse coepere; quod quidem Angliae non cessit in
10 bonum. Illis quippe diutinae concertationis pertaesis et mollius
agentibus, provinciales discordantium procerum motus efferbuere.
Castella quoque per singulas provincias studio partium crebra
surrexerant, erantque in Anglia quodammodo tot reges, vel potius
tyranni, quot domini castellorum, habentes singuli percussuram
15 proprii numismatis, et potestatem subditis regio more dicendi juris.
Cumque ita singuli excellere quaererent ut quidam superiorem,
quidam vel parem sustinere non possent, feralibus inter se odiis
disceptantes, rapinis atque incendiis regiones clarissimas corrup-
erunt et, in fertilissima olim patria, fere omne robur panis ab-
20 sumpserunt. Aquilonalis vero regio quae in potestatem David regis
Scottorum usque ad flumen Tesiam cesserat, per ejusdem regis
industriam in pace agebat.

[William of Newburgh 1.22; as in Rolls Series, vol. 82A, p. 69; also
Stubbs, op. cit., pp. 138-9]

In l.2 **imperatrix** is Matilda, daughter of Henry I, who was the
widow of Henry V, Emperor of Germany (hence her title) and now
married to Geoffrey of Anjou.

In l.7 **certatum est** is an impersonal passive, literally 'it was
fought'.

In ll.10-11 **Illis ... pertaesis ... agentibus** is an ablative absolute.

In l.19 the phrase **robur panis** is a rather odd way of saying 'the
power to produce bread', i.e. all the corn crops were destroyed.

In l.20, the word **aquilonalis** ('northern') comes from the word
aquilo, a northerly wind.

*

Matthew Paris was a monk at St Albans, a Benedictine cathedral
which had about a hundred monks in Matthew's time. Matthew
became the Chronicler at the cathedral in 1235, succeeding Roger of
Wendover whose *Flores Historiarum* was a history of the world from
the creation to 1235; Matthew thus had a tradition of historiography
to follow. He wrote several historical works, the finest being the
Chronica Majora which covers the period from Roman Britain to his
own day.

6. Domesday Book; Historians after 1066

In the following excerpt (printed here with some omissions) Matthew describes the events leading up to the granting of the Magna Carta by John.

6(1) Rex tenuit curiam suam ad Natale Domini apud Wigorniam vix per spatium unius diei; deinde cum festinatione Londinias veniens apud Novum Templum hospitio sese recepit. Venientesque ad regem ibidem supradicti magnates, in lascivo satis apparatu militari,
5 petierunt quasdam libertates et leges regis Eadwardi cum aliis libertatibus sibi et regno Angliae et ecclesiae Anglicanae concessis confirmari, prout in carta regis Henrici primi et legibus praedictis ascriptae continentur. Audiens autem rex postulabat inducias usque ad clausum Paschae. Rex autem interim volens sibi praecavere
10 in posterum, fecit sibi soli contra omnes homines fidelitatem per totam Angliam jurare, et homagia renovare; et ut sibi melius provideret, in die Purificationis beatae Mariae Crucem Domini suscepit. In hebdomada Paschae convenerunt apud Stamford magnates cum equis et armis, qui jam in sui favorem universam fere
15 totius regni nobilitatem attraxerant; et exercitum inaestimabilem confecerunt, eo maxime quod rex exosum semper se omnibus exhibuit. Aestimati sunt namque in exercitu illo duo millia militum, praeter equites servientes et pedites. Erat autem rex eo tempore apud Oxoniam. Die Lunae proxima post octavas Paschae barones
20 memorati in villa de Brakeleie pariter convenerunt. [Rex] misit ad eos archiepiscopum Cantuariensem et Willelmum Mareschallum comitem de Penbrock sciscitans ab eis quae essent leges et libertates quas quaerebant. At illi nunciis praelibatis cedulam porrexerunt quae ex parte maxima leges antiquas et regni consuetudines contin-
25 ebat. Tunc archiepiscopus cum sociis suis cedulam illam ad regem deferens capitula singula coram ipso memoriter recitavit. Cum itaque archiepiscopus et Willelmus Marescallus regem ad consensum inducere nullatenus potuissent, ad jussionem regis ad barones sunt reversi. Magnates constituerunt Robertum filium Walteri prin-
30 cipem militiae, appellantes eum marescallum exercitus Dei et sanctae ecclesiae, et sic singuli ad arma convolantes versus Norhamptunam acies direxerunt. Infecto negotio ad castrum de Bedeford perrexerunt. Venerunt itaque ad eos ibidem nuncii ab urbe Londoniarum, secretius eis indicantes quod, si vellent urbis ingres-
35 sum habere, cum festinatione illuc venirent. Ad Wares usque venerunt. Nono kalendas Junii Londoniensium civitatem sine aliquo tumultu intraverunt. Favebant enim baronibus divites civitatis, et ideo pauperes obloqui metuebant. Et a civibus jam dictis accepta

securitate, miserunt litteras ad comites, barones et milites illos qui
40   adhuc per Angliam regi, licet ficte, adhaerere videbantur. Hi omnes
cum mandatum baronum accepissent, maxima pars eorum
Londinias profecti, confoederati sunt magnatibus supradictis, regem penitus relinquentes. Cessaverunt placita scaccarii et vice-
comitatuum per Angliam, quia nullus inventus est qui regi censum
45   daret vel in aliquo obediret. Statuerunt regi diem ut veniret contra
eos ad colloquium in pratum inter Stanes et Windlesores situm,
decimo quinto die Junii. Convenerunt itaque. Tandem igitur cum
hinc inde varia sorte tractassent, rex Johannes, vires suas baronum
viribus impares intelligens, sine difficultate leges et libertates con-
50   cessit.

[Matthew Paris, *Chronica Majora*, under MCCXV; as in Rolls Series, vol. 57B, p. 584ff.; text as above taken from Stubbs, op. cit., pp.
273-4]

The narrative style is uncomplicated and clear. In his commentary
on events Matthew often uses a more elaborate style, but the above
passage is fairly typical of his narrative technique.

The grammar of place names was never fixed in Medieval Latin,
and writers had their own tastes in how far they should latinise
them. In this passage Matthew uses **Wigornia** (l.1) for Worcester,
Londiniae (fem. pl.) for London (ll.2, 34, 42), **Oxonia** (l.19) for
Oxford, and **Norhamptuna** (l.32) for Northampton, all of which
decline as Latin nouns, but other place names he leaves in their
English forms without a Latin ending.

In l.4 the word **magnates (magnas-atis)** is a medieval invention
based on the classical Latin adjective **magnus-a-um**. It means 'a
great person', and is, of course, still occasionally found in English as
'magnate'.

Also in l.4, the word **lascivus** is something of a 'false friend'. It
can mean 'lascivious, wanton', but it also means 'playful', and in a
bad sense 'impudent, blatant', which is what it means here.

In ll.8-9 there are two rather rare usages. **Induciae** (or **indu-
tiae**) normally means 'truce', but it can have the associated meaning
of 'delay', 'pause in negotiations'. **Clausus** is here used for 'close' in
the sense of 'end'.

In l.12 the Purification of the Blessed Virgin Mary is on 2 February. John therefore presumably had a long period of penance
('**Crucem Domini suscepit**') until Easter.

In l.19 **octavas Paschae** are the 'octaves' (eight-day periods) associated with Easter and which last until Pentecost.

In 1.20 **Brakeleie** is Brackley in Northamptonshire, about twenty miles north of Oxford.

In 1.23 **cedula**, or in its more common form **schedula**, is a classical word meaning any piece of paper with writing on it.

In l.35 **Wares** is Ware, three miles east of Hertford.

In 1.36, **nono kalendas Junii** is 24 May on the old Roman calendrical system.

In l.46 Matthew does not here mention the name of the **pratum**, which was, of course, Runnymede, roughly equidistant between Staines and *Old* Windsor.

7

Other Material: Maps, Monuments, Letters

Maps

The copperplate printing of maps began in the early 16th century and quickly developed into a considerable industry in many parts of Europe. British map-makers played a prominent part in this development, though by the later 16th century Flemish cartographers and publishers had become the leaders in the field. Latin was frequently used on these maps until well into the 18th century, though in England John Speed's famous county maps from 1610 onwards were printed with an English text. In the 17th and 18th centuries whether or not to use Latin was clearly a marketing decision: if the map was intended for international distribution the text was in Latin, and for national distribution the national language was a better bet provided literacy was fairly widespread, as it was now fast becoming in most of western Europe.

One of the earliest British mapmakers was George Lily, a Catholic who spent much of his adult life living in exile in Italy. It was Lily who published what was probably the first printed map of the British Isles produced from a copperplate engraving. The first edition was printed in Rome in 1546, and a later edition came out in London in 1555, probably when Lily had returned to England after the accession of Queen Mary. Other editions were produced in Rome and Venice until 1589. Unfortunately copies of Lily's map are now quite rare, though it has been reproduced often in modern books (e.g. C. Moreland and D. Bannister, *Antique Maps: A Collector's Guide*, Phaidon Christie's, 3rd ed. 1989, Plate I, opp. p. 182). The text added to the map is wholly in Latin. There is a title and two blocks of text, as follows:

7(a) BRITANNIA INSULA QUAE DUO REGNA CONTINET ANGLIAM ET SCOTIAM CUM HIBERNIA ADIACENTE

BRITANNIA insularum in Europa existentium maxima a meridie ad septentrionem protenditur, formam fere habens triangularem cuius
5   circuitus continet milliaria 1720. Nam a Douero Cantij parte ad

Cathenesiam extremam Scotiae partem intersunt 600 milliaria. Ab eodem loco ad extremum Cornubrae promontorium milliaria sunt 320. A quo rursus ad supremam extremitatem Cathenesiae inveniuntur 800. Distat a Gallia milliaria 30. Duo continet regna, Angliam

10   solo fertiliorem urbibus frequentiorem et magis morigeratam, ac Scotiam asperiorem et ob frigus infertiliorem. Dirimuntur ab invicem ad orientem Tueda ad occidentem Solueo fluminibus, in medio vero a Cheviota monte. Obiacent Scotiae ad occidentem 43 insulae Eboniae seu Hebrides dictae quarum prima et antiquissima

15   Druidum memoria Mona erat. Ad septentrionem sunt Orcades Insulae 31 satis angusto freto a Cathenesia divisae quarum prima magnitudine ceteras vincens est Pomonia. Ultima in ditione Scotiae est Thule polum elevatum habens gradibus 63. In qua sole existente in Cancro tenebrae vel nullae vel brevissimae adsunt. Dividunt

20   Angliam in tres veluti regiones tria ingentia flumina, Tumesis, Sabrina, Humbrus; Scotiam item tria, Cluda, Forthea, Tau.

HIBERNIA Insula non longe a Britannia in Oceano sita est a Circio in Euro-austrum protensa, longitudine milliaria 260 latitudine 100. Ab ortu Britanniam a meridie Galliam, ab occidente et septentrione

25   Oceanum fere infinitum habet. Forma oblonga et ovo non dissimilis. In regiones quatuor dividitur, scilicet in Laginiam, Mononiam, Conaciam et Hultoniam. Laginiam a Mononia separat Suirus flumen, ab Hultonia Boandus, Mononiam a Conacia discriminat Sineus. Hic coeli mira est temperies, adeo ut nihil enatum gignat nec aliunde

30   importatum nutriat.

George Lily was evidently a home-loving Englishman.

    Geographical names, in a latinised medieval form, can be difficult to recognise. Most of these are not too bad, though **Sabrina** for the River Severn (1.21) and **Pomonia** for Mainland Orkney (1.17) may be a bit of a surprise.

    In ll.14-15 the phrase **prima et antiquissima Druidum memoria** is somewhat vague. It is probably intended to mean 'first and most ancient because of the memory of the Druids', i.e. because the island was associated with the Druids. In fact the Romans used the name **Mona** to refer to Anglesey (as in Tacitus, *Annals* 14.29 and *Agricola* 14 and 18), and in the early days of Roman Britain Anglesey was certainly a stronghold of the Druids, so George Lily may be confusing the reputation of the two islands. But from the 16th century, maps produced in Britain consistently use **Mona** of the Isle of Man. For Lily to say that the Isle of Man was in the

Hebrides is a strange notion, though it was still in Lily's time thoroughly Celtic-speaking.

In l.18 **Thule** is presumably the Shetlands, though 63 degrees is 2 degrees too far north. 63 degrees fits the Faroes better, but these were Danish by this time. The name had been used by classical writers for some (or rather any) land in the far north, and it has been variously interpreted to mean Scandinavia, the Faroes, Iceland, or (with greater probability, as here) the Shetlands.

In l.22 the word **Circio** (from **Circius**) is a good classical word for a WNW wind, and in l.23 **Euro-auster** is a SSE wind. In fact on his map Lily has Ireland lying slightly inclined NNE to SSW.

ll.28-30 present a very strange view of the fertility of Ireland.

*

Christopher Saxton's maps of the counties of England and Wales produced between 1574 and 1578 (price 4d each) have been justly famous since their appearance for their fine cartography and their beautiful design. All the maps were published together as an atlas in 1579, the first set of printed county maps in this country. The text on the maps is entirely in Latin, though Saxton identified towns on his maps by the English names by which they were known in his day. The main sections of introductory text are given below, together with the text which accompanies the maps as far as Gloucestershire. The order is that found in William Ravenhill, *Christopher Saxton's 16th Century Maps: The Counties of England and Wales*, Chatsworth Library, 1992. Abbreviations are mainly given in their full form, and punctuation has been standardised.

7(b)   *Frontispiece* (picture of Queen Elizabeth I)

Clemens et regni moderatrix iusta Britanniae hac forma insigni conspicienda nitet.

Tristia dum gentes circum omnes bella fatigant
caecique errores toto grassantur in orbe,
5   pace beas longa, vera et pietate Britannos,
iustitia moderans miti sapienter habenas.
Chara domi, celebrisque foris, longaevaque regnum
hic teneas, regno tandem fruitura perenni.

This is written in the classical hexameter form (the metre used by Vergil and Ovid, among many others). It is hardly up to Vergil's standard, but it does at least scan correctly. It was a feature of classical poetry that adjectives were frequently separated from their nouns, and the author of this little piece (probably not Saxton himself) has followed this practice with some enthusiasm. Just to help a little, in l.3 **tristia** qualifies **bella**, and **omnes** qualifies **gentes**; in l.4 **toto** qualifies **orbe** (and **caeci** *does* qualify **errores**); in l.5 **pace** qualifies **longa**, and **vera** qualifies **pietate**; in l.6 **miti** qualifies **iustitia**; and in l.8 **perenni** qualifies **regno**.

7(c)   *Index*

Indicem huic operi tripartitum adiecimus. Primo, alphabetico ordine singulos comitatus. Secundo, nostrae distributionis ac tabularum seriem. Tertio, iudicum itineraria, initia, et dierum iuridicorum ac locorum ad iudicia tam civilia quam criminalia exer-
5 cenda constitutorum definitum tempus (vulgus circuitus ac assisas vocat) reperies.

A point of style which permeates the rest of the Latin text of the maps is evident here: in nearly every case where the genitive case is used (and this occurs on nearly every map) it precedes the nominative/accusative. So we have here **nostrae distributionis ac tabularum seriem** (ll.2-3), **iudicium itineraria, initia**, and **dierum ... ac locorum ... tempus**. We shall see that the word **descriptio** in all the maps follows what it is that the map is a description of. This has the effect, of course, of putting the county names prominently at the beginning of the title for each map, though in the genitive case.

7(d)   *Catalogue*

Catalogus urbium, episcopatuum, oppidorum mercatoriorum, castrorum, ecclesiarum parochialium, fluviorum illustrium, pontium, lucorum, saltorum, septorumque omnium quae per totam Angliam Walliamque in unoquoque comitatu continentur, quemadmodum
5 suis locis in chirographicis Angliae Walliaeque tabulis (ubi suum cuique nomen adjicitur) illustrissime referuntur. Numerus vero eorum omnium quae in hac serie colliguntur ad imum huius indicis designatur, sicuti infra videre licet.

However, here the nominative (**Catalogus**) *precedes* the list of genitives! At the foot of each column in the Catalogue is a helpful translation into English of the categories listed in ll.1-3 (given here with some abbreviations extended) – 'Cities, Bishoprics, Market Towns, Castles, Parish Churches, Rivers, Bridges, Chases, Forests, Parks'.

7(e) | *England*

ANGLIA hominum numero, rerumque fere omnium copiis abundans, sub mitissimo Elizabethae, serenissimae et doctissimae reginae, imperio, placidissima pace annos iam viginti florentissima.

5   Animadvertendum nos propter locorum angustias urbes tantum oppida mercatoria castella et loca quaedam celebriora hac tabula inclusisse.

The county maps then follow, some maps containing more than one county. The amount of text on the county maps varies considerably. Most have somewhere on the map **Christopherus Saxton descripsit** and also the name of the engraver in the form ... **sculpsit**. Several different engravers were employed, and it is interesting to note the slight differences of style. In the examples given below, most of the Latin text which appears on the maps is given, but a few small items have been omitted.

7(f) | *The County Maps: England*

Kent, Sussex, Surrey, Middlesex, London
Cantii, Southsexiae, Surriae, et Middlesesiae comitatuum, una cum suis undique confinibus, oppidis, pagis, villis et fluminibus in eisdem, vera descriptio.

   Cantium, praeter metropoliticam Angliae civitatem, quae Britannicis temporibus Kairkent, Romanis Dorobernia, Saxonicis Canterbury appellata est, habet etiam Roffensem urbem, oppida mercatoria 17, ecclesias parochiales 398.

   Anno Domini 1575 et Dominae Elizabethae Reginae anno 17.

Hampshire
Southamptoniae comitatus (preter insulas Vectis, Jersey et Garnsey quae sunt partes eiusdem comitatus) cum suis undique confinibus, oppidis, pagis, villis et fluminibus, vera descriptio.

   Southamptoniae comitatus (preter civitatem Wincestriam) habet oppida mercatoria 18, pagos et villas 248.

   Anno Domini 1575 [added to the coat of arms].

The next few are decidedly shorter, though Saxton felt obliged to give each county a different introduction. He was apparently sometimes pushed to think of anything distinctive to say.

Dorset
Dorcestriae Comitatus vicinarumque regionum nova veraque descriptio. Anno Domini 1575.

Wiltshire
Wiltoniae Comitatus (harbida planitie nobilis) hic ob oculis proponitur. Anno Domini 1576.

Somerset
Somersetensem Comitatum (agri fertilitate celebrem) hec ob oculis ponit tabula. Anno 1575 et Domine Elizabethe Regine anno 17.

Devon
Devoniae Comitatus rerumque omnium in eodem memorabilium recens, vera particularisque descriptio. Anno Domini 1575.

Cornwall
Promontorium hoc in mare proiectum Cornubia dicitur. Factum est hoc opus anno Domini 1576 et Domine Elizabethe Reginae 18.

Essex
Essexiae Comitatus nova, vera ac absoluta descriptio. Anno Domini 1576.

Hertfordshire
Hartfordiae Comitatus nova, vera ac particularis descriptio. Anno Domini 1577.

Oxfordshire, Buckinghamshire and Berkshire
Oxonij, Buckinghamiae et Berceriae Comitatuum, una cum suis undique confinibus, oppidis, pagis, villis et fluminibus in eisdem vera descriptio. Anno Domini 1574.

Oxonium preter Academiam ac villam Oxoniensem habet oppida mercatoria 9, ecclesias parochiales 208. Buckinghamia continet in se oppida mercatoria 11, ecclesias parochiales 185. Berceria continet in se oppida mercatoria 11, ecclesias parochiales 139 [given as 140 in the Catalogue].

7. Other Material: Maps, Monuments, Letters

All the information in this last paragraph was in fact in the Catalogue, but on the map it helped to fill in an otherwise blank corner.

Gloucestershire

Glocestriae sive Claudiocestriae Comitatus (Claudij Caesaris nomine adhuc celebratur) verus tipus atque effigies. Anno Domini 1577.

This is a piece of false etymology by Saxton. The name Gloucester actually derives from a native British name, Glev (meaning 'bright place'), with the addition of the Latin 'castra' (camp), since the town was a legionary base in the Roman period.

Hereafter the text on the maps is very much modelled on those above, with the occasional addition of a snippet of information about the county. Nevertheless, every county does have a different text, even though some are very close to being repeats of others.

*

Maps which illustrate the exploration and colonisation of the 15th-17th centuries are frequently accompanied by Latin texts. Few of these were in fact produced in Britain; Flemish and Dutch cartographers dominated this particular field. The popularity of these maps in recent years has been high, both because of their contribution to the understanding of the history of the period and because of their artistic merit. The texts on these maps are often very important sources of information, frequently underused even by cartographic specialists, not all of whom know Latin. The following selection illustrates the kind of information which is commonly to be found on maps of this period.

Johann Ruysch's world map published in Rome in 1508 was one of the earliest world maps to include the New World. At this stage there was still confusion about how the new discoveries fitted in with China and South East Asia, and Ruysch's map shows this confusion, though at least he acknowledged the imperfect state of understanding. A copy of the map can be found in A.E. Nordenskiold, *Facsimile Atlas to the Early History of Cartography*, Dover Publications 1973, Plate XXXII. The following passages come from the parts of the map which describe South America; the north coast and part of the east coast had been explored and fairly accurately mapped, but the exploration was still proceeding. The text on the map is in small, very neat capitals, though there are frequent abbreviations; the texts which follow are transcribed in expanded form.

7(g) *Terra Sancte Crucis sive Mundus Novus*

Passim incolitur haec regio, quae a plerisque alter terrarum orbis existimatur. Feminae maresque vel nudi prorsus vel intextis radicibus aviumque pennis varii coloris ornati incedunt. Vivitur multis in commune nulla religione, nullo rege. Bella inter se conti-
5   nenter gerunt, humanaque captivorum carne vescuntur. Aere adeo clementi utuntur ut supra annum 150 vivant. Raro aegrotant, tunc-que radicibus tantum curantur herbarum. Leones hic gignuntur, serpentesque et aliae foedae belluae sylvae. Insunt montes flumi-naque. Margaritarum atque auri maxima copia. Avehuntur hinc a
10   Lusitanis ligna brasi alias verzini et cassiae.

[At the southernmost part of the map, on the east coast of South America] Naute Lusitani partem hanc terre huius observarunt et usque ad elevationem poli antarctici 50 graduum pervenerunt, non-dum tamen ad eius finem austrinum.
15   [Along the undrawn north-western coast of South America] Hu-cusque naute Hispani venerunt et hanc terram propter eius magnitudinem mundum novum appellarunt, quia vero eam to-taliter non viderunt nec usque in tempore hoc longius quam ad hunc terminum perlustrarunt, ideo hic imperfecta reliquitur, presertim
20   cum nescitur quo vergitur.

In ll.3-4 **vivitur multis** is an impersonal passive expression, liter-ally 'it is lived by many'.

If the figure of 50 degrees south given in l.13 is correct (and there is no reason to believe it is not at least fairly close to what was observed), then the Portuguese had already reached within 150 miles or so of the Straits of Magellan. This probably reflects infor-mation brought back by Amerigo Vespucci on his voyage in 1502. It was not until 1520 that Magellan sailed through the straits into the Pacific.

ll.15-20 are apparently based on the fourth voyage of Columbus in 1502-4, and perhaps also on the voyage of Pinzon in 1507-8. On his map Ruysch guessed that there was an ocean on the west side of South America, but he made no attempt to draw a coastline. It was not until 1513 that Bilbao crossed the isthmus of Darien in Panama and saw the Pacific.

In 1630 Henricus Hondius, the Latin name of a Flemish carto-
grapher from Ghent, produced in Amsterdam an elegant map of
Bermuda. It has now found its way onto coffee tables and trays
because of its clarity and detail and as an outstanding example of
the mapmaker's art. It contains an interesting little note as well as
the usual geographical details in Latin. I actually first transcribed
this from an excellent reproduction on a coffee table, but then found
it reprinted (in black and white) in C. Moreland and D. Bannister,
op. cit., p. 254 (though a good magnifying glass is needed to read the
texts in this copy).

7(h)   Mappa Aestivarum Insularum, alias Barmudas dictarum, ad ostia
Mexicani aestuarij jacentium in latitudine graduum 32 minutorum
25, ab Anglia Londino scilicet versus Libonotum 3500 miliaribus
Anglicanis, et a Roanoack (qui locus est in Virginia) versus Eurono-
5   tum 500 mill., accurate descripta.
    Circa solstitium aestivum anno 1616 solvere ex his insulis quin-
que viri in scapha superne aperta, trium doliorum majorum
capacitatis, et post septem hebdomadarum navigationem omnes
incolumes in Hiberniam appulerunt, quale ab hominum memoria
10   vix accidisse creditur.

In l.7 a **dolium** is literally a 'tun', a large barrel, which when used
as a standard measure was 216 gallons (of ale), which is near
enough one ton. The meaning here is apparently a boat of three tons
capacity – not very big.

Monuments

The most common use of Latin on inscriptions from the Anglo-Saxon
period up to the 19th century was on memorials of various kinds in
churches. Most churches built before 1800 have some Latin inscriptions on such memorials, and a few Latin inscriptions are found
even into the 20th century. They range from the very simple to the
highly elaborate, some from the late 17th and on into the 19th
century being in very florid style and displaying the writer's classical education.
    The following are some of the formulae frequently found:

Hic iacet [sepultus] ... Here lies [buried] ... (followed by the name in the nominative)

In [piam] memoriam ... In [pious, loving] memory ... (followed by the name in the genitive)

In hoc monumento [tumulo] requiescit [conditur] ... In this monument [tomb] rests [lies buried] ... (name in the nominative)

Hoc monumentum [marmor] ponendum curavit ... [Name of person, usually wife, son or daughter of the deceased] had this monument [marble] set up (**curare** with a gerund or gerundive construction is a frequent way in both Classical and Medieval Latin to express the idea of 'to have/get something done')

Obiit (much commoner than **mortuus est**) – died.

Coniunx (or often **coniux**), **maritus, pater, mater, filius, filia** are, of course, common words on these inscriptions, often with adjectives such as **fidissimus, pius, amans, moerens**. The genitives which these relationships require can get complicated, especially if the deceased is also in the genitive after **in memoriam**. It is useful to remember that the words **coniunx, maritus, filius**, etc. will normally occur *after* the genitive with which they belong. A genitive is often dependent on another genitive in apposition to a preceding noun – which sounds complicated, but see the first line of the example below, where FILII is a genitive in apposition to JOHANNIS, and has two genitives, MICHAELIS and AGNETIS, attached to it:

IN PIAM MEMORIAM JOHANNIS BROWN MICHAELIS ET AGNETIS BROWN FILII ELIZABETHA JOHANNIS FILIA FIDISSIMA HOC MONUMENTUM PONENDUM CURAVIT

[In loving memory of John Brown, son of Michael and Agnes Brown, Elizabeth the most faithful daughter of John had this monument set up]

Full stops and commas are often lacking, and where they do occur they are often less than helpful. It often requires more than a little patience to sort out who was whose what.

The style of memorial inscriptions is very ancient, much of the wording going back ultimately to the classical period. The introduction of Christianity brought specifically Christian vocabulary into the repertoire, but there was nevertheless a continuous tradition of funerary style from the time of the Roman Republic. On a recent visit to Lyon in the south of France I noticed in the Gallo-Roman Museum the following inscription dating from AD 493:

7(i)   IN HOC TUMULO QUIESCIT
BONE MEMORIAE URSUS
QUI VIXIT IN PACE ANNUS
X & OBIET II NON MARCIAS ...

The style altered little throughout the whole medieval period. Even the inconsistencies in spelling are a regular feature of such short inscriptions, since they were done locally by people whose command of written Latin was not always perfect. In this case we have BONE MEMORI*AE* (l.2), ANNUS instead of ANNOS (l.3), and OBIET instead of OBIIT (l.4).

*

Cathedrals, medieval churches and ruined abbeys are good hunting grounds for what are usually fairly simple and expressive inscriptions of the pre-renaissance period. Many are to be found in the surrounds of monumental brasses, like this one from Lincoln Cathedral:

7(j)   HIC IACET RICARDUS DE GAYNSBURGH OLIM CEMENTARIUS ISTIUS ECLESIE [*sic*] QUI OBIIT DUODECIM KALENDARUM IUNII ANNO DOMINI MCCC

Richard was the master mason responsible for designing and building the famous Angel Choir in the cathedral.

*

In the abbey church at Thornton Abbey in north Lincolnshire (a house of Augustinian Canons, and a large and wealthy one) there are the remains of several tombs, of both canons and lay people. Most are from the 15th century and are in a simple style typical of the period. The following selection illustrates the Latin of the inscriptions:

7(k)   HIC IACET ROBERTUS GUDYK QUI OBIIT PRIMO DIE MENSIS OCTOBRIS ANNO DOMINI MCCCCLXII ET JOHANNA UXOR EJUS QUORUM ANIMABUS PROPICIETUR DEUS AMEN

HIC IACET DOMINUS WILELMUS MEDELEY ABBAS HUJUS MONASTERII XII
5 QUI OBIIT XII DIE MENSIS DECEMBRIS ANNO [DOMINI MILLESIMO QUADRINGENTESIMO] SEPTUAGESIMO TERCIO CUJUS ANIME PROPICIE-TUR DEUS AMEN

HIC IACET DOMINUS JOHANNES HOTON QUI OBIIT XIIIIo DIE MENSIS SEPTEMBRIS ANNO DOMINI MILLESIMO QUADRINGENTESIMO VICESIMO
10 NONO CUJUS ANIME PROPICIETUR DEUS AMEN

There was obviously an abbey style for funerary inscriptions, and one finds the same phenomenon elsewhere.

In ll.5-6 the words in square brackets are missing from the inscription, but can be easily reconstructed since the dates when William Medeley was abbot are known from the monastic records.

       *

Such inscriptions were in fact among the latest manifestations of the use of Latin for records in this country. Most Latin inscriptions which are to be seen in churches today date from the 17th and 18th centuries, when most people who could afford a sizeable monument made sure it was inscribed in Latin; and, of course, monuments from this period are still surviving in good condition. From the later 18th century the use of Latin on this kind of monument declined.

This next example comes from Heversham church in the south of Cumbria:

7(1)

IN PIAM MEMORIAM
TAM OPTIMAE QUAM DILECTISSIMAE MATRIS
ANNAE PRESTON
ANNO MDCCLXVII DEFUNCTAE
5 HOC MARMOR
PONENDUM CURAVIT
FILIUS MAERENS GUL.s PRESTON
FERNENSIS EPISCOPUS

The grammatical subject, as so often in funerary inscriptions, is at the end (FILIUS ... in ll.7-8). William Preston was Bishop of Ferns (FERNENSIS in l.7) in County Wexford in Ireland.

In l.2 TAM ... QUAM means literally 'as ... as ...', though sometimes (as here) it means little more than 'both ... and ...'.

*

The next is rather more complex. It comes from the parish church in Gainsborough, Lincolnshire, and the writer can quote Vergil – though he also makes a grammatical error!

7(m)

JOHANNES SYMPSON A.M.
VIR DOCTUS SACERDOS PIUS
HOC OPPIDO NATUS
DIE IV FEBRUARII A.D. MDCCLV
5   OPTIMO MARITO
SAXEM POSUIT
ANNA
CONIUX FIDISSIMA
VERBA DICTAVIT
10   ET NOMEN ADSCRIBI VOLUIT
IN MEMORIAM MUTUAL. AMICITIAE
JACOB CALTON
PATRI ADIACENT
SEPTEM INFANTULI
15   QUOS ... AB UBERE RAPTOS
ABSTULIT ATRA DIES ET FUNERE
MERSIT ACERBO

The construction is a little loose, and the lack of punctuation does not help. The most likely way to format the text seems to be as follows: the first four lines are a kind of nominative phrase; ll.5-8 describe what Anna his wife has done; ll.9-12 add the involvement of Jacob Calton; and ll.13-17 give the sad story of the seven children. Infant death was, of course, much commoner then than now, and such information is frequently found on inscriptions, more especially on memorials to mothers.

In l.1 A.M. is for 'Artium Magister', later usually reversed to the immediately recognisable 'M.A.'

In l.4 it seems that the date is more likely to be the date of death rather than the date of birth, since there is no other date given; perhaps one needs to assume 'OBIIT'.

In l.6 SAXEM should be SAXUM (2nd declension neuter, not 3rd declension m/f)

In l.11 MUTUAL. is an abbreviation for MUTUALIS.

The last three lines are a quotation from Vergil, *Aeneid* 6.428-9.
The dots indicate a few missing words.

*

The following two inscriptions both come from the ruined cathedral
at Elgin in Scotland. Both date from the 17th century when the
cathedral was already disused and falling into disrepair. The first is
quite short, but illustrates the problem of genitives mentioned
above:

7(n)

(i) HIC QUIESCUNT EXUVIAE MARGARETAE MCKALEY MURDOCHI MISERA-
TIONE DIVINA MORAVIENSIS QUONDAM NUNC ORCADUM EPISCOPI
CHARISSIMAE CONIUGIS QUAE FATIS CONCESSIT MENSE MAIO ANNO
DOM 1676

The following is more elaborate, and includes six lines of verse in
the classical elegiac couplet metre, which do scan, though with a bit
of a strain.

(ii) MEMORIAE CHARISSIMAE CONIUGIS ELIZABETHAE PATERSON DIGNIS-
SIMIS PARENTIBUS ECCLESIAE SCOTICANAE MINISTRIS FIDELISSIMIS
PROGNATAE MONUMENTUM HOC EXTRUENDUM CURAVIT SUPERSTES
MARITUS D. IACOBUS THOMSON PASTOR ELGINENSIS.

5   CORPORE PRAESTANTI VULTUQUE ANIMOQUE SERENA
    ET BIS NUPTA VIRO HIC SUAVIS ELISA IACET
FEMINA LABE VACANS PIISQUE PARENTIBUS ORTA
    VIRTUTUE MERITIS LAUDE & HONORE NITENS
TER DENOS VIXIT SEX ET FERME INSUPER ANNOS
10   FIDA VIRIS MUNDO MORTUA CHARA DEO

DECESSIT 12 AUG 1698 AETATIS 36

In l.1 MEMORIAE CHARISSIMAE is dative instead of the more usual IN
MEMORIAM ... Presumably Paterson was Elizabeth's maiden name.

In l.2 PARENTIBUS apparently means 'ancestors' and not 'parents',
since they are referred to as 'ministers of the Church of Scotland'.
Parentes not infrequently has this extended meaning in both
Classical and Medieval Latin.

Again the grammatical subject is at the end of the sentence –
SUPERSTES MARITUS ... in ll.3-4.

In l.5 the ablatives CORPORE ... ANIMOQUE are 'ablatives of description'.

In l.6 the writer could not get ELIZABETHA to fit the metre, so he cut her down to ELISA.

l.9 has quite a remarkable way of saying 'nearly thirty-six'.

In l.11 the word ANNO is to be understood before AETATIS.

Letters

Considerable quantities of letters in Medieval Latin survive. Churchmen usually communicated in Latin, and diocesan archives contain many examples up to the 17th century. After the Renaissance most educated people could write fair Latin, often based on the newly discovered classical authors, and many used it as their preferred medium for letters. Perhaps the most famous international scholar of his day was Erasmus (1466-1536). He was born in Rotterdam of obscure parentage (he was apparently illegitimate), and his real name appears to have been Gerrit Gerritszoon. He became an Augustinian monk, studied theology at Paris, and spent several years in England, some of them at Cambridge as Professor of Divinity and Greek. The later years of his life were spent at Basel in Switzerland. Erasmus' published output was prodigious, and was mainly in the fields of theology and philosophy. He edited the first reliable edition of the New Testament in Greek. He also wrote large quantities of letters to his numerous friends around Europe, and most of these have survived; they fill eight volumes in a modern edition. They are written in an impeccable style and with a wide range of vocabulary, and are a lively and invaluable commentary on the intelligentsia of his day and on many aspects of everyday life. His classical references, however, often come thick and fast, and assume the kind of thorough knowledge of the classical world which the recipients of his letters undoubtedly had.

The following letter was written in 1499 to an Italian friend, currently living in France. It was probably written from Bedwell in Hertfordshire where the father-in-law of Erasmus' friend and pupil Lord Mountjoy (they had met in Paris) had a country house. Erasmus had been invited to stay in England by Lord Mountjoy. This was Erasmus' first visit to England; hence his amusement at English manners. The text is from P.S. Allen, *Selections from Erasmus*, 2nd ed., Oxford 1918, repr. 1961, p. 23.

141

7(o) Erasmus Fausto Andrelino Poetae Laureato.

Nos in Anglia nonnihil promovimus. Erasmus ille, quem nosti, iam
bonus propemodum venator est, eques non pessimus, aulicus non
imperitus, salutat paulo blandius, arridet comius, et invita Minerva
5 haec omnia. Tu quoque, si sapis, huc advolabis. Quid ita te iuvat
hominem tam nasutum inter merdas Gallicas consenescere? Sed
retinet te tua podagra; ut ea te salvo pereat male. Quamquam si
Britanniae dotes satis pernosses, Fauste, ne tu alatis pedibus huc
accurreres; et si podagra tua non sineret, Daedalum te fieri optares.
10 Nam ut e plurimis unum quiddam attingam, sunt hic nymphae
divinis vultibus, blandae, faciles, et quas tu tuis camenis facile
anteponas. Est praeterea mos numquam satis laudatus. Sive quo
venis, omnium osculis exciperis; sive discedis aliquo, osculis dimit-
teris; redis, redduntur suavia; venitur ad te, propinantur suavia;
15 disceditur abs te, dividuntur basia; occurritur alicubi, basiatur affa-
tim; denique quocumque te moves, suaviorum plena sunt omnia.
Quae si tu, Fauste, gustasses semel quam sint mollicula, quam
fragrantia, profecto cuperes non decennium solum, ut Solon fecit,
sed ad mortem usque in Anglia peregrinari. Cetera coram io-
20 cabimur; nam videbo te, spero, propediem.

Vale, ex Anglia. Anno MCCCCLXXXXIX.

Poeta Laureatus in l.1 is not 'Poet Laureate' in the modern
English sense, but more literally 'prize-winning poet'.

In l.4 **invita Minerva** is an ablative absolute in form, literally
'Minerva [being] unwilling'. Minerva was the goddess of wisdom,
and Erasmus means that all this was a matter of show and perhaps
not entirely appropriate for a man of learning.

In l.6 the word **nasutus** means literally 'having a big nose', but
it came to mean 'witty'. In the same line **merda** is not quite in
Erasmus' style; perhaps he was quoting his friend's view of
France!

Ne in l.8 is not the **ne** of negative commands and purpose clauses,
but the interjection 'surely'.

The reference to **Daedalus** in l.9 is to the myth about Daedalus
and Icarus who escaped from captivity in Crete by making wings
and flying away.

The **camenae** of l.11 are Italian water nymphs and muses of
poetry – especially apt for the devotion of an Italian poet.

In ll.13-16 Erasmus uses three words for 'kiss', **osculum**,
suavium, and **basium**. According to Servius, the 4th century com-

mentator on Vergil, in his note on *Aeneid* 1.260, 'sciendum osculum religionis esse, savium [= suavium] voluptatis; quamvis quidam osculum filiis dari, uxori basium, scorto savium dicant' – 'one should know that an "osculum" is a matter of reverence, "suavium" a matter of pleasure; though some say that an "osculum" is given to one's sons, a "basium" to one's wife, and a "suavium" to a prostitute'. Clearly Erasmus is not following all these nice distinctions, though it seems he implies that one does begin with the perfunctory 'osculum' before moving onto the more familiar 'basium' and 'suavium'. I have not attempted to convey these subtleties in the translation!

In ll.14-5 **venitur**, **disceditur**, **occurritur**, and **basiatur** are all impersonal passives (literally 'it is come', etc.).

In l.18 the reference is to Solon, the 6th century Athenian politician who decided to leave Athens for ten years after introducing his new constitution.

*

The collection of Erasmus' correspondence also contains many letters to Erasmus from his numerous friends. The following letter is from John Fisher, bishop of Rochester, and was written probably in 1517, not long after the publication of Erasmus' edition of the Greek New Testament and also soon after Erasmus had left Cambridge. John Fisher was not only Bishop of Rochester but also Chancellor of Cambridge University, where he had learned some Greek from Erasmus. He was later to fall foul of Henry VIII, and this culminated in his refusal in 1535, along with Thomas More, to swear to Henry's Acts of Succession and Supremacy. Both were executed in the Tower of London. In 1935 John Fisher was canonised. The text can be found in G.S. Facer, *Erasmus and his Times*, Alpha Classics 1951, pp. 40-1.

7(p)   Episcopus Roffensis Domino Erasmo S.P.

Quantum erat molestum audire tuae navigationis discrimen, tantum sane laetor quod salvus incolumisque evaseras. Iustum quidem erat ut poenam dependeres tantae properationis tuae a me, apud
5   quem tutus ab omni iactatione pelagi quiescere potuisti ....

In Testamento Novo per te ad communem omnium utilitatem traducto nemo qui sapit offendi potest, quando non solum innumera in eo loca tua eruditione plurimum illustrasti, verum etiam universo operi integerrimam adhibuisti commentationem, ut nunc multo

143

10 quam ante gratius multoque iucundius ab unoquoque et legi et
    intellegi possit. At vereor sane ne crebrius dormitarit impressor.
    Nam ipse me exercitans in lectione Pauli iuxta praeceptiones tuas,
    repperi saepenumero dictiones Graecas illum omisisse, ac nonnun-
    quam sententias integras. Tibi et istud debeo, Erasme, quod
15 conicere aliquousque possum, ubi non omnino Latinis Graeca
    respondeant. Utinam aliquot menses licuisset habere te praecep-
    torem.

Felix vale ex Roffa.
Discipulus tuus Io. Roffensis.

In l.1 **S.P.** stands for '**salutem plurimam**', 'fullest greeting'. The
verb **dicit** ('says') is understood. Both the greeting and the abbreviation are from classical Latin.

The **quantum** ... **tantum** of l.2 form a pair of correlatives,
literally 'how much ... so much'. Such clauses are often difficult to
translate fully into English since we do not often use clausal com-
parisons in quite this way. Fisher means that he was as happy to
hear that Erasmus was safe as he was sad to hear about the
problems of his voyage.

In l.3 **evaseras** is pluperfect tense. This is a very classical
'epistolary' usage, in which tenses are sometimes used from the
point of view of the recipient of the letter; where one would expect
present tenses describing events at the time the writer was writing
the letter one finds instead the imperfect or perfect (e.g. 'I am
writing this letter on 4th October' becomes 'I was writing OR I wrote
...') and the pluperfect was used to describe events which *had* taken
place before the writer wrote his letter (e.g. 'I saw Maria yesterday'
becomes 'I had seen ...'). But the usage was never entirely consistent.

In l.7 **quando** is used as a conjuction and not as an interrogative
word, and it therefore means 'since' (and not 'when ...?').

In l.11 **dormitarit** is a shortened form of **dormitaverit**, the
perfect subjunctive of **dormitare**, a derivative of **dormire**, with the
sense 'to be drowsy, to nod off'. Fisher has carefully followed the
classical rule for the sequence of tenses, using a perfect subjunctive
after a primary main verb (**vereor**, in the present tense).

Roffa in l.18 is Rochester, and **Roffensis** in ll.1 and 19 is the
adjectival form. The Saxon name was Hrofaescaestir, the latter part
being, of course, the Latin **castra**, fort. As in many names with

144

'-chester' or '-caster' it was the regular practice in Medieval Latin to omit this termination and form a Latin word from the first element.

8

Resources

This section is not intended as a bibliography of Medieval Latin, or even as an exhaustive coverage of the kind of resources available to anyone who wishes to cope effectively with texts in Medieval Latin. It is rather a guide to some of the essential tools and to other sources of specialist help, together with what I hope will be some useful ideas on further study. The focus is very much on the needs of a historian rather than of a linguist.

Language

It was pointed out in Chapter 1 that the *morphology* of Latin did not change substantially from Classical to Medieval. Therefore a good Classical Latin grammar will give all the noun, adjective, pronoun and verb forms which will be encountered in Medieval Latin, though one has to remember that Classical **ae** will usually appear in Medieval Latin as **e**, and that the Perfect and Pluperfect Passives will often be formed with **fui** and **fueram** in Medieval Latin instead of with **sum** and **eram**. A good short grammar, always available in print, is

> B.H. Kennedy, *The Shorter Latin Primer* (rev. by Sir James Mountford), Longman 1974

There are differences, as we have frequently noticed, between Classical and Medieval Latin in *syntax*. There is no readily available comprehensive treatment of Medieval Latin syntax in English, but several introductory books do cover it well enough for most purposes. Perhaps the most systematic available at the moment is

> Eileen A. Gooder, *Latin for Local History*, Longman 1961 (2nd ed. 1978)

Dictionaries present something of a problem. A new and very full dictionary is currently being produced:

Dictionary of Medieval Latin from British Sources, ed. R.E. Latham/D.R. Howlett, Oxford 1975 onwards

The first five of the ten planned fascicules have been published, so we have a very full dictionary down to the letter L. This dictionary is designed to include all words used in British sources, whether of classical or later origin, and when complete will doubtless be a great asset for British medieval studies – though the complete dictionary will cost £500 at 1997 prices.

For practical purposes (and certainly for words beginning with any letter after L) one is faced with using two dictionaries, one to check on any Classical Latin words and the other on any specifically Medieval Latin words. There is a very full Classical Latin Dictionary –

The Oxford Latin Dictionary, Oxford 1968 onwards

– though this deals only with authors to the end of the 2nd century AD, and specifically excludes 'Christian Latin'. For medievalists therefore the much older

Lewis and Short, *Latin Dictionary*, Oxford 1880 (and often reprinted)

offers a wider range of vocabulary likely to be found in medieval texts.

For specifically medieval words the most convenient work is

R.E. Latham, *Revised Medieval Latin Word-list from British and Irish Sources*, Oxford 1965 (reprinted with Supplement 1980)

This gives the first known date for the use of each word and includes many variant spellings, though it does not give quotations or references to texts.

For those whose knowledge of Latin is still fairly modest it can be frustrating to have to consult two dictionaries – and as often as not you consult the wrong one first! After a while, however, even non-classicists get the feel of whether a word is likely to be classical or medieval, and the frustration reduces.

It is worth adding that the vocabulary given at the back of Eileen Gooder's *Latin for Local History* is very useful. It gives around 2,800 of the more frequently occurring words, including classical words. Also useful and doing a very similar job is

> Janet Morris, *A Latin Glossary for Family and Local Historians*, Federation of Family History Societies (Publications) Ltd, 1989 and reprints

This little book gives about 3,500 words, mainly taken from deeds, wills and parish records. It is not a full dictionary, of course, but any student who knows the words given here will find reading Latin records much easier.

Historians and chroniclers

The historians from Gildas to the 14th century vary greatly in accessibility, and it would be impossible here to try to summarise those currently available in published form. In the 19th and 20th centuries many editions have been made of the more important Medieval Latin historians and monastic chroniclers, though nearly always in very small print-runs, and they are usually to be found only in major academic libraries and sometimes in county record offices.

Still a major and convenient source of the Latin text (no translation is given) of many of the historians, chroniclers and sundry other important documents is

> The Rolls Series (or more accurately *Chronicles and Memorials of Great Britain and Ireland from the Invasion of the Romans to the Reign of Henry VIII*), Brown, Green, Longmans and Roberts, London 1858-93

which contains some 250 volumes.

A modern work with extensive bibliography on the historians and chroniclers is

> Antonia Gransden, *Historical Writing in England*, vol. 1 c. 500-1307; vol. 2 c. 1307-early 16th century, Routledge 1974 and 1982

To find out what is available in printed form the following are invaluable:

E.C.L. Mullins, *A Guide to the Historical and Archaeological Publications of Societies in England and Wales*, 1901-1933, Athlone Press 1968

E.L.C. Mullins, *Texts and Calendars: Analytical Guide to Serial Publications*, vol. 1 up to 1957, vol. 2 1957-1982, Royal Historical Society 1958 and 1983

As a taster of what the historians and chroniclers have to say on different reigns it is useful to consult

Stubbs' *Select Charters from the Beginning to 1307*, Oxford, 9th ed. 1913, reprinted several times.

'Excerpts' from relevant historians are given under each reign. Stubbs gives no translation for Latin texts, though he does for texts in Anglo-Saxon and Norman French.

The Domesday Book is available in a modern edition, consisting of 38 volumes (including indices):

Domesday Book Series, general editor John Morris, Phillimore 1976-1992

Charters, deeds, court rolls and other local records

Stubbs (op. cit.) has, of course, a good selection of Latin charters. Though Stubbs does not contain translations of the Latin texts, several of the charters found in Stubbs are translated in

J.J. Bagley and P.B. Rowley, *A Documentary History of England*, vol. 1 (1066-1540), Penguin 1966

There are other published collections (see E.L.C. Mullins, op. cit.), but many charters are held as individual items either by the Public Record Office in London or by county and diocesan record offices. Archivists will advise on what is available for their area.

For those interested in local or family history it is again to the local county record office or diocesan record office that one needs to turn, and indeed to the professional staff of these offices, since the cataloguing systems for archive materials are necessarily geared to the kind of archive holdings in each office, and the help of a professional archivist can save hours of fruitless labour. Until the 15th century most deeds, wills and accounts are in Latin, ecclesiastical records are mostly in Latin until the Reformation, and court rolls, as we have seen, are normally in Latin until 1733. If research involves land transactions before the dissolution of the monasteries then monastic cartularies are likely to be important, if they are available. Many of these have been published, which gets over the problem of transcription, and they are usually well indexed which helps greatly in identifying the main focuses of research, but few have been fully translated.

Court rolls in Latin have rarely been translated or even transcribed, let alone indexed, but they are usually available in considerable bulk, at least for the 17th and early 18th centuries. They do present quite a challenge, but they remain a largely untapped resource for local and family history. In preparing the material from the Kendal Record Office for Chapter 5 I came across the names of several families who are still well known in the area – though they may not be too keen to resurrect these particular records!

For manorial records of the 13th-16th centuries county record offices are again the main repository, and archivists will advise on exactly what is available in their collection. A very helpful book on actually reading manorial records is

Denis Stuart, *Manorial Records*, Phillimore 1992

This covers palaeography and interpretation of most types of manorial records (courts, rentals, accounts, custumals), and there are full transcriptions of the examples quoted together with grammatical tables and vocabulary.

We have not been concerned in the present book with palaeography, but those interested in original deeds, court rolls and other local records will undoubtedly have to become familiar at least with the palaeography relevant to their needs. There are now many excellent books available. The following three cover most of the ground:

F.G. Emmison, *How to Read Local Archives 1500-1700*, Historical Association 1967 and later reprints

K.C. Newton, *Medieval Local Records: A Reading Aid*, Historical Association 1971

C.T. Martin, *The Record Interpreter*, Phillimore 1982 (repr. of 1910 ed.)

Inscriptions, usually in churches, can be very useful sources of family and local history, and, as we have seen, these were often in Latin until the 17th century or even later. They often give a brief summary of the career of a prominent person as well as his (sometimes her) family connections, and this information can be difficult to obtain from other sources. Such inscriptions are very rarely recorded in printed form, though some county libraries have collections of transcripts (e.g. Lincoln); but usually one has to go and find them in situ.

Translations

These translations are written as an aid to understanding the Latin passages included in the text and they have therefore been kept close to the Latin. They are not, however, word-for-word translations and sometimes more literal renderings, or words added for the sake of clarity or English idiom, have been included in square brackets where additional help was thought useful.

Chapter 2: The Anglo-Saxon Period

2(a) Nennius' Account of Arthur

At that time the Saxons were growing strong in number and increasing in Britain. But when Hengist died, Octha, his son, crossed from the left part of Britain to the kingdom of the Canti [in Kent], and from him descended the kings of the Canti. At that time Arthur was fighting against them in those days together with the kings of the Britons, but he himself was war-leader [lit. 'leader of the wars']. The first battle [lit. 'war', and so throughout this passage] was at the mouth of a river which is called Glein. The second and third and fourth and fifth [were] on another river, which is called Dubglas, and is in the region of Linnuis. The sixth battle [was] on a river which is called Bassas. The seventh battle was in the forest of Celidon, that is Cat Coit Celidon. The eighth battle was in the fortress of Guinnion, in which Arthur carried the image of the holy Mary, perpetual virgin, upon his shoulders, and the pagans were turned in flight on that day, and there was a great slaughter upon them through the power of our Lord Jesus Christ and through the power of the holy virgin Mary, his mother. The ninth battle was waged in the city of the Legion. He waged the tenth battle on the bank of a river which is called Tribruit. The eleventh battle took place on a hill which is called Agned. The twelfth battle was on the hill of Badon, on which nine hundred and sixty men fell on one day from one attack of Arthur; and no one overthrew them except himself alone, and he was victor in all the battles. And when they were defeated in all the

153

battles, they kept seeking help from Germany, and they continually increased [their numbers] many times over, and they brought kings from Germany to rule over them in Britain until the time when Ida reigned, who was the son of Eobba. He was the first king in Beornica, that is in Berneich.

2(b) The Welsh Annals: The Battle of Badon

[516]: Year 72. Battle of Badon, in which Arthur carried the cross of our Lord Jesus Christ for three days and three nights on his shoulders, and the Britons were the victors.

1. Arthur, C. King Arthur, B.
2. ...... On his shoulders [ablative case], B.
3. Following words read: and he was the victor, C; In that battle fell Colgrinus and Radulphus, leaders of the Angles, B.

2(c) William of Malmesbury: The Battle of Badon

But when he [Vortimer] died, the strength of the Britons withered, their hopes diminished and flowed backwards; and indeed they would have gone to ruin at that very time [lit. 'already then'], if Ambrosius, the sole survivor of the Romans, who was monarch of the kingdom after Vortigern, had not crushed the rising [power of the] barbarians with the outstanding assistance of the warrior [lit. 'warlike'] Arthur. This is the Arthur about whom nonsensical stories of the Britons are current even today; [yet] he is clearly worthy not of dreamt up false stories, but of being recorded as true history [see notes in text for a more literal translation], since he sustained his failing country for a long period, and sharpened the broken minds of his countrymen to war; finally, in the siege of Badon Hill, relying on the image of the Lord's mother, which he had stitched onto his equipment, he alone attacked nine hundred of the enemy and destroyed them with incredible slaughter.

2(d) Matthew Paris: Concerning the victory of Arthur on the Hill of Colidon

In the year of grace 518. Boniface sat in the Roman [papal] throne for two years and seven days. During this time Arthur, king of the Britons, having collected a large army, headed for the city of Kaerlindcoit, which is now called Lincoln, where he found the Saxons and created unheard of carnage among them; for on one day six thousand of them fell, ending their lives wretchedly, some [lit. 'partly'] drowned in rivers, some run through with weapons, some slaughtered in flight. But Arthur followed them as they fled and did not rest until they came to the wood of Colidon, and there they came together from their flight and tried to resist Arthur, defending themselves manfully. When Arthur saw this, he ordered trees around that part of the wood to be cut, and the trunks to be placed around it in such a way that any way out was completely denied to them; for he wanted to besiege them in the place for a long time, until they all perished from hunger. But the Saxons, not having anything to feed on, asked for permission to leave, on the condition that they should be allowed to make for Germany completely unarmed [lit. 'at least with naked bodies'; **nudus** in military contexts often means 'unarmed']. Then Arthur, having sought advice, agreed to their request, and retaining their possessions and spoils, and hostages for the payment of tribute, he granted only [that they could] retreat.

2(e) Matthew Paris: Concerning the famous battle of king Arthur against the Saxons

In the year of grace 520. The Saxons Colgrinus, Baldulphus and Cheldricus regretted that they had made an agreement with Arthur; therefore returning to Britain they landed on the shore of Toton [near Southampton?], and finally besieged the city of Badon. So when the news had spread, Arthur ordered their hostages to be hanged; then he headed for the siege and ordered everyone to take up arms; he himself [was] dressed in a corslet and had a helmet on his head with a picture of a dragon; also on his shoulders he hung a shield with the name Pridwen, on which there was depicted an image of the holy mother of God, [and] he very frequently recalled her to his mind; he was girded also with his excellent sword Caliburn, [and] he adorned his right hand with a lance by the name of Rou. Then having positioned his forces he bravely attacked the pagans. They resisted manfully the whole day, and continually destroyed the Britons. At length, as the sun began to set [lit. 'inclined towards its setting'], the Saxons seized the next hill, intending to hold it as a fortress. But when the following day dawned [lit. 'when the following sun brought back the day'], Arthur went up to the top of the hill with his army, but in ascending he lost many of his men, for the Saxons, running at them from the top, more easily

inflicted wounds. However, the Britons, having occupied the top of
the hill with very great bravery, wrought most dreadful slaughter
on the enemy, though the Saxons confronted them [lit. 'presented
their chests to them'] and continued to resist them with every effort.
And when they had spent much of the day in fighting, Arthur,
finally drawing his sword Caliburn, called upon the name of the
blessed virgin Mary, and thrusting himself in a rapid attack amidst
the dense lines of the enemy, he annihilated whoever he met with a
single blow. He did not cease to make his attack until he [had] killed
eight hundred and forty men with his sword alone. Colgrinus and
his brother Baldulphus fell there, and with them many thousands
of the barbarians. But Cheldricus, seeing the danger of his allies,
turned to flight with the remains of the army. So the king ordered
Cador, the leader of Cornubia [Cornwall] to pursue them, and
finally, when no means of defence remained, with their forces torn
to pieces, they made for the island of Thanet. The leader [i.e. Cador]
pursued them there, and did not rest until he annihilated
Cheldricus and received the surrender of the rest. The same year
John sat on the Roman [papal] throne for two years.

2(f) Gildas: The Battle of Badon

From that time, now our countrymen, now the enemy were victori-
ous, so that in this people the Lord could make trial, in his customary way, of his latter-day Israel, [to see] whether it loved him or not;
until the year of the siege of Badon Hill, and almost the last
slaughter of the villains, and not the least. And the fortieth year
[since then?] began one month ago [lit. 'one month now having
elapsed'] (as I know), and this was also [the year] of my birth.

2(g) Gildas: 'The Bear'

Why have you too been rolling in the long-standing filth of your
iniquity since the years of your youth, [you] the Bear, who sit on
many, the driver of the chariot of the Bear's stronghold, despiser of
God, and oppressor of his dispensation, Cuneglasus, in Latin 'Red
Butcher'.

2(h) Bede: St Gregory and the Angles

A story which has been handed down to us by the tradition of older
generations about the blessed Gregory should not be passed over in

silence. It was in fact the reason [lit. 'warned in fact by which cause'] that he took such diligent care for the salvation of our nation. They say that one day merchants had recently arrived and many goods had been brought together in the forum for sale, and many people had gathered to buy; and Gregory himself came among the others and saw some boys up for sale among the other goods, white-skinned and with beautiful faces, the appearance of their hair also striking. When he saw them, he asked, so they say, from what region or land they had been brought, and it was said that [they came] from the island of Britain, whose inhabitants were of such an appearance. He again asked whether these same islanders were Christians, or were still enveloped in pagan errors. And it was said that they were pagans. But he, drawing long sighs from the depths of his heart, said, 'Ah! what sadness that the author of darkness should possess people of such shining countenance, and that such grace of appearance should hold a mind empty of internal grace!' So he asked again what was the name of that people. The reply was given that they were called Angles. But he said, 'Rightly, for they also have angelic faces, and it is right that such people should be fellow-heirs of the angels in heaven. What name does the province have from which they were brought?' The reply was given that the same provincials were called Deiri. But he said, 'They are rightly [called] Deiri, saved from wrath [Latin **de ira**] and called to the mercy of Christ. What is the king of that province called?' The reply was made that he was called Aelli. But he, making play on the name, said, 'Alleluia! The praise of God the Creator should be sung in those parts.'

2(i) Bede: Caedmon (I)

In the monastery of this abbess there was a certain brother especially notable by divine grace, because he was accustomed to compose songs appropriate to religion and piety, so that whatever he learned from holy scripture through those who expounded them, he could produce in his own language, that is the language of the Angles, after a very short time in poetic words composed with very great sweetness and sadness. By his songs the minds of many were often stirred to contempt of the world and to a search for the heavenly life. And indeed others also after him among the people of the Angles tried to compose religious poetry, but no one could compare with him. For he did not learn from men, nor was he trained by a man in the art of singing, but by divine aid [lit. 'divinely helped'] he received the gift of singing for nothing. Therefore he could never compose anything frivolous or superfluous in his poems, but only those things which are concerned with religion befitted his religious tongue. Although he was settled in secular life until the time of advanced age, he had learned nothing of singing at any time. So sometimes at a feast, when it was decided as an entertainment that all should sing in turn, when he saw the harp approaching him he used to get up in the middle of the meal, go out and walk back to his house.

2(j) Bede: Caedmon (II)

When he did this on one occasion, and he had left the house of the feast and gone out to the horses' stables, whose custody had been assigned to him that night, and there at the appropriate time he had gone to sleep [lit. 'had given his limbs to sleep'], someone stood by him in his dream. Greeting him and calling him by his name he said, 'Caedmon, sing something to me.' But he replied and said, 'I do not know how to sing; for that very reason I left the feast and came out here, because I could not sing.' Again the person who was speaking to him said, 'Nevertheless, you shall sing to me [see note in text].' 'What must I sing?' he said. He said, 'Sing of the beginning of [all] creatures.' When he received this reply, he immediately began to sing verses in praise of God the Creator, which he had never heard, of which this is the sense: 'Now we must praise the maker of the heavenly kingdom, the power of the Creator, and his purpose, the works of the Father of glory; how he, since he is the eternal God, was the maker of all miracles; who, the almighty guardian of the human race, first created heaven as a roof for the sons of men, then the earth.' This is the sense, but not the actual order of the words which he sang in his sleep. For poems, however excellently composed, cannot be translated from one language to another word for word without loss of their grace and dignity. Rising from his sleep, he retained in his memory all the things that he had sung while sleeping, and soon added to them more words in the same style of poetry worthy of God.

2(k) Bede: Caedmon (III)

And coming early in the morning to the reeve who was in charge of him, he told him what gift he had received, and having been taken to the abbess he was told to describe the dream and say the poem, with many learned men present, so that by the judgement of all of them what he was reporting and where it came from could be assessed. And it seemed to everybody that a heavenly grace had been granted to him by the Lord. And they explained to him some passage of sacred history or doctrine, ordering him, if he could, to translate this into a measure of verse. He undertook the task and went away, and returning in the morning rendered what had been ordered composed in excellent verse. So the abbess soon grasped the grace of God in the man and told him to leave the secular life and take on the monastic way of life. He was taken into the monastery with all his possessions and she admitted him to the community of brothers, and ordered him to be taught the events of sacred history. Everything that he could learn by listening, by recalling it to himself and by ruminating [upon it] like a cow chewing the cud [lit. 'like a clean animal'; see note in text] he turned it into the sweetest poetry. And by repeating it more pleasantly he made his teachers in turn into his audience. He sang about the creation of the world, about the origin of the human race, about the whole story of Genesis, about the exodus of Israel from Egypt and their entry into the promised land, about many other events of sacred scripture, about the Lord's incarnation, passion, resurrection and ascent into heaven, about the coming of the Holy Spirit, and the teaching of the apostles. Likewise he made many poems about the terror of the future judgement, and the horror of the punishment of hell, and the joy of the heavenly kingdom, but also very many others about divine blessings and judgements, in all of which he took care to pull men away from the love of wickedness, and in fact to rouse them to the love and practice of good action. For he was a very religious man, and humbly submitted to the disciplines of the monastic rule, but against those who wished to do otherwise [he was] inflamed with a zeal of great fervour; whence he also brought his life to a close with a beautiful end.

2(1) Bede: Cuthbert (I)

But divine providence, wishing to demonstrate more widely in what great glory Cuthbert, the man of the Lord, lived after his death, whose illustrious life before his death was also marked by frequent signs of miracles, when eleven years had passed after his burial, put into the minds of the brothers that they should raise his bones, which, in the manner of the dead, they thought should be found dry, the rest of the body by now being wasted away and reduced to dust; and that they should place them concealed in a new coffin, in the same place in fact but upon the paved area, so that he could be duly venerated [lit. 'for the sake of worthy veneration']. When they reported to Eadbert, their bishop, that this is what they wanted, he approved their plan and told them that they should remember to do this on the day [i.e. the anniversary] of his burial. They did so, and opening the tomb they found the whole body as complete as if he were still alive, and with the joints of his limbs flexible, much more like in sleep than in death; but also all the clothes in which [the body] had been dressed appeared not only unspoiled but also in their former newness and amazingly brightly coloured. When the brothers saw this they were struck immediately with great fear and rushed to report what they had found to the bishop, who at the time was by chance staying as a solitary in a place quite remote from the church, surrounded on all sides by ebbing waves of the sea. For he was accustomed always to spend the time of Lent in this [place], and [lit. 'in this (place)' repeated] to pass the forty days before the Lord's Nativity in great devotion of abstinence, prayer and tears; in which [place] also his venerable predecessor Cuthbert used sometimes to serve the Lord alone before he went to Farne Island.

2(m) Bede: Cuthbert (II)

But they also brought to him a part of the garments which had covered the holy body. When he was thankfully receiving these gifts and listening willingly to these miracles (for he was kissing the garments themselves with obvious feeling as if they were still around the body of the father), he said, 'Put new garments around the body for these that you have removed, and thus put it back in the coffin which you have prepared. For I know for certain that that place will not remain empty for long, which has been sanctified by such great grace of a heavenly miracle; and how blessed he is to whom the Lord, the author and bestower of all happiness, will consider it fitting to present an opportunity of resting in it.' When the bishop had finished these [words] and more of this kind with many tears and great sorrow and also with trembling tongue, the brothers did as he had ordered, and they placed the body, wrapped in new clothing and concealed in a new coffin, upon the paved area of the sanctuary. Very soon after [lit. 'and no delay'] God's beloved bishop Eadbert was attacked by a severe illness, and it increased day by day and the heat of his fever became much worse; not long after, that is on the day before the Nones of May [i.e. on 6 May] he also departed to the Lord. Placing his body in the tomb of the blessed father Cuthbert, they put it on top of the coffin in which they had placed the undecayed limbs of the same father. The miracles of healing also done several times in that place bear witness to the merits of both, and we have previously entrusted to memory some of these in the book of his life. But we have thought it appropriate to add in this History too some things which we happen to have heard recently.

Chapter 3: Grants, Deeds, and Other Legal and Ecclesiastical Documents

3(a) Charter of Geoffrey de Thorlay

Let all present and future know that I Geoffrey de Thorlay have given, granted, and by this my present charter confirmed to Sarah, my daughter, and to her heirs four bovates of land with my messuage pertaining to them in the territory of Stallingborough, with meadows and with pastures and with all other easements within and without the aforesaid vill, namely those four bovates of land with appurtenances which I held from Gilbert de Tours; to have and to hold from me and my heirs in fee and hereditarily, freely and without disturbance, quietly and peacefully, paying thence annually to me and my heirs six shillings for all service, namely at the feast of St Botolph [17 June] three shillings, and at the feast of St Andrew [30 November] three shillings. Moreover, I have given, granted, and by this my present charter confirmed to the same Sarah and her heirs a third part [dower] consisting of two bovates of land in the aforesaid territory, with all appurtenances, namely that part which Matilda the daughter of Robert formerly held; to have and to hold, freely, without disturbance and quietly, free from all service, except foreign service. And I and my heirs will guarantee all the aforesaid land with all its appurtenances to the aforesaid Sarah and her heirs against all people in perpetuity. These being witnesses: Geoffrey Nevil, Thomas de Tours, etc.

3(b) Notification of Gift, Mountnessing, Essex, c. 1152

To the lord Ralph, by the grace of God dean of the church of St Paul, London, and to Richard, archdeacon of the same church, and to the chapter of the whole church, and to all the faithful of the church of St Mary, Michael Capra [sends] greeting in Christ. You should know that I have given and granted and by my charter confirmed, in perpetual alms for the soul of my father and of my mother and of all my ancestors, to God and to the church of St Mary and of St Leonard in my wood in Ginges and to the brothers serving God there, both future and present, the church of St Giles of Ginges and all appurtenances to the same church, just as they have ever quite rightly belonged. Namely in the lands and tithes of the wood and of the meadow and of the orchard, with all freely held customary dues pertaining to the aforesaid church. These being witnesses: William parson of the same church who has agreed to this, Gilbert his vicar, and William son and heir of the same Michael who also granted this [OR who also agreed to this], Robert de Mounteney, Robert bailiff of the Hundred, Richard Lepuhier, Jordan his brother, Alwin the smith, Robert Morel, Jordan Rufus, Richard son of William.

3(c) Institution of a priest, Canwick in the diocese of Lincoln

Canwick (valued at 20 marks). Alan of Canwick, chaplain, presented by the said Prior and the convent of the Hospital of Lincoln, has been admitted to the perpetual benefice of vicar of the said church; and in the same, etc. [see note on text], which consists of the total altarage and of six acres of arable land in the fields of Bracebridge, with a toft next to the church of Canwick on the north side and of another toft towards the south side of the church, to make a courtyard for [lit. 'of'] the vicar. And the benefice of the vicar is valued at 4 marks and rather more. The Prior will respond as above.

3(d) Grant of Land, Fryerning, Essex, c. 1170

Be it known to [all men] both present and future that I Margaret de Munfichet have granted and given to Fulk five acres of land which Godfrey le Fuchel held and another five acres which Roger son of Aldiva held in my vill of Ginges in return for his service, to hold from me and my heirs, himself and his heirs, by paying annually one pound of pepper on the eve of St John the Baptist [23 June] in return for all service, except the king's service. And he shall pay this aforesaid pound of pepper to the church of the blessed John of Ginges. These being witnesses: Warren of Bassingbourne, Alexander his brother, William chaplain of Ginges, Serlo chaplain of Ginges, Roger of Thriplow, Warren of Barrington, Eustace his brother and Richard his brother, John the son of Eustace, William of the Chamber.

3(e) Grant of Land, Marbury, Cheshire, c. 1170

Be it known to all both present and future that I Richard of Marbury have given and granted to William my brother of Marbury, and have confirmed by this my present charter, all the land of Marbury with all its appurtenances in woodland, in open ground, in meadows, in pastures, in mills, in fish-ponds, and in all other places belonging to the same vill, to hold and to have for him and his heirs in fee and inheritance in perpetuity, freely and quietly and undisturbed, from me and my heirs, himself and his heirs paying to me and my heirs annually at Easter four barbed arrows in return for all service pertaining to me and to my heirs. But on condition that the aforesaid William my brother must do the same service for the lord Warin of Vernon as I myself did for my lord or my father before me did for his lords. This I have done with the consent and agreement of the lord Warin of Vernon and of my heirs. And I transfer from me and my heirs all my right concerning the aforesaid land to William my aforesaid brother and to his heirs in perpetuity in return for three and a half marks which William my aforesaid brother has given to me, part in the presence of the whole county of Chester and part in the court of my lord Warin of Vernon and part in the presence of the Wapentake of Halton. Witness: Lidulph of Twemlow, Hamo of Bartington, Gilbert son of Nigel, Robert of Stochal, Radulph the chaplain, Richard of Vernon, Raer of Stanthorne, Gilbert of Bostock, and all the county of Chester.

3(f) Deed of Land Exchange, Takeley, Essex, c. 1212

Let [all men] present and future know that I William de Hautville, son of William, have granted and given and by the present charter confirmed to the church of St John the Baptist of Colchester and to the abbot and monks of the same place Helya the son of Gilbert and his whole tenement in Takeley, namely his messuage and three crofts of land which lie between the aforesaid messuage and the land of the church of Takeley, and one acre which lies between Le Wardbrock and between the land of Arnold Berard, and one acre of pasture which lies between the land of Arnold and the land of Hardwin, and the whole field from my domain which is called Newenhale, with all their appurtenances in Takeley except the mill situated in the same field, in pure and perpetual alms; and I have given these aforenamed tenements to the aforesaid abbot and monks of Colchester in exchange for eighty [lit. 'four times twenty'] acres of land which William my father had previously given them in his park of Takeley in pure and perpetual alms. Moreover I have made this gift for the salvation of the soul of the lord king John and of his ancestors and successors and for the salvation of my soul and of all my ancestors and of my heirs. And I and my heirs shall guarantee to the aforesaid church of St John and to the abbot and monks of Colchester the aforenamed tenements in pure and perpetual alms quit from all secular service and tax against all men and women. These being witnesses: Geoffrey son of Peter, Earl of Essex, Aubrey de Ver, Earl of Oxford, William son of Fulk, Robert de Cantelu, Roger de la Dune, Ralph de Berners, Master Robert of Kent, William de Haya, Alexander son of Osborn, Richard son of Payn, William of Takeley, Nicholas son of Gerard, Nigel of Hawkeston, Richard son of Ralph, Richard of Bumpstead, Lawrence of Takeley, Raymond of Selford, Roger Testard, Robert de Camps, Roger de Tey, and many others.

3(g) Quitclaim to Lanercost Priory, c. 1255

Deed of Agnes daughter of William son of Jonetta of Carlisle concerning the quitclaim of Cumquenecath.

To all the faithful of Christ to whom the present document shall come, Agnes daughter of William son of Jonetta of Carlisle greeting in the Lord. All of you should know that I, for the salvation of my soul and the soul of my father and my mother and of all my ancestors, have granted and on behalf of myself and my heirs have quitclaimed in perpetuity to the prior and convent of Lanercost all the right and claim that I had or that I and my heirs shall be able to have at any time in Cumquenecath with all its appurtenances, in such a way namely that neither I nor my heirs shall in future be able to demand or to assert any right or claim on the aforesaid Cumquenecath with its appurtenances. And if I had, or any of my heirs at any time shall be able to have any [claim], that [claim] I have completely abjured by touching the holy gospels. In witness of this matter I have placed my seal on this document. These being witnesses: the lords Robert of Muncaster and John of Ireby, Ada of Bassenthwaite, Radulf of Pocklington, then Sheriff of Cumbria, Patrick of Ousby, Matthew the clerk, Jakelin of Carlisle, John of Burton, clerk, Walter son of Warren, Robert of Carwinley, and many others.

3(h) Grant of Land, Little Waltham, Essex, c. 1275

Let [all men] present and future know that I William de la Grave of
Little Waltham have granted, given and by this my present charter
confirmed to William Russel merchant of Chelmsford, in return for
his homage and service and for twenty-four shillings of silver pennies which he has given me in payment, two acres of my land with
all their appurtenances in Little Waltham, lying in a certain croft
which is called Langecroft as it is enclosed by hedges and ditches,
between the land of John of Belsted [in Broomfield, just to the south
of Little Waltham] which is called la Reden [apparently in Great
Waltham, a mile to the west of Little Waltham] on one side and the
lane leading from the king's highway to the grove of Geoffrey of
Belsted on the other, whereof one headland abuts on the yard of the
said John and the other headland on my messuage, to have and to
hold for the said William and his heirs or his assigns or their heirs
from me and my heirs or my assigns, and whenever and to whomso-
ever he shall wish to give, sell, bequeath, mortgage or in any way
assign the said two acres of land with their appurtenances, except
to religious men and Jews, freely, quietly, properly and in peace, by
right and hereditarily in perpetuity, paying for this annually to me
and my heirs or my assigns, himself and his heirs or his assigns
eight pence at two terms of the year, namely at Easter four pence
and at the feast of St Michael [29 September] four pence, for all
secular services, customary dues, attendances at the courts and all
secular demands, except service of the lord king when it falls due, at
more or less one farthing. And I the said William and my heirs or
my assigns shall guarantee, defend and acquit the said two acres of
land with their appurtenances to the said William and his heirs or
his assigns or their heirs as is aforesaid through the aforenamed
service against all men and women in perpetuity. And so that this
my grant, gift and my confirmation may remain right and stable in
perpetuity I have set my seal to this present deed. These being
witnesses: Robert of Haylesden, Roger of Wimbish, Geoffrey of
Belsted, Richard Koc, Sewell of Springfield, Richard of Munchanesy,
Stephen le Franceis, and others.

3(i) Gift by Robert I to Melrose Abbey, 1315

Robert by the grace of God king of the Scots to all upright men of his
whole land both clerical and lay, greeting. You should know that we,
for the salvation of our soul and for the salvation of the souls of all

our ancestors and successors the kings of Scotland, have given, granted and by this our present charter confirmed to God and to the church of the blessed Mary of Melrose, to the abbot and monks serving God there and who will serve in perpetuity all our land and tenement of Lessuden with appurtenances. To hold and to have for the said abbot and monks and their successors in perpetuity as free, pure and perpetual alms throughout all their proper boundaries and borders with the due and customary services of the freeholders and with the villeins of the said land at the time of our predecessor the lord Alexander king of Scotland of good memory, recently deceased, and of the lady Mary queen of Scotland, his mother, and with all other freedoms, produce, fishing rights, mills, easements, and their lawful appurtenances both named and unnamed, as free and quietly, fully and honourably as any alms is held or possessed quite freely or quietly, fully or honourably in the kingdom of Scotland, save only the support of devoted prayers for us. In witness of which thing we have ordered our seal to be set to our present charter. Witnesses: the venerable fathers William and Robert by the grace of God bishops of St Andrews and Glasgow, Edward of Bruce, Earl of Carrick, and lord Galwydie our brother, Thomas [son] of Ranulph, Earl of Moray, our grandson, Patrick, Earl of March, James, Lord of Douglas, and Robert of Keith, our marshal. At Ayr on the first day of May in the tenth year of our reign.

3(j) Deed of Income for a Chantry, Harlow, Essex, 1324

Let [all men] present and future know that I William of Mashbury in the county of Essex have given, granted and by this my present charter confirmed to Master John of Stanton, clerk, three shillings of annual rent to be received annually at two terms of the year by equal portions at the feast of St Michael [29 September] and at Easter from John son of Stephen of Paris for twelve acres of arable land and two acres of meadow which he held from me in the vill of Great Parndon lying in the field called Wedhey in the said vill between Parndon Wood on one side and the land of Walter Cook on the other. And one headland abuts on Farnhel and the other headland on the common road which leads from Ryhel [Rye Hill] towards Waltham. To have and to hold the aforesaid three shillings with homages, guardianships, escheats, reliefs, marriage rights [see text for a definition of these] and all other things pertaining to the said rent, for the said Master John of Stanton, his heirs and assigns, concerning the chief lord of that fief through the services due and customary by right for this. And I the aforesaid William of Mashbury, my heirs and assigns shall guarantee against all people in perpetuity the aforesaid three shillings of annual rent with homages, guardianships, escheats, reliefs, marriage rights and all other things pertaining to the said rent to the said Master John of Stanton, his heirs and assigns. In witness of which thing I have set my seal to this present deed. These being witnesses: Thomas de Cann, Gilbert at Chamber, Geoffrey Maulle, James of Weald, John Campion and others. Given at Harlow on the ninth day of April in the seventeenth year of the reign of king Edward son of king Edward.

3(k) Will of William Felton, Knight

In the name of God, Amen. I William of Felton, knight, of healthy memory and sound mind, on the Monday next before the feast of the Nativity of the Blessed Virgin Mary AD 1358, make my will in this fashion. Firstly I grant and bequeath my soul to almighty God and to the Blessed Mary and to all the saints; and my body to be buried in the church of the blessed John the Baptist of Edlingham. Likewise [I bequeath] 40 shillings as an offering. Likewise [I bequeath] 100 shillings for a light around my body on the day of my burial. Likewise I grant and bequeath to Isabella my wife five silver dishes and a silver chalice. Likewise I grant and bequeath to Master Peter, vicar of Edlingham, 20 shillings. Likewise I grant and bequeath the whole residue of my goods, moveable and immovable, and all that is owed to me by anyone to Master William, my son, after my debts have been paid in full. And so that these things may be faithfully performed and implemented I ordain, make and establish these as my executors: the aforesaid Master William of Felton, my son and heir, Isabella my wife, and the aforesaid Master Peter, vicar of the church of Edlingham. These being witnesses: William Clerk, William Zole, and William of Crokisdon and others.

3(l) Will of the Lady Margaret de Eure widow of John de Eure, Knight

... Likewise to Elizot, my maidservant, one coverlet of red and grey, one pair of sheets, likewise 1 bench cover. Likewise to the same 1 gown furred with black; likewise to the same 10 shillings. Likewise to Margaret Egleston one coverlet with tapestry decorated with vines and grapes. Likewise 1 canvas, 1 pair of sheets, 2 blankets, 2 cloths, 2 towels, 1 hood well furred, another hood furred with purydmenev.(?). Likewise to Radulph of Lumley 1 coverlet with 4 tapestries decorated with parrots. Likewise to Robert Heron 1 complete bed of Parisian work …

3(m) John Pickering

Inventory of all the goods moveable and immovable of Master John Pickering, chaplain, recently deceased, valued by 4 fitting and prudent men, whose names are these: Richard Patterson, Henry Coniers, John Tranome, John Wilkinson; which John Pickering died on the 10th day of the month of October AD 1472.

HALL. First of all, neither in the hall nor in the bedrooms was anything found [lit. 'is found'] to the value of 1d, except only the clothes [in which] he had been dressed every day; which is to say that everything inside, namely the pots, pans, dishes, linen and woollen garments, and the other ornaments were removed by a most wicked woman.

IN THE STABLE. One mare with a foal to the value of 10s. Another mare 8s. One horse 5s.

IN THE BARN. 24 quarters of wheat, the price of one of which 3s 4d. 20 quarters of oats, the price of one of which 20d. Peas, 10 quarters, the price of one of which 20d. Hay 16s.

IN THE FIELD. Six bovates of corn, the price of one bovate 10s. One plough 10s.

LIVESTOCK. Six oxen 54s. Five bullocks and six heifers, the price of one 4s 2d. Four cows with calves, the price of one 9s. 23 sheep, the price of one 12d. 6 pigs 6s 8d.

Total sum: £19 6s 8d. [see note on text]

3(n) Oxfordshire

Manesser Arsic renders the account concerning the taxation of Oxfordshire.
In the treasury £76 13s 6d in assayed money, in two tallies.
In respect of the alms determined for the Knights of the Temple, one mark.

And in respect of the payment determined for thirteen sick people, £19 15s 5d, and for the same 65s towards clothing.

And in respect of gifts to the abbot of Osney, 9s 5d; and to the canons of St Frideswide, 25s for the customary service of the festival.

And to the same 17s 7d concerning the new donation.

And in respect of the payment determined to William son of Baldwin, 102s 6d, through the writ of the King.

And in respect of the lands granted to Engelger de Bohun, £20 in assayed money in respect of Bloxham; and to the same man in respect of the vill of Richard de Luci, £20 in unassayed money.

And to the Count of Flanders £76 in assayed money in respect of Barton (?), with 100 shillings from Wicha (?). And to Hugo de Plugeno, £42 10s in assayed money in respect of Headington. And to the abbess of Godstow 100 shillings in assayed money in respect of the same vill. And in respect of the same vill to Henry of Oxford 50 shillings in assayed money.

And to Gilbert Angevin £10 in unassayed money in respect of Besenton (?). And in respect of the same vill to the abbess of Godstow 100 shillings in unassayed money.

... And in respect of the running of the houses of the sick of Oxford, 60 shillings. And for the scything of meadows and the preparation of hay and taking it to Woodstock, 60 shillings.

3(o) Manorial Survey, Thaxted, c. 1395

Thomas Tewe holds 6 acres of pasture and does common suit [see note on this passage] and pays annually				1d
The same John Benge holds one grove recently [the property] of Roger atte Welde and pays annually	1½d			1½d
William Yerdele holds one messuage and one acre of land	4d	4d	4d	4d
John Proude holds 4 acres of land from the tenement of James, which tenement in fact owes common suit and pays annually	4d	4d	4d	4d

Henry Boyton holds one messuage and 30 acres of land, meadow and pasture, and owes common suit and pays	15s		15s	
The same Henry holds half a virgate of land from the tenement formerly [the property of] Goldsmith, and owes common suit, and he makes 3 cartloads of corn and hay recovering from the lord $4\frac{1}{2}$d, or he shall give the lord 6d, and he pays annually	$20\frac{1}{4}$d	$20\frac{1}{4}$d	$20\frac{1}{4}$d	$20\frac{1}{4}$d
William Symond holds 3 acres of land and pays annually	$4\frac{1}{2}$d 1 capon	$4\frac{1}{2}$d	$4\frac{1}{2}$d	$4\frac{1}{2}$d
Thomas May holds 6 acres of land and one right of encroachment, and pays	$4\frac{1}{4}$d	$4\frac{1}{4}$d	$4\frac{1}{4}$d	$4\frac{1}{4}$d
Walter Ewayn holds 6 acres of land and one piece of meadow and pays	$2\frac{1}{4}$d	$2\frac{1}{4}$d	$2\frac{1}{4}$d	$2\frac{1}{4}$d
John Herry, butcher, holds 1 acre of land and pays	1d	1d	1d	1d
John Thrower, John Dod hold one acre of land and pay annually	1d	1d	1d	1d

Chapter 4: Charters

4(a) Charter of Archbishop Thurstan to Beverley, c. 1130

Thurstan, by the grace of God Archbishop of York, to all the faithful of Christ both present and future, greeting and the blessing of God and of himself (i.e. Thurstan).

Let it be known to you that I have given and granted, and on the advice of the chapter of York and of Beverley and on the advice of my barons have confirmed by this charter, to the people of Beverley all freedoms by the same laws that those of York have in their city. Moreover let it not escape your notice that the lord Henry our king has granted to us the power to do this out of his good will, and by his charter has confirmed our statutes and our laws according to the form of the laws of the citizens of York, saving the dignity and honour of God and of Saint John and of ourselves and of the canons, so that in this way indeed he may exalt and promote the honour of the mercies of his predecessors with all these free customs.

I wish my citizens of Beverley to have their guildhall, which I give to them, and I grant that there they may conduct their statutes to the honour of God and of St John and of the canons and to the betterment of the whole township, by the same law of freedom as those of York have in their guildhall. I also grant to them [the power to raise] import duty in perpetuity in return for eight marks annually; moreover on the three feasts on which the duty concerns [i.e. is at the discretion of] us and [our] canons, namely on the feast of St John the Confessor in May [St John at the Latin Gate, 6 May ?], and on the feast of the Translation of St John [i.e. John of Beverley, 25 October], and on the Nativity of St John the Baptist [24 June]; truly on these three feasts I have released all the citizens of Beverley [to be] free and quit of all import duty. Also by witness of this charter I have granted to the same citizens free entry and exit in the town and outside the town, on open land and in woodland and in marshland, on roads and on paths and in other meeting places, except in meadows and cornfields, in such a way that someone may at some time be able to grant and confirm better, freer and wider rights; and know that they are free and quit of all import duty throughout the whole county of York just as those of York. And I wish that anyone who disregards this may be cursed, just as the custom of the church itself of St John asserts and as has been decreed in the church of St John.

These are witnesses: Geoffrey Murdac, Nigel Fossard, Alan de Percy, Walter Espec, Eustace Johnson, Thomas the Reeve, Archdeacon Thurstan, Canon Herbert, William Toleson, William of Bayeux; in the presence of the whole family of the archbishop, clerical and lay, in York.

4(b) Charter of King Stephen concerning the freedoms of the Church of England and the kingdom

I Stephen by the grace of God [and] by the assent of the clergy and people appointed as king of England, and consecrated by William

Archbishop of Canterbury and by the legate of the holy church of Rome, and confirmed by Pope Innocent of the holy Roman see, by respect and love of God I grant that the holy church be free and confirm to it due reverence.

I promise that I shall neither do nor permit anything by way of simony in the church or in ecclesiastical matters. I assert and confirm that justice concerning ecclesiastical persons and all clerics and their goods, and the power and distribution of ecclesiastical honours is in the hands of the bishops. I decree and grant that the dignities of the churches confirmed by their privileges, and their customary dues held by ancient tenure, shall remain inviolate. I grant that all possessions and holdings of the churches which they had on that day on which king William my grandfather died [lit. 'was living and dead'] be for them free and without condition, without any challenge of claimants. But if a church hereafter claims back anything of what it held or possessed before the death of the same king, [but] which it now does not hold, I reserve to my indulgence and dispensation either to restore or to investigate it. But whatever has been contributed to them after the death of the same king by the generosity of kings or by the gift of princes, by way of offering or by purchase, or by any exchange of the faithful, [this] I confirm. I promise them that I shall make and preserve, as far as I am able, peace and justice in all things.

I reserve to myself the forests which William my grandfather and William my uncle established and held. All the rest which king Henry added to them I return and grant immune to the churches and the kingdom.

If any bishop or abbot or other ecclesiastical person before his death reasonably shall have distributed or shall have determined the distribution of his goods, I grant that it remains firm. But if he dies prematurely [lit. 'will have been overtaken by death' i.e., presumably, before he has made a will], for the salvation of his soul on the advice of the church the same distribution may take place. But while offices are vacant of their own pastors, the offices themselves and all possessions associated with them I entrust in the hands and guardianship of the clergy or of upright men of the same church, until a pastor is legally appointed.

I utterly root out all exactions and injustices and misjudgments which have been wrongly perpetrated by sheriffs or by any others.

I shall observe good laws and ancient and just customs, in murders and lawsuits and in other cases, and I order and decree [such] to be observed. I grant and confirm all these, save my royal and just dignity [i.e. provided my royal and just dignity is not assailed].

Witnesses W. Archbishop of Canterbury, etc.

At Oxford, in the 1136th year from the Incarnation of the Lord, but in the first of my reign.

4(c) Charter of Henry II to Lincoln, c. 1157

Henry by the grace of God, etc., to the bishop of Lincoln, justices, sheriffs, barons, ministers and all his faithful [subjects] of Lincoln, French and English, greeting. You should know that I have granted to my citizens of Lincoln all their freedoms and customary dues and laws which they had in the time of Edward and William and Henry, kings of England, and their merchant guild of men of the city and of other merchants of the county, just as they had it quite fully and freely in the time of our aforesaid predecessors the kings of England. And all men who stay and carry on trade within the four boundaries of the city may enjoy [lit. 'be at ...'] the gilds and customs and taxes of the city just as fully as in the time of Edward, William and Henry, kings of England. I grant to them also that if anyone has bought any land within the city of the burgage of Lincoln, and has held it for one year and one day without challenge, and he who has bought it can show that a claimant existed in the territory of England within the year and did not claim it, from then on he may hold it fully and in peace as before without plea. I also confirm to them that if anyone has stayed in the city of Lincoln for one year and one day without challenge of any claimant, and he has paid his customary dues, and the citizens can show by their laws and the customary dues of the city that a claimant has existed in the territory of England and has not challenged him, from then on he may remain in peace as before in my city of Lincoln as my citizen. Witnesses Ph. Bishop of Bayeux, Ern. Bishop of Lisieux, Thomas the Chancellor, Count Reginald, Ric. de Humes, Constable, H. of Essex, Constable. At Nottingham.

4(d) Charter of Henry II to Nottingham, c. 1157

Henry, king of England, etc. You should know that I have granted and by this my charter confirmed to the citizens of Nottingham all those free customs which they had in the time of Henry our grandfather; namely market dues and the right to warranty from a thief and the right to punish thieves and the right to tax, from Thurmaston as far as Newark, and concerning all those crossing the Trent as fully as in the town of Nottingham, and on the other side from the brook beyond Rampton as far as the water of Radford in the north. Also men from Nottinghamshire and from Derbyshire should come to the city of Nottingham on Fridays and Saturdays with their wagons and pack-animals; and no one should trade in dyed cloth within a radius of ten leagues [probably around 15 miles] of Nottingham, except in the town of Nottingham. And if anyone, wherever he may come from, has stayed in the town of Nottingham for one year and one day, in time of peace, without challenge, no one afterwards except the king shall have right over him. And whoever of the townspeople shall buy a neighbour's land and possess it for a whole year and one day without claim from the parents of the seller, if they shall have been in England, afterwards shall possess it with immunity. And let no answer be given to the reeve [i.e. a defendant does not need to appear in court] of the town of Nottingham charging any of the citizens unless there shall be another accuser in the case. And whoever shall stay in the town, from whichever fief he may be, he must pay feudal taxes at the same time as the citizens and contribute to the expenses of the town. Also all who shall come to the market of Nottingham, from Friday evening until Saturday evening, may not be distrained except for the king's tax. And the passage of the Trent must be free for those sailing as much as one perch measures from each side of the stream of the river. Wherefore I wish and order that the aforesaid citizens should have and hold the aforesaid customary rights rightly and in peace, freely and with immunity, and honourably and fully and wholly, just as they had in the time of king Henry my grandfather.

4(e) Articles of the Barons, sections 4 and 17

Let not a widow give anything for her dower or her dowry [see notes in text for definitions] after the death of her husband, but let her remain in her house for forty days after his death, and within that period let her dower be assigned to her; and let her have her dowry and her inheritance immediately.

Let not widows be compelled to marry, as long as they shall wish to live without a husband; in such a way however that they shall make a guarantee that they will not marry without the consent of the king, if they hold [property] from the king, or of their lords from whom they hold [property].

4(f) Magna Carta, sections 7-8

Let a widow after the death of her husband immediately and without difficulty have her dowry and her inheritance, and let her not give anything for her dower or for her dowry or for her inheritance, which inheritance her husband and she herself shall have held on the day of the death of the same husband, and let her stay in the house of her husband for forty days after his death, within which her dower should be assigned to her.

No widow should be compelled to marry as long as she shall wish to live without a husband, in such a way however that she should make a guarantee that she will not marry without our assent, if she holds [property] from us, or with the assent of her lord from whom she holds [property], if she holds [property] from another.

4(g) Articles of the Barons, sections 31 and 33

That merchants should have safe passage in going and coming to buy or to sell, without all wrongful taxes, through ancient and proper customary rights.

That any person should be allowed to go out of the kingdom and to return, saving the security of the lord king, except in time of war for some short time for the common benefit of the kingdom.

4(h) Magna Carta, sections 41-2

Let all merchants have a safe and secure passage in going out of England and coming into England, and in staying and travelling in England, both by land and by sea, to buy and to sell, without all wrongful taxes, through ancient and proper customary rights, except in time of war, and if they are from a land at war against us; and if such are found in our land at the beginning of the war, let them be arrested without damage to their persons or goods, until it is known from us or from our chief justice how merchants of our land are being treated who shall be found in the land at war with us; and if our people are safe there, let the others be safe in our land.

Moreover let any person go out from our kingdom and return safely and securely by land and by sea, saving our security, except in time of war for some short time for the common benefit of the kingdom, except for prisoners and outlaws according to the law of the kingdom, and people from a land at war against us, and merchants concerning whom let it be done as has been aforesaid.

4(i) Charter granted by Alexander, King of Scots, to Elgin

Alexander by the grace of God King of the Scots to all upright men of his whole land, greeting. You should know that we have granted and by this our charter confirmed to our citizens of Elgin that for the betterment of our town of Elgin they should have in the same town their own merchant guild as freely as any of our citizens in the whole of our kingdom has his guild quite freely. Witnesses Alan the Ostiary, Reginald le Chen, chamberlain, Hugh of Abernethy, William and Bernard of Mowat, Alexander of Moray, and William Byset. At Elgin, on the 28th day of November, in the twentieth year of our reign.

In the year 1234
(incorrectly for 1268; see text)

4(j) Charter of the Prince of Wales, 1301

For Edward, the king's son

The king to the Archbishops and the others, greeting. You should know that we have given, granted and by this my charter confirmed to Edward our dearest son all our lands of North Wales, Anglesey and of Hope [in Clwyd, 5 miles north of Wrexham] with all our lands and holdings existing within the four cantreds, and also all our lands of West Wales and of South Wales, namely in the counties of Carmarthen and of Cardigan the castles and manors of Haverford and of Builth, all the lands and holdings which were of Rhys ap Meredydd and which are in our hand through forfeit of the same Rhys, together with all our other lands and holdings in those parts existing in our hand on the day of the completion of the present charter, excepting the castle and town of Montgomery with appurtenances which we have assigned as a dower to our dearest consort Margaret Queen of England. We have also given and granted to our same son all our county of Chester, together with our manors of Macclesfield and of Overton and all our land of Meilor Seisnek ['the English Mellor'] with all its appurtenances, to have and to hold, with castles, towns, manors, freedoms, customary dues, homages, services, rents, fiefs of knights, advowsons of churches [i.e. the right to allocate benefices], escheats [i.e. properties which fall to the feudal lord when there is no heir], mines, shipwrecks, and all other things pertaining to the lands and holdings above mentioned, by whatever name they are recorded, for our aforesaid son and his heirs the kings of England in perpetuity, as wholly and fully as we have held those lands and holdings with all their appurtenances, saving for our aforesaid consort the castle and town of Montgomery with appurtenances which we have assigned to her as a dower as was aforesaid; doing for us on behalf of the counties and lands and holdings above mentioned such service as it will be found that we did for lord Henry of celebrated memory formerly king of England our father on behalf of the counties and cantreds aforesaid while we held them from the grant of our same father. Wherefore we wish and firmly command that our aforesaid son and his heirs the kings of England in perpetuity should have and hold all the aforesaid lands [and] holdings with the aforesaid counties, together with castles, towns, manors, freedoms, customary dues, homages, services, rents, fiefs of knights, advowsons of churches, escheats, mines, shipwrecks, and all other things pertaining to the lands and holdings above mentioned, by whatever name they may be recorded, as wholly and fully as we held those lands and holdings with all their appurtenances, saving for my aforesaid consort the castle and town of Montgomery with appurtenances which we have assigned to her as a dower, doing for us on behalf of the counties and lands and holdings above mentioned such service as it will be found we did for lord Henry of celebrated memory formerly king of England our father on behalf of the counties and cantreds aforesaid while we held them from the grant of our same father as was aforesaid. These being witnesses: the venerable fathers R. Archbishop of Canterbury, J. of Lincoln, S. of Salisbury, J. Norwich, W. of Coventry and Lichfield, and J. Carlisle, Bishops; John de Warenne, Earl of Surrey, Roger le Bigod of Norfolk and Marshal of England, Radulf de Montehermer of Gloucester and Hereford, Guy de Beauchamp of Warwick, and Richard Arundell, Earls; John de Britain, Reginald de Grey, John de Saint, John de Hastings, and others. Given by our hand at Nettleham 7th day of February.

4(k)

The king to his dear and faithful Philip ap Howel, guardian of the castle, town and land of Builth, greeting. Since by our charter we have given and granted to Edward our dearest son the castle, town and lands aforesaid with all their appurtenances to have and to hold for himself and his heirs the kings of England in perpetuity just as is contained fully in the aforesaid charter, we order you that you should free to our aforesaid son the castle, town and land with their appurtenances whatsoever without delay to have and to hold according to the form of the aforesaid charter, with witnesses as above.

Similar letters are sent to William Chykum, guardian of the castle and town of Aberconwy, John de Havering, guardian of the castle of Beaumaris and of the land of Anglesey, Thomas de Macclesfield, guardian of the manors of Macclesfield and of Overton with appurtenances and of the land of Mailor Seisnek, and Walter Hachit, guardian of the castle and town of Haverford, with witnesses as above.

Chapter 5: Court Rolls

5(a) Manor Court Roll from Great Waltham, Essex, 1318

View of Frankpledge in the same place [i.e. Great Waltham], on the day and year aforesaid.

Common payment:	All the chief sureties give as part of [lit. 'from'] the common payment
5s 1d	5s 1d
	All the chief sureties present that William Heynon made an encroachment by digging up the land in a certain lane which leads from the house of John Cook towards Chatham Green, therefore he is in mercy, on the surety of John Cook and
Fine: 3d	John Little.
	Likewise they present that William Mot has made an encroachment by putting manure in the common street to the annoyance of the lord and of the neighbours.
Fine: 3d	Therefore he is in mercy.
	Likewise they present that Robert Leuelif has made an encroachment with one wall by stopping up a certain course of water to the annoyance of the neighbours, therefore he is in mercy, on the surety of John Cook and William Heynon. And an order has been made to remove the said
Fine: 6d	wall.

Payment: 2s

And afterwards the said Robert made a payment so that the said wall could stand in peace since it does not stand to great annoyance, on the surety of the aforesaid John Cook and William Heynon.

Fine: 3d

Likewise they present that Robert Leuelif has made an encroachment by putting manure in the common street to the annoyance of the neighbours, therefore he is in mercy, on the surety of John Cook and William Heynon.

Fine: 2d
Order made

Likewise they present that Thomas Randolf has made an encroachment with a certain hedge near Colkeslane to the annoyance of James de la Hyde and others, therefore he is in mercy, on the surety of Adam Rat and Richard Whitbread. And an order has been made to remove the said encroachment.

Order made

Likewise they present that the lord ought to clean the ditch near the lane below his Courthouse because the neighbouring road in wintertime is completely submerged to the annoyance of the neighbours.

Fine: 3d

Likewise they present that Richard, son of Richard Whitbread, has made default, therefore he is in mercy.

5(b) Manor Court Roll from Antingham, Norfolk, 1438

Paragraph: Court held in the same place [i.e. Antingham] on Wednesday next after the feast of Exaltation of the Holy Cross [14 September], in the seventeenth year of the reign of king Henry the sixth.

Paragraph: Jurors by virtue of their office present that Richard Jonyour has gravely damaged his messuage of the

Fine: 6d

villeinage of the lord in Antingham so
that they are [sic] in danger of falling
down through lack of roofing, plastering
and carpentry. Therefore [he is] in mercy.
And he is ordered to repair the said
messuage well and sufficiently before the
next Court under penalty of 6s 8d. And
since he is unable to repair the said
tenement as it is said, therefore it has
been ordered to take possession into the
hand of the lady [see introductory
paragraph in text], etc.

5(c) Act Books of the Ecclesiastical Court of Whalley, 10 May 1532

Inquisition against John Cronkshay. It is noted that he had carnal knowledge of Emmota, the wife of Richard Cronkshay, and that he himself is married and is related to the said Richard Cronkshay in the second and second degrees of consanguinity and affinity [i.e. in the second degree of consanguinity and the second degree of affinity]. The man appeared [in court]. And [the case] is adjourned until Thursday, as above, and afterwards the woman appeared [in court], and they were warned to be present on the Thursday next after the feast of Pentecost.

... Agnes Marsden of Bowland was made pregnant as a result of illicit intercourse by a certain James Cutler, who lives outside the jurisdiction [of the court]. The woman appeared [in court] and she admits the charge. And she is under oath to carry out the penances specified [lit. made] for her, etc. And she has been ordered to go round the parish church of Chipping on one day in procession and in penitence with a wax candle in her hand, costing one penny. And similarly on one day around the chapel of Saint Michael within the castle of Clitheroe before [lit. this side of] the feast of Mary Magdalen [22 July].

5(d) Kendal Quarter Sessions, Christmas 1694
(i)

The jury on behalf of the lord king upon their oath present that Lancelot Lancaster of Ambleside in the aforesaid county, yeoman, on the thirtieth day of October in the sixth year of the reign of King

William and of the late Queen Mary of England etc. violently [lit. 'by force and arms'] [and] feloniously in Ambleside in the aforesaid county took, stole and carried away a ewe of a certain Thomas Ellis valued at five shillings which he recently found there, and other enormities etc., to the grave loss etc. and against the peace etc.

> Witnesses: George Fisher
> Thomas Dixon
> Thomas Ellis
> under oath

(ii)

The jury on behalf of the lord king upon their oath present that George Brown of Troutbeck in the county of Westmorland, gentleman, on the tenth day of June in the sixth year of the reign of the lord King William and of the late lady Queen Mary of England etc. violently broke and entered the close of a certain Rowland Cookson called Hindwick Moss at Troutbeck in the aforesaid county and deposited (in English 'did lay') diverse quantities of hemp (in English 'hemp'), namely five cartloads of hemp, in the aforesaid close, to the grave loss of the same Rowland and against the peace of the lord king, now etc.

> Witness: Rowland Cookson
> under oath

(iii)

The jury on behalf of the lord king upon their oath present that, since a certain George Brown, gentleman, and all those whose estate he himself owns, from a time of which there is no contrary memory of men, for a long time and legitimately had possessed and still is in possession of and in an ancient turbary (in English 'a peat moss') in a certain place called Hindwick in Troutbeck in the aforesaid county, and no persons whatsoever dug turves in the same without the permission of the same George, a certain Robert Hoggart of Applethwaite in the aforesaid county, yeoman, and Mary his wife, on the twentieth day of June in the sixth year of the reign of King William and of the late Queen Mary of England etc. violently entered the aforesaid turbary and dug diverse cartloads of turves (in English 'peats') and carried them away, to the grave loss of the same George and against the peace etc.

> Witness: George Brown, gentleman
> under oath

(iv)

The jury on behalf of the lord king upon their oath present that, since a certain George Brown, gentleman, and all those whose estate he himself owns, from a time of which there is no contrary memory of men, for a long time and legitimately had possessed and still is in possession of and in an ancient turbary (in English 'a peat moss') in a certain place called Hindwick in Troutbeck in the aforesaid county, and no persons whatsoever dug turves in the same without the permission of the same George, a certain Rowland Cookson of Applethwaite in the aforesaid county, and John Birkett of the same, on the seventeenth day of October in the sixth year of the reign of King William and of the late Queen Mary of England etc. violently entered the aforesaid turbary and dug diverse cartloads of turves (in English 'peats') to the grave loss of the same George and against the peace etc.

> Witness: George Brown
> under oath

(v)

The jury on behalf of the lord king upon their oath present that Thomas Jackson of Storth in the aforesaid county, yeoman, and Thomas Burrow of Beetham in the aforesaid county, yeoman, on the second day of January in the sixth year of the reign of William by the grace of God lord king of England, Scotland, France and Ireland, defender of the faith etc. violently at the aforesaid Storth in the aforesaid county took and carried away a ewe of a certain Thomas Burrow senior and committed other enormities against him to the grave loss of the same Thomas and against the peace of the said lord king, his crown and his dignity etc.

> Witnesses: Ellias Johnson
> Thomas Burrow
> Richard Fell

(vi)

The jury on behalf of the lord king upon their oath present that Margaret Straker wife of John Straker of Kirkby Kendal in the aforesaid county on the eleventh day of January in the sixth year of the reign of the lord King William now of England etc. at Stainton in the aforesaid county, contriving and falsely and maliciously intending to bring a certain Richard Holme then and there into disrepute with his neighbours and to slander the good name of the same Richard [lit. 'to oppress the same Richard in his good name'] concerning the same Richard then and there in the presence and hearing of several liege and faithful subjects of the said lord king, spoke declared and made public these following false, fictitious, scandalous and reproachful words in English, namely: Thou (meaning the same aforesaid Richard) has my trunk (meaning the same aforesaid Margaret's) and is an unworthy man for not bringing it out before this. By reason of the speaking and declaration of the said scandalous words the good name of the same aforesaid Richard Holme has been seriously damaged [lit. 'the same aforesaid Richard Holme has been seriously damaged in his good name'] to the grave loss of the same Richard and against the peace etc.

> Witnesses: Thomas Swanson
> Katherine Swanson
> Mary Jackson
> under oath

(vii)

The jury on behalf of the lord king upon their oath present that Nicholas Towanson of Docker in the aforesaid county, yeoman, William Towanson of the same in the aforesaid county, yeoman, and John Towanson of the same in the aforesaid county, yeoman, on the twenty second day of December in the sixth year of the reign of King William and of the late Queen Mary of England etc. left open (in English 'suffered to lye open') the fences and gates of the farm of the same Nicholas, gentleman, of New Hutton in the aforesaid county, called Woodheads. By reason of the opening of the fences and gates in the aforesaid farm the goods and chattels of the same Nicholas went away and fled from there and trespassed (in English 'did trespass') upon the common called Docker Common and ate and consumed grass and pasturage, and the aforesaid William and John chased the aforesaid goods and chattels from the aforesaid farm of the same Nicholas as far as the common called Docker Common, to the grave loss of Brian Wykeman and against the peace etc.

> Witnesses: James Mallinson
> Brian Wykeman
> under oath

(viii)

The jury on behalf of the lord king upon their oath present that Peter Collinson of Kirkby Lonsdale in the aforesaid county, yeoman, on the twentieth day of December in the sixth year of the reign of the lord King William and of the late Queen Mary of England etc. at the aforesaid Kirkby Lonsdale in the aforesaid county, contriving and falsely and maliciously intending to bring a certain Robert Dineley then and there into disrepute with his neighbours and to slander the good name of the same Robert concerning the same Robert then and there in the presence and hearing of several liege and faithful subjects of the said lord king and lady queen, spoke declared and made public these following false, fictitious, scandalous and re-proachful words in English, namely: I (meaning the same aforesaid Peter) want my mare, and thou (meaning the same aforesaid Robert) has stolen her. By reason of the speaking and declaration of the said scandalous words the good name of the same aforesaid Robert has been seriously damaged, to the grave loss of the same Robert and against the peace etc.

Witness: Robert Dineley

Chapter 6: Domesday Book; Historians after 1066

6(a) Robert of Hereford, for the year 1086

This is the 20th year of William, king of the English, by whose order in this year a census was made of the whole of England on the lands of each county, on the possessions of each nobleman, on their lands, on their households, on their men both slaves and free, both on those living only in huts and on those possessing houses and lands, on ploughs, on horses and other animals, on the service and tax of the whole property of everybody. Groups of investigators were sent one after another, and into counties they did not know, so that some could criticise the census of others and accuse others before the king. And the land was troubled by many disasters resulting from the gathering of the royal monies.

6(b) Domesday Book: the Customs of Chester

The city of Chester in the time of King Edward paid tax for 50 hides. Three hides and a half which are outside the city, that is, one hide and a half beyond the bridge, and two hides in Newton and Redcliff and in the bishop's stronghold, these were taxed with the city.

In the time of King Edward there were in the same city 431 houses paying tax. And besides these the bishop had 56 houses paying tax. At that time this city returned ten and a half marks of silver. Two parts (thirds) were the king's and a third the earl's. And these were the laws there:

If the peace made by the hand of the king or by his writ or through his commissioner was broken by anyone, then the king had 100 shillings. But if the same king's peace was broken after being made on his order by the earl, of the hundred shillings which were given for this the earl had the third penny [i.e. a third part]. However, if the same peace was broken after being made by an official of the king or by a reeve of the earl, there was a fine of 40 shillings, and the third penny [the third part] was the earl's.

If any free man breaking the king's peace killed a man in his house, his land and money were entirely the king's, and he himself became an outlaw. The earl received this same [fine] only in the case of his own man making this forfeiture. But nobody could grant pardon [lit. return peace] to any outlaw except through the king ...

If a widow had intercourse illegally with anyone, she paid a fine of 20 shillings; however, a girl [paid] 10 shillings for a similar case.

Whoever in the city seized the land of another and could not prove it was his paid a fine of 40 shillings. Similarly also he who then made a complaint, if he could not prove that it ought to be his.

He who did not pay the rent he owed by the appointed date paid a fine of 10 shillings.

If fire burned the city, the person from whose house it came paid a fine of 3 ores of pennies, and to his near neighbour he gave 2 shillings. Of all these fines 2 parts were the king's and a third the earl's.

6(c) Domesday Book: Pampisford, Cambridgeshire

Pampisford was assessed for 5 hides and 22 acres in the time of King Edward, and [likewise] now. Of these 5 hides and 22 acres the Abbot of Ely holds two hides and three and a half virgates. There is land for six ploughs there. One hide and one and a half virgates and two ploughs are in the demesne. Four ploughs are for the villeins; there are twelve villeins, five bordars, three slaves; one mill of twenty shillings; a meadow of one plough. There are thirteen cattle not used for draught; ninety-five sheep, twenty-three pigs. In total it is valued and was valued at seven pounds. This land lies and lay in [the demesne of] the church of St Etheldreda of Ely.

And of these 5 hides and 22 acres Radulf de Scamnis and Radulf Brito hold one hide and twenty-two acres from Earl Alan. There is land there for two ploughs and for two oxen. One plough is in the demesne and the other plough is for the villeins. There are two villeins, two bordars; two acres and a half of meadow. There are four cattle not used for draught; thirty-seven sheep; thirty-nine pigs. In total it is valued at thirty shillings; and at one time it brought in ten shillings and in the time of King Edward thirty shillings. Almar, Eddiva's man, held this land. He could give it and sell it to whoever he wished in the time of King Edward. But Eddiva held the soc.

And of these 5 hides and 22 acres Radulf de Scannis holds three virgates from Picot the sheriff from the king's fief. There is land there for one plough, and there is a plough; there are two and a half acres of meadow. This land is valued and was valued at ten shillings. Edric, Aluric Child's man, held this land. He could give his land to whoever he wished in the time of King Edward.

And of these 5 hides and 22 acres Hardwin holds ten acres from the abbot. There is land for one ox; it is valued and was valued at twelve pence. Suelling holds this land and held it in the time of King Edward, and he could not leave it. And in the same vill Picot holds five acres from Eudo the Steward; it is valued and was valued at six pence. Burro held this land from Aluric Camp; he could leave it when he wished. In the same vill Hardwin holds half an acre from the king's fief; there is land for two oxen. This land is valued and was valued at four ores. Two tenants in socage held this land, King Edward's men, and they found watchmen [see note on l.34]; they could leave. And in the same vill a certain priest holds half a virgate from the countess Judith; there is land for two oxen. A tenant in socage, Earl Gurd's man, held this land; he could not leave.

6(d) Land of the Abbacy of Ely

... In Pampisford the same abbot holds 2 hides and 3 virgates and a half. There is land for 6 ploughs. In the demesne [there is] 1 hide and 1 virgate and a half and there are 2 ploughs. [There are] 12 villeins there and 5 bordars with 4 ploughs. [There are] 3 slaves there and one mill of 20 shillings. [There is] a meadow of 1 plough. It is valued and was valued at seven pounds. This land lay and lies in the demesne of the church of Ely.

... In the same vill Hardwin holds from the abbot 10 acres. [There is] land for 1 ox. It is valued at 12 pence. Suelling held this land from the abbot, but he could not leave it.

6(e) William of Malmesbury: the English

However, the study of literature and religion had fallen into disuse in the preceding age, not many years before the arrival of the

Normans. The clergy were content with second-rate literature and could scarcely stumble through the words of the sacraments; anyone who knew his grammar was seen by the rest as an amazing miracle. Monks with their refined clothing and showing no discrimination in the kind of foods [they ate] made a mockery of their rule. The nobles, devoting themselves to gluttony and to sex, did not attend church in the morning in the Christian fashion, but in their bedrooms and amid the embraces of their wives they gave only half an ear to [lit. tasted with their ears] the solemnities of matins and the mass [given] by a hurrying priest. The common people were without protection [lit. exposed in the middle] and were prey to the more powerful, so that, either when their possessions were exhausted or when they had even been torn away bodily to distant lands, they [the more powerful] could pile up heaps of treasure.

In short, at that time the English were simply dressed in garments which came half-way to the knee, their hair was close cropped, their beards shaved, their arms weighed down with golden bracelets, their skin decorated with painted designs; in food they brought on sickness, in drink they encouraged ulcers.

6(f) William of Malmesbury: the Normans

Moreover the Normans, to speak of them as well, were at that time and still are well dressed with garments to incite envy, in food they are fastidious and avoid excess [lit. 'this side of any excess']; they are a people accustomed to warfare and they scarcely know how to live without war. They go for the enemy energetically, and when their strength has proved inadequate they destroy no less effectively by trickery and bribery. At home, as I have said, their huge buildings consume only moderate expenditure, they envy their equals, they want to surpass their superiors, they protect those subject to them from others; they are faithful to their lords, but soon become unfaithful at a slight offence. They look upon disloyalty fatalistically, they change their opinions according to who pays them [lit. 'with money']. However, of all nations they are the most kindly in treating foreigners with the same honour as themselves; they also enter into marriage with their subject peoples. By their arrival they revived the standard of religion which had died out everywhere in England; you can see churches rising everywhere in the towns, and monasteries in the villages and cities, in the new style of building, and the land flourishing in the fresh observance [of religion], so that every rich person thinks he has wasted a day when some splendid magnificence does not shine upon it.

6(g) William of Malmesbury: the accession of Stephen

When he [Stephen] was accepted as king by the people of London and Winchester, he also brought over to his support Roger, bishop of Salisbury, and William de Ponte Arcus, the custodians of the royal treasury. However, so that the truth is not hidden from posterity, all his efforts would have been in vain had not his brother Henry, bishop of Winchester, who was now legate of the papal see in England, given him his compliant assent, apparently persuaded by the fervent hope that Stephen would maintain the ways of his grandfather William in the moderation of his reign, and especially in the discipline of the vigour of the church. Therefore, having drawn up a tightly worded oath which William, archbishop of Canterbury, demanded of Stephen concerning the return of liberty to the church and its continued preservation, the bishop of Winchester appointed himself as mediator and surety.... So Stephen was crowned king of England on the 11th day before the kalends of January [22 December], a Sunday, with three bishops present (the archbishop, and the bishops of Winchester and Salisbury), no abbots, and very few nobles, on the 22nd day after the death of his uncle, in the 1135th year of the Lord's Incarnation.

6(h) William of Malmesbury: Eilmer

Not long after, a comet, a star so they say portending changes of kingdoms, appeared trailing its long fiery tail [lit. hair] across the sky. Therefore a certain monk of our monastery called Eilmer, cowering at the sight of the terror of the blazing star, said wisely, 'You have come, you have come, you who are to be mourned by many mothers. It is a long time since I saw you, but now I behold you much more terrible, threatening the destruction of this country.' He was a well educated man for those times, of advanced age, having attempted in his early youth a deed of great daring, for he had fastened wings to his hands and feet by some means or other so that he could fly like Daedalus, accepting the legend as true, and having collected the air from the top of a tower he flew for a furlong and more. But shaken by the violence of the wind and the air current, and at the same time by the consciousness of his rash deed, he fell and forever thereafter he was lame and had damaged legs. He himself used to give as the reason for his failure that he forgot [to add] a tail to the rear part.

6(i) William Fitzstephen: the death of Thomas Becket

Somebody struck him with the flat of his sword between the shoulder blades, saying, 'Go, you are dead'. He stood his ground unmoved, and offering his neck he commended himself to the Lord; and he had the holy bishop martyrs on his lips, the blessed Denis and the holy Alphege of Canterbury. Some said, 'You are captured, you will come with us,' and laying their hands upon him they wanted to drag him from the church. He replied, 'I shall go nowhere; you will do here what you want to do and what you have been ordered to do,' and as far as he could he resisted and the monks tried to hold him back. With them was also master Edward Grimm, who also put his arm in the way and received the first sword blow which was directed by William de Tracy at his head; and [both] were seriously wounded by the same blow, the archbishop on his bowed head and Edward himself in the arm ...

The archbishop wiped away with his arm the blood flowing from his head and when he saw it he gave thanks to God, saying, 'Into your hands, Lord, I commend my spirit.' A second blow was landed on his head, and at this he fell onto his face, first kneeling down, and putting his hands together and extending them to God, near the altar of St Benedict which was there. And he took care, or had the grace, to fall becomingly, covered with his cloak down to his ankles, as if about to adore and to pray. He fell on his right side, about to go to the right hand of God.

6(j) Henry of Huntingdon: the promises of Stephen

From there Stephen went to Oxford, where he repeated and confirmed the agreements which he had made to God and the people and the holy church on the day of his coronation, which are these: first he vowed that on the deaths of bishops he would never retain churches in his hands, but would immediately agree to selection by the rules of the church and grant them to the bishops. Secondly he vowed that he would not retain in his hands the forests of any cleric or lay person, as King Henry had done, who each year brought any persons to trial if they had either hunted in his own forests, or if they had uprooted them or diminished them for their own purposes ... Thirdly he vowed that he would forever remit the Danegeld, that is [the tax of] two shillings per hide, which his predecessors were accustomed to receive every year. These were the main things which he vowed to God, and [there were] others, but he stood by none of them.

6(k) William of Newburgh: the reign of Stephen

And at first in fact it seemed that the kingdom of England had been split in two, with some favouring the king and some the empress, not because either the king or the empress commanded their side effectively, but because each individual was striving for the warlike ends of his own party according to the circumstances. For neither was able to act effectively over their own people and to exercise the power of discipline, but each curried the favour of their followers, so that they would not defect from them, by denying them nothing. Indeed there was long hard fighting between the two parties, with alternating fortunes. But as time went by there began to be less forceful interchanges between them as they experienced ever more frequently the fickleness of fortune; but this did not actually turn out well for England. In fact as they became wearied by the daily struggle and began acting more moderately, disturbances blazed up in the shires among squabbling nobles. In each county also castles had frequently risen in support of the parties, and there were in England pretty well as many kings, or rather tyrants, as there were lords of castles, each minting his own coinage and holding the power of dictating the law over his subjects like a king. And as they all individually sought to dominate, so that some could not bear anyone above them and some could not even bear any equal as they disputed amongst themselves with fierce hatred, they destroyed with their plundering and burning the most productive regions, and in a land that was once extremely fertile they destroyed almost all power to produce food. But the northern region, which had fallen into the power of David, king of the Scots, as far as the River Tees, through the industry of the same king enjoyed peace.

6(l) Matthew Paris: Magna Carta

The king held his court at the Nativity of the Lord at Winchester for scarcely the space of one day; then he came to London with great speed and rejoined his household at the New Temple. And coming to the king there the above mentioned leading nobles, in quite blatant military dress, demanded that certain liberties and laws of

King Edward together with other liberties granted to them and to the kingdom of England and to the English church be confirmed, as are contained in the charter of King Henry I and included in the aforesaid laws. Hearing this the king demanded a postponement until the end of Easter. But the king meanwhile, wishing to take precautions for the future, insisted on the swearing of an oath of loyalty throughout the whole of England to himself alone against all men, and on the renewal of homages; and in order to provide better for himself, on the day of the Purification of the blessed Mary he took up the Cross of the Lord. In the week of Easter the leading nobles met at Stamford with horses and arms, and by now they had attracted almost all the nobility of the whole realm to their side; and they got together an army of incalculable size, most particularly because the king constantly showed himself hostile to them all. For in that army it was estimated that there were two thousand knights, besides the cavalry, the feudal tenants and the footsoldiers. The king was at that time at Oxford. On the Monday next after the octaves of Easter the barons mentioned above likewise came together in the town of Brackley. The king sent to them the Archbishop of Canterbury and William Marshall, Earl of Pembroke to find out from them which were the laws and liberties that they wanted. But they handed to the aforesaid emissaries a document which contained in large measure the ancient laws and customs of the realm. Then the Archbishop with his colleagues, taking that document back to the king, recited the chapters one by one from memory in his presence. Therefore, when the Archbishop and William Marshall had been totally unable to bring the king to agree, on the order of the king they returned to the barons. The leading nobles appointed Robert son of Walter as leader of the armed forces, calling him 'Marshall of the Army of God and of the Holy Church', and thus all of them took to arms jointly and directed their forces towards Northampton. But achieving nothing there they headed towards the castle of Bedford. And messengers from the city of London came to them there, indicating to them in some secrecy that if they wanted to have access into the city they should come there with haste. They came as far as Ware. On the ninth day before the kalends of June [24 May] they entered the city of the people of London without any disturbance. For the wealthy people of the city supported the barons, and for this reason the poor were afraid to speak against them. And having been assured of safety from the already mentioned citizens, they sent letters to those earls, barons and knights who were throughout England apparently still, though feignedly, on the side of the king. When all these had received the directive of the barons, the greatest part of them set out for London and allied themselves with the above leading nobles, completely abandoning the king. The courts of the exchequer and of the sheriffs ceased throughout England, since no one could be found who would pay tax to the king or would obey in any matter. They fixed a day for the king to come to them for a conference, in a meadow situated between Staines and Windsor, on the fifteenth day of June. And so they met. Finally therefore when they had discussed [matters] from both sides with varying success, King John, realising that his power was inferior to that of the barons, without obstruction granted the laws and liberties.

Chapter 7: Other Material: Maps, Monuments, Letters

7(a) George Lily's Map of the British Isles

BRITAIN, AN ISLAND WHICH CONTAINS TWO KINGDOMS, ENGLAND AND SCOTLAND, WITH IRELAND LYING NEARBY

Britain, the largest of the islands which exist in Europe, stretches from the south to the north, having almost the shape of a triangle whose circumference is 1720 miles. For from Dover, a part of Kent, to Caithness, the furthest part of Scotland, it is 600 miles. From the same place to the furthest promontory of Cornwall is 320 miles, and again from here to the furthest extremity of Caithness it is 800 miles. It is 30 miles from France. It contains two kingdoms, England [which is] more fertile in its soil, more populous in its cities and of a pleasanter character, and Scotland [which is] harsher and less fertile because of the cold. They are divided from one another in the east by the River Tweed and in the west by the River Solway, and in the middle by the Cheviot Hill[s]. To the west of Scotland there lie 43 islands called the Eboniae or Hebrides, of which the foremost and most ancient because of the memory of the Druids was Mona [the Isle of Man]. To the north are the 31 Orkney Islands, separated from Caithness by quite a narrow straight, of which the foremost in size exceeding the rest is Pomonia [Mainland]. The last [land] under the jurisdiction of Scotland is Thule [the Shetlands], having the pole elevated at 63 degrees. Here when the sun is in Cancer there is either very little night or none at all. Three huge rivers, the Thames, the Severn and the Humber, divide England into three regions, as it were; three rivers likewise [divide] Scotland, the Clyde, the Forth and the Tay.

The island of Ireland is situated in the [Atlantic] Ocean not far from Britain, extending from the NNW to the SSW 260 miles in longitude and 100 miles in latitude. It has Britain to the east, France to the south, and almost endless ocean to the west and north. Its shape is oblong and not unlike an egg. It is divided into four regions, namely into Laginia [Leinster], Mononia [Munster], Conacia [Connacht] and Hultonia [Ulster]. The River Suir separates Leinster from Munster, the Boyne [separates it] from Ulster, and the Shannon divides Munster from Connacht. Here the temperature of the climate is remarkable, so that it brings nothing to fruit that sprouts and nourishes nothing that is imported from elsewhere.

7(b) Christopher Saxton: Frontispiece

The gentle and just governess of the kingdom of Britain shines forth in full view in this distinguished form.

> While all nations wage sorrowful wars all around
> and blind errors prowl about in all the world,
> you gladden the British with long peace and true piety,
> wisely controlling the reins with mellow justice.
> Beloved at home, famous abroad, may you long hold your
>   kingdom here,
> to enjoy at last the everlasting kingdom.

7(c) Index

We have added an index to this work in three parts. Firstly, all the counties in alphabetical order. Secondly, the table of our organisation [of the counties] and of the maps. Thirdly, you will find the circuits of the judges, the opening days and prescribed time of the law-court days and of their locations assigned for the conduct of trials both civil and criminal (commonly called the circuits and assizes).

7(d) Catalogue

Catalogue of cities, bishoprics, market towns, castles, parish churches, well-known rivers, bridges, chases, forests, and of all the parks which are contained in each county throughout the whole of England and Wales, just as they are recorded most clearly in their own places in the hand-drawn maps of England and Wales (where the name of each is added). The number of all those which are collected together in this table is indicated at the foot of this index, as can be seen below.

7(e) England

England, abounding in the number of its people and in the provision of almost all things, most flourishing now for twenty years in most tranquil peace under the most gentle rule of Elizabeth, the most serene and learned queen.

It should be noted that because of the restrictions of space we have included on this map only cities, market towns, castles and certain more famous places.

7(f) The County Maps

Kent, Sussex, Surrey, Middlesex, London
A true description of the counties of Kent, Sussex, Surrey and Middlesex, together with their boundaries on all sides, towns, districts, villages and rivers in the same.

Apart from the archbishop's city of England, which was called Kairkent in British [i.e. pre-Roman] times, Dorobernia in Roman times and Canterbury in Saxon times, Kent also has the city of Rochester, 17 market towns and 398 parish churches.

In the year of the Lord 1575 and in the 17th year of the lady Queen Elizabeth.

Hampshire
A true description of the county of Southampton (except the islands of Wight, Jersey and Guernsey which are parts of the same county) with its boundaries on all sides, towns, districts, villages and rivers.

The county of Southampton has (apart from the city of Winchester) 18 market towns and 248 districts and villages.

In the year of the Lord 1575.

Dorset
A new and true description of the county of Dorchester and of the neighbouring regions. In the year of the Lord 1575.

Wiltshire

The county of Wiltshire (well-known for its grassy plain) is here put forward before your eyes. In the year of the Lord 1576.

Somerset

This map places before your eyes the county of Somerset (celebrated for the fertility of its land). In the year 1575 and in the 17th year of the lady Queen Elizabeth.

Devon

A recent, true and detailed description of the county of Devon and of all memorable things in the same. In the year of the Lord 1575.

Cornwall

This promontory which projects into the sea is called Cornwall. This work was done in the year of the Lord 1576 and in the 18th year of the lady Queen Elizabeth.

Essex

A new, true and complete description of the county of Essex. In the year of the Lord 1576.

Hertfordshire

A new, true and detailed description of the county of Hertfordshire. In the year of the Lord 1577.

Oxfordshire, Buckinghamshire and Berkshire

A true description of the counties of Oxfordshire, Buckinghamshire and Berkshire, together with their boundaries on all sides, towns, districts, villages and rivers in the same. In the year of the Lord 1574.

Oxfordshire has, apart from the university and town of Oxford, 9 market towns, 208 parish churches. Buckinghamshire contains within it 11 market towns, 185 parish churches. Berkshire contains within it 11 market towns 139 parish churches.

Gloucestershire

A true print and representation of the county of Gloucestershire or Claudiocestershire (it is still known by the name of Claudius Caesar). In the year of the Lord 1577.

7(g) The Land of the Holy Cross or the New World

This region is everywhere inhabited; it is considered another world by most people. Women and men go either completely naked or dressed in woven fibres and birds' feathers of various colours. Many live together with no religion and no king. They constantly wage war amongst themselves. They feed on human flesh of captives. They have such a mild climate that they live beyond their 150th year. They are rarely ill, and when they are they are healed simply by the roots of herbs. Lions live here and snakes and other dreadful beasts of the forest. There are mountains and rivers. There is a great quantity of pearls and gold. Timber of brasil [used for red dye], also called 'verzin', and cassia are exported from here by the Portuguese.

Portuguese sailors have observed this part of this land and reached as far as the 50th degree of latitude south [lit. as far as the elevation of the antarctic pole of 50 degrees]. However, [they did] not yet [reach] its southern tip.

Spanish sailors came as far as this and called this land the New World because of its size, since indeed they did not see it all, nor up to this time have they surveyed further than this limit. Therefore here it is left unfinished, especially since it is not known in which direction it tends.

7(h) Henry Hondius' Map of Bermuda

Map of the Summer Islands, otherwise called the Bermudas, accurately described, lying at the mouths of the Mexican Gulf at a latitude of 32 degrees 25 minutes. From England, that is London, [it is] 3500 English miles towards the SSW, and from Roanoke (which is in Virginia) [it is] 500 miles towards the SE.

Around the summer solstice in the year 1616 five men set sail from these islands in an open boat, with a capacity of three tons, and after a voyage of seven months they all reached Ireland safely. Such a thing it is believed has rarely happened within the memory of men.

7(i) Inscription from Lyon, AD 493

In this tomb rests Ursus of good memory who lived in peace for 10 years and died on the 2nd day before the Nones of March [probably 5th March is intended] ...

7(j) Inscription from Lincoln Cathedral

Here lies Richard of Gainsborough, formerly Mason of this church, who died on the 12th day before the Kalends of June [21 May] in the year of the Lord 1300.

7(k) Inscriptions from Thornton Abbey, Lincolnshire

Here lies Robert Gudyk who died on the first day of the month of October in the year of the Lord 1462, and Joan his wife. May God have mercy on their souls. Amen.

Here lies Master William Medeley, the 12th Abbot of this monastery, who died on the 12th day of the month of December in the year of the Lord 1473. May God have mercy on his soul. Amen.

Here lies Master John Hoton, who died on the 14th day of the month of September in the year of the Lord 1429. May God have mercy on his soul. Amen.

7(l) Inscription from Heversham, Cumbria

In loving memory of both an excellent and most beloved mother, Anne Preston, died in the year 1767, her grieving son William Preston, Bishop of Ferns, had this marble set up.

7(m) Inscription from Gainsborough, Lincolnshire

John Simpson, Master of Arts, a learned man and devout priest, born in this town, [died ?] on the 4th day of February AD 1755. Anna, his most faithful wife, placed this stone for her excellent husband. Jacob Calton dictated the words and wished his name to be added to the inscription in memory of their mutual friendship. With their father lie seven small infants, 'whom ... torn from the breast a dark day stole away and plunged in bitter death'.

7(n) From Elgin Cathedral
(i)
Here lie the remains of Margaret McKaley, dearest wife of Murdoch by divine mercy formerly Bishop of Murray and now Bishop of the Orkneys, who yielded to the fates in the month of May in the year of the Lord 1676.

(ii)

To the dearest memory of his wife Elizabeth Paterson, descended from most worthy ancestors, most faithful ministers of the Church of Scotland, her surviving husband Master James Thomson, Pastor of Elgin, had this monument erected.

Here lies sweet Elisa, superior in body and serene in countenance
    and mind, and twice married to a husband,
A woman lacking any blemish and born of devout parents, shining
    forth in her virtue, merits, praise and honour.
She lived three times ten and almost six years more, faithful to her
    husbands in this world and dear to God in death.

Died 12 August 1698 in her 36th year.

7(o)

Erasmus to Faustus Andrelinus, Prize-winning Poet.

We have made some progress in England. The Erasmus whom you knew is now almost a good huntsman, not the worst of horsemen, and a not inexperienced courtier; he pays his respects a little more charmingly, he smiles at people more affably, and all this without the help of Minerva [the goddess of wisdom and learning]. If you have any sense you too will hurry here. Why are you so content, you a man of such wit, to grow old amid the shit of France? But your gout prevents you. I wish it would disappear [lit. 'perish badly'] and leave you well. Though if you knew well enough the delights of Britain, Faustus, you would surely run here with wings on your feet. And if your gout did not allow it, you would wish that you could become Daedalus.

For let me mention just one point out of many. There are here nymphs with divine faces, charming, good natured, and whom you would easily prefer to your native Italian muses [camenae]. There is also a custom which is never praised enough. If you arrive anywhere, you are welcomed with kisses from everybody; if you leave, you are sent off with kisses; you return, you are given kisses; people come to your house, you are toasted with kisses; when they leave, kisses are exchanged; when you meet anywhere, there is an abundance of kisses; finally wherever you go, everything is full of kisses. If you had once tasted how tender and fragrant they are, Faustus, you would indeed wish to stay abroad not just for ten years, as Solon did, but to stay in England until you died. We'll have a joke about the rest face to face, for I shall see you very soon, I hope.

Goodbye, from England. In the year 1499.

7(p)
The Bishop of Rochester to Master Erasmus, fullest greetings.

It was so annoying to hear of the danger of your voyage, but I am of course so glad that you escaped safe and sound [see note on text for the Latin constructions here]. It was indeed right that you should pay some penalty for your very hasty departure from me, with whom you could have rested safe from every tossing of the sea ...

In the New Testament, translated by you to the common utility of all, no one who has any sense could be displeased, since not only have you shed great light on innumerable passages in it by your learning, but you have also added a most complete commentary to the whole work, so that now it can be read and understood much more pleasingly and pleasantly than before by every single person. But in fact I fear that the printer has rather frequently dozed off. For while I was exercising myself in the reading of Paul in accordance with your orders, I found that on numerous occasions he had omitted Greek words, and sometimes whole sentences. To you I also owe this, Erasmus, that I can to some extent conjecture, where the Greek does not altogether agree with the Latin. I wish that I had been allowed to have you as a teacher for several months.

Best wishes from Rochester.
    Your pupil John [Bishop of] Rochester.